Traveling Economies

Traveling Economies

American Women's
Travel Writing

* * *

JENNIFER BERNHARDT STEADMAN

THE OHIO STATE UNIVERSITY PRESS
Columbus

Library of Congress Cataloging-in-Publication Data

Steadman, Jennifer Bernhardt, 1971–
Traveling economies : American women's travel writing / Jennifer Bernhardt Steadman.
    p. cm.
Includes bibliographical references and index.
ISBN 978–0–8142–1066–6 (cloth : alk. paper)—ISBN 978–0–8142–9143–6 (cd-rom) 1.
Travelers' writings, American—History and criticism. 2. American prose literature—
Women authors—History and criticism. 3. American prose literature—19th century—
History and criticism. 4. Women travelers—United States—History—19th century. 5.
Women travelers—United States—Social conditions—19th century. 6. Women authors,
American—19th century—Political and social views. 7. Women travelers in literature. 8.
Feminism in literature. 9. Travel in literature. I. Title.
PS366.T73S72 2007
810.9'320922—dc22
            2007013298
Paper (ISBN: 978-0-8142-5689-3)
Cover design by Amy Bernhardt and Hallie Steele.
Text design and typesetting by Jennifer Shoffey Forsythe.
Type set in Adobe Palatino.

· Contents ·

· *Acknowledgments* ·

$\mathcal{I}$ owe a special debt of thanks to the traveling women whose lives and writing inspired this project and who continued to captivate me with their spirit and often with their wit through the long process from research to dissertation to book. Mentors at Emory University's Institute for Women's Studies helped to start me on the right path, and I am deeply grateful for the guidance of Martine Watson Brownley, Mary Odem, Kimberly Wallace Sanders, and Mark Sanders. Especially, I am indebted to Frances Smith Foster for providing me with a model of scholarship and professionalism that I will carry with me. I offer special thanks to the librarians and staff members who have helped me in my own travels to recover these women at Duke University's Sallie Bingham Center for Women's History and Culture in the Rare Book, Manuscript, and Special Collections Library; Howard University's Moorland-Spingarn Research Center; Trinity College's Watkinson Library; and Harvard University's Schlessinger Library. I am grateful to my editors at The Ohio State University Press, Heather Miller and Sandy Crooms, copyeditors Maggie Diehl and Ben George, as well as to the anonymous readers who offered excellent advice and feedback.

The insightful critiques offered by friends and colleagues have improved this manuscript at every turn; I thank Chloe Wheatley, Todd Vogel, and Laura Micham especially for their time, energy, and scholarly generosity. Elizabeth Engelhardt has filled the roles of mentor and best friend with style and inspiration. Without almost daily long-distance phone calls I would not have had the energy to keep going.

Without her critical reading and editing, her hands-on tours of archives, and her advice on writing conference papers, book reviews, and articles, I would be a much poorer scholar—thank you so very much for sharing the brain.

"Over the Rainbow" was the song my mother and grandfather sang to me, offering promises of adventure and of a home that would always welcome me after my travels. My mother, Melody Bernhardt, shared books and stories and heroines with me, and I still love Jo March and Edna St. Vincent Millay because they are our secret. My dad, Lee Bernhardt, taught me to take risks and to celebrate my discoveries. Without him, I never would have believed I could make a layup or hit a three wood or send postcards home from a café overlooking the Cinque Terre. My sister, Amy, has taught me that travel and adventure should figure in our lives on a regular basis. She lent her skill, vision, and style to the book's cover, and I am honored by her generous gift. Amy and I inherited our travel bug from our grandfather, Buck Schaub, who explored as much of the world as he could and taught us to be endlessly curious. From my grandmother Lillian Schaub I learned to make a chocolate cake that tastes like her kitchen, and every time I make it, which is often, I am reminded that home and family sustain me. My grandparents Marie and Otto Bernhardt gave me Southern roots, which sent me first to Wake Forest and then to Atlanta. Beryl Steadman, my mother-in-law and research assistant, shares my passion for literature and has even shared my trips to archives and libraries.

My most special thanks is reserved for my husband, Tim Steadman, who has made our family and my work our shared priority and made it possible for me to write and think and teach. He offers the special gift of his love and support when he backs up my computer, when he lovingly puts our daughter, Emily, to bed on nights when I teach—and in too many other ways to count. Emily has been my inspiration for finishing the book—I hope someday she will be inspired to set off on her own adventures and maybe even to write about them. I am sure that her baby brother, Lucas, will follow close behind, and I can't wait to see where they go.

Economies of Travel

*I*n its lushly illustrated parody of women's travel and travel writing, *Harper's New Monthly Magazine* invites its readers to laugh at heroine Impulsia Gushington's pretensions to independence, self-sufficiency, and world travel. The September 1863 feature titled "An Unprotected Female in the East" mocks Impulsia's travel mishaps as she journeys from Alexandria to Cairo and in the process is abandoned by her travel companion, robbed by locals of everything except her undergarments and hoopskirt, fleeced by fellow travelers and servants, charmed by dubious suitors, and deceived by fake relatives. At her first Eastern port of call, Impulsia is the stereotypical picture of a middle-class tourist, surrounded by mountains of luggage, dressed for the heat in full skirt and long cloak, and carrying a tiny dog as an inappropriate travel accessory. Her conspicuous consumption of tourism matches her clichéd musings on the liberating effects of travel. Later in her story, as she enjoys the romance of her first camel ride, Impulsia gushes: "My camel proved to be gentle, easy, and docile . . . The lovely scene, the balmy air, the sense of freedom, the relief from hateful associations, all combined to soothe and calm my spirit . . . I compared the flat conventionalities of civilized existence with the piquant charm of my present situation." The camel, despite its gentleness, provides her with a chance to imagine herself as the daring heroine of her own epic travel narrative, a welcome respite from her "flat" everyday experience of domestic comfort. "The sense of freedom" she feels relaxes her

Figure 1. Impulsia Gushington's runaway camel ride. Lady Dufferin, "An Unprotected Female in the East." *Harper's New Monthly Magazine* No. 160, Vol. 27 (September 1863): 445 (Courtesy of the Watkinson Library, Trinity College).

"spirit" rather than inspiring further adventure; it is clear that her tour and her newfound freedom are only temporary and that she will return to "civilized existence" refreshed but unchanged by her travels.[1]

Impulsia's camel has other ideas, however, and his sudden speed bounces her out of her travel daydreams:

> Good gracious! What spirit of evil had taken possession of my gentle camel? I found myself bounding over the sandy plain at a pace which threatened dislocation of all my members!
>
> It was in vain that I grasped the horn of the saddle (which is the principal security of one's seat on a camel) with a mad desperation that only served to fatigue my arms: these tremendous bounds lifted me out of the seat . . . My serviceable little hat flew like a rocket

from my head; my parasol mounted like a balloon . . . On and on
we rushed; the scared cranes screamed above my head; the sand
seemed all on fire beneath my camel's feet; the low hills fleeted by
like dreams; the wind deafened me by its rush and roar against my
ears . . . I found myself (when conscious) bruised indeed and shaken,
but sound and whole in limb, upon a heap of drifted sand. (443–44)

The accompanying illustration is meant to amplify Impulsia's florid
prose and the joke (see figure 1); it also emphasizes the parody's underlying message about women's travel. The mobility and autonomy to
which women gain access through travel challenge status quo gender
norms, particularly for white, middle-class women. *Harper's* and its
audience, larger American society, attempt to neutralize the threat by
discouraging other would-be Impulsias. Readers are meant to learn that
her impulsive decision to travel has endangered not only her finances
but also her reputation—and the camel ride increases the stakes by risking her life. Her middle-class femininity is what is truly at stake as the
markers of her social status—her fashionable hat and parasol—literally
fly away while she careens across the desert. With her hair and shawl
flying behind and her parasol already gone, Impulsia is undone, left
with no protection against the desert sun and no husband, father, or
brother to rescue her. In the next scene her dress is stolen, a final punishment for her enjoyment of "the sense of freedom."[2]

Although slowed by the Civil War, the travel writing and tourism
of white, middle-class women steadily increased from midcentury and
would only grow after the 1863 publication of the *Harper's* parody.[3]
The rising popularity of not only tourism but also women's published
travel writing provides the fodder for *Harper's*—the audience needs
to recognize the subject of the parody for the joke to work. The vivid
Harper's portrait amplifies the stereotype, not merely repeating it but
reinforcing it as well. The ultimate effect of this popular representation,
then, is the erasure of other models of earlier female travelers—be they
workers, activists, or journalists—such as those found in the pioneering journeys and outspoken social commentary of the women studied
here. The black and white women travel writers featured in *Traveling
Economies* present an alternative vision of women's mobility, autonomy,
and competence that at the time was far more threatening to gender,
race, and class norms than the female tourists *Harper's* mocks. Recovering their travels and their writing invites us to rethink where and how
women went and what they wrote in antebellum America.

Economies of Travel

In fact, it is the very act of traveling, whether by camel or by today's corporate ladder, that often reveals the continuing constraints women face. Assumptions about gender, race, and class that are often masked or invisible for women who do not openly transgress social boundaries are laid bare in the lives and writings of traveling women. Nineteenth-century women's travel writing reveals the social structures designed to keep women in their place, while simultaneously dismantling those hierarchies in their lives and texts.

Women who did not travel already blurred the boundaries between public and private in their own neighborhoods, where they worked for pay, formed literary societies and temperance leagues, or even wrote for local newspapers. Traveling served to raise the stakes, as each town along the stagecoach route was confronted with the reality of a mobile, independent woman traveler and with the prospect of the town's own mothers, sisters, and wives climbing on board to join her. The transgressions that could be tolerated on the local level were much more threatening on a potentially national and transnational scale. The reactions of railroad companies or other travelers to the presence of women and African-Americans reinforced cultural, social, and political ideas about their proper place. Segregated railroad cars and steamship cabins institutionalized cultural anxiety about free black citizenship and worked to limit the circulation of black bodies and labor. Unwanted chivalrous attention from concerned fellow passengers thinly disguised an intention to monitor women's movement and conveyed the cultural consensus that they were unfit for independence and self-determination, much less the rigors of travel. However, black and white women could and did travel and lay claim to agency by moving beyond these confining definitions of womanhood, blackness, and class.

Travel can be a term so broad and all-encompassing as to be rendered almost meaningless. At times including the European tour of the wealthy socialite, the desperate running of the fugitive slave, and the forced migration of the Trail of Tears, definitions of travel fundamentally express movement, mobility from place to geographical place, regardless of whether the mobility was forced or chosen. *Traveling Economies* focuses on travel between the extremes of wealthy tourism and forced removal in order to examine travel that is often overlooked—the elected journeys of women who traveled for work. Work for these travelers encompassed a wide range of economic, social, and political activities. "Ragged-edge travel" is my designation for these work-motivated trips that made use of rapidly improving transportation technologies, but at bargain rates without the benefits of chaperones, first-class accommodations, or guided tours. Ragged-edge travelers undertook their journeys to support themselves, to serve their communities, to enter national and international political debates, to criticize social and political institutions, and to demonstrate their own and their gender's and race's fitness for the rigors of public life. Analyzing how—and, even more important, why—they went opens up new routes to understanding the diversity of women's experience in the nineteenth century.

Travel can be a difficult, uncomfortable, alienating, and frightening experience, for contemporary women and for their historical predecessors. It is tempting to romanticize what we imagine today as the glamour and boldness of their pioneering journeys. However, *Traveling Economies* approaches nineteenth-century women's travels from a critical perspective that does not simplistically equate travel with agency. Rather, travel is a strategy that works with a series of other attempts to at least survive and at best subvert and reconstruct systems of power that depend on women's exploitation and stasis.

Women authors' discussions of the multiple and complex motivations behind their decisions to travel point us to a more-complicated theory of women's travel. Travel becomes not just an occasion to confront social systems, but to record their effects on women's lives and to mark a course for women who might follow. Analyzing what I will call the Economies of Travel—women travel authors' evaluation of the risks and rewards of travel, the subsequent freedom and danger they experienced, and finally the strategies of writing and publication they employed—interrogates the meaning of women's mobility for travelers and for the larger culture. Getting themselves to St. Petersburg, the free soil of Toronto, the new world with its new democracy and possibilities for women, or even to the top of Pikes Peak involved confronting danger women travelers could imagine, such as exploding steamship engines and "colored cabins." However, there were also dangers they did not conceive of, such as sinkholes and beatings. While women tried to evaluate the virulence of these threats before they left, the realities of threats at home often trumped the imagined dangers of traveling. The threat of capture and enslavement sanctioned by the Fugitive Slave Law, or the impossibility of surviving on a schoolteacher's salary, or the insufferable control of a guardian rendered home an unsafe space for these traveling women, making the risk of travel an appealing option or a last desperate resort. Outcomes could be good or bad, but women's narratives of their journeys ultimately reveal the social power structures that made them consider leaving in the first place, and that continued to operate as they traveled.

Traveling Economies begins by analyzing how women travel authors' discussions of race, class, and gender as well as their representations of their own unconventional travels reveal both the inhospitable social and economic climate for white and black ragged-edge women in the northeastern United States and the potential liberation and danger associated with the alternative of travel. Chapter 1 compares the travel texts of Amy Morris Bradley and Nancy Prince to analyze how two very different women navigate early-nineteenth-century economies of travel. Broadening the initial focus on the material motivations and conditions of women's journeys, *Traveling Economies* then explores the communities and constituencies that women travelers claim to represent and advocate for through the pages of their travel texts, ultimately claiming authority to articulate a vision for a nation they can call home. Chapters 2 and 3 focus on Anne Royall and Mary Ann Shadd Cary, who both endeavor to redefine home, nation, and citizen in their journalistic travel texts. Traveling female social critics are often not welcome in the places they visit; chapter 4 of this study examines the hostile responses generated by one woman traveler, Frances Wright, and the way the society she challenged reinscribed her into existing ideologies of race, class, and gender. Finally, chapter 5 considers the contexts of publication for ragged-edge women's travel narratives, specifically Julia Archibald Holmes and the *Sibyl,* and investigates how travel texts and women travelers circulated in antebellum culture and provided an alternative model of femininity that reached a wide and diverse audience.

Before I embark, I want to use the remainder of this introduction to explain the theoretical and methodological underpinnings of *Traveling Economies*. Briefly surveying the field of scholarship on women's travel writing, I will summarize how it has been studied and how *Traveling Economies* expands and complicates current scholarly conversations on the subject. I have divided the following discussion into rubrics labeled Economies of Gender, Race, Class, Publication, and Nation, but the inadequacy of those categories is immediately apparent: Where do we put conversations about black women's insistence on their proper femininity? Does a discussion of acceptable jobs for white, middle-class women fit under "gender" or "class"? Does the chivalry that white women enjoy work to separate white and black women as effectively as segregated train cars? The overlap and overflow argues in support of one of the primary goals of this study, the production of nuanced and complicated comparisons of the writing and experience of white and black women. Careful comparisons do more than recover neglected women's texts and biographies; they offer more-complex pictures of a nineteenth-century world consumed with anxiety about race and gender. And while *Traveling Economies* explores the cultural contexts that resonate throughout women's texts, the analysis focuses on how those influences impact the literary strategies women travel writers employ. Thinking about how those texts reached their audience and who read women's travel writing connects the figure of the woman traveler back to cultural ideas about new roles for women.

Economies of Gender:
Negotiating Femininity at Home and Abroad

Once they opted to go, whether their traveling outfit consisted of petticoats or bloomers, the travelers in this study brought their female bodies and the additional baggage of gender expectations with them. Constructions of gender in the early nineteenth century or today cannot be packed in their own discrete suitcase, neatly separated from constructions of race and class and sexuality. Rather, gender, race, class, and sexuality interacted and intersected in complex ways, and required female travelers constantly to negotiate shifting social expectations, changing statuses of privilege and discrimination. The unseemliness of wandering the street begging for charity or loudly expressing political opinions could deny a traveler the benefits of white, middle-class femininity. While white women could lose status because they traveled and wrote, some black women travelers experienced greater freedom and mobility because their skin color automatically excluded them from the rigid expectations of feminine behavior and limitations to solely domestic space that often afflicted white women.

Feminist body theory, with its insights into the ways in which cultural norms of gender, race, and class are projected onto the bodies of women and minorities, offers a useful lens through which to read women travelers' literal and textual negotiations of social ideologies. Theorist Susan Bordo describes how a social gaze leveled at women's bodies effectively monitors, controls, and limits women within a patriarchal system, an experience that the authors in *Traveling Economies* repeatedly represent. Social scrutiny regulates women's behavior by identifying and isolating evidence of difference from the norm of the wealthy, white, masculine body. For both white and black women travelers of the nineteenth century, their bodies were not expected to be moving around, autonomous, partaking of the power and prerogatives of mobile, powerful, independent white male bodies. In a nineteenth-century world where urbanization and industrialization replaced neighborhood networks of kin and friendship, increasing reliance on visual cues of status fed the explosion of freak shows. Such visual entertainment, disability-studies theorist Rosemarie Garland Thomson argues, taught audiences about difference, race, gender, and national identity. I argue that the same gaze that eager audiences leveled at displays of bearded ladies and African "savages" was also directed at the unexpected figure of the female traveler, with her disruption of emerging constructions of femininity and domesticity. Women travelers negotiated the social scrutiny that registered what theorists Jennifer Terry and Jacqueline Urla term their "embodied deviance" and worked both to deflect negative responses to their unorthodox behavior and unexpected presence and to revise the cultural meanings written on their bodies.[4] At moments emphasizing their proper femininity, women travelers also performed "unfemininity," my term for their representation of their own strength, intelligence, and travel savvy that effectively revised cultural ideas about what women could do.[5]

The rhetorical violence generated by Frances Wright's travel and public participation (which I will discuss in chapter 4) illustrates the very gendered terms that often framed criticism of women travelers. Wright was infamous as an early feminist, abolitionist, public lecturer, and advocate of free love, as well as a published travel writer. Her public life and travels made her a target for critics who had less-progressive ideas about women's political and social participation or who opposed her programs of gender, labor, or abolition reform. Portrayed in a popular cartoon as a quacking, nagging goose or decried as the "Red Harlot of Infidelity," Wright's trespass into the public realm of politics, speaking, and writing violated many critics' ideas of appropriate femininity. Descriptions of Wright's "great masculine person" take the criticism a step further, literally inscribing her social deviance onto her body to emphasize the extent of her inappropriate behavior, ideas, and mobility.[6]

Scholars previously explored nineteenth-century gender roles using the framework of separate spheres (women relegated exclusively to domestic rather than public life); however, subsequent critical approaches demonstrate the limits and inadequacy of separate-spheres formulations of women's experience, instead arguing for more-complex understandings of the ways in which women participated in public life. Women travelers present a particularly salient counterexample confirming that the strict confinement of women only to the home may have never accurately represented the actual experience of women, instead functioning primarily, but nevertheless powerfully, on the level of rhetoric and ideology. The wide-ranging travels of the diverse group of women discussed here, as well as the crucial fact of their travel publications, suggest the range of models of mobility and autonomy available to women to counteract the ideological mandates of separate spheres. Thus, thinking about traveling women invites us to modify our understandings of women's experience in the last century to consider the constant and complex negotiations individual women entered into between gendered expectations and the lived reality of their participation in private and public.[7]

Even as these women's experiences of gender are complicated and multiple, their textual representations of gender add still another layer of complexity. As they do in their lives, women travel authors negotiate gender expectations constantly in their texts. On one page they may be critiquing women's subordination and relegation to domesticity in their narratives, only to assert their proper femininity and claim the privileges of appropriate womanhood (protection, authority, audience acceptance) on another page. Black women authors both analyze the devastating effects of stereotypes that dehumanize, degrade, segregate, and disempower black women and represent themselves as fitting within standards of white femininity to gain reader sympathy despite their "transgressive" behavior (be it traveling or writing). Gender becomes something women authors both negotiate and strategically deploy in service to their representation of themselves and their travels.

Economies of Race:
Black Women and the Risks of Travel

Race is also negotiated and represented in women travelers' lives and texts, regardless of whether the travelers are black or white. White women are often discussed only in terms of their race privilege, the benefits accorded to them on the basis of their white skin. However, whiteness could often bring with it restrictions in the form of heightened expectations of appropriately feminine behavior and reprisal for unladylike traveling and writing. Whiteness frequently constituted another set of baggage women travelers had to carry, a marker that was at once invisible (because all women were presumed to be white) and yet able to be used against women perceived to be breaking the rules. However, some women travelers embraced their whiteness, deploying it strategically in their texts, drawing on stereotypes of racial difference to build a case for their transgressive presence. At moments when their own traveling, writing, speaking, or public behavior was unfeminine, they sometimes represent racially different women in a negative way to divert attention from themselves or to justify their behavior. Interestingly, black women travel writers also use this strategy in their texts, deflecting readers' attention from their transgressive writing and traveling by contrasting their appropriately feminine behavior with the morally suspect behavior of the white women they include in their narratives.

Although black women travel writers sometimes employ racial difference in these ways, race also operates very differently in their texts. As mentioned earlier, traveling black women directly challenge nineteenth-century and even present-day definitions of black experience. The institution and ideologies of chattel slavery declaimed that black people were unfit for freedom, and even the nominally "free" North reacted with discrimination and racism when confronted with the reality of free blacks in competition for scarce jobs in their communities. Twenty-first-century scholarly attention focusing on nineteenth-century black travel narratives has so far helped to recover the broad range of free black experience and to insert the histories of free blacks into our syllabi, our textbooks, and our collective cultural memory. Scholars and historians have appropriately analyzed the central role that travel plays in slave narratives, primarily as the defining journey from slavery to freedom. However, critical analysis of narratives of elected travel by free blacks (whether or not that travel was in some sense forced by the hostile economic and social conditions of the free North) illuminates the continuum of black experiences in America—from the confinement of slavery to the mobility and autonomy of traveling black activists and writers. Moreover, as Farah Griffin and Cheryl Fish have demonstrated with their anthology, *A Stranger in the Village: Two Centuries of African-American Travel Writing*, black authors have consistently contributed to the American travel genre. The recent special issue of *BMa: The Sonia Sanchez Literary Review* titled "Black Travel Writing" claims to be "the first book-length collection of fully-fledged scholarly articles on black travel writing ever to have been published," and includes Jennifer Young's analysis of Phillis Wheatley's travel poems, Kenneth Speirs's discussion of black cowboy Nat Love, and Kimberly Blockett's reading of itinerant preacher Zilpha Elaw's "moving subjectivities," as well as my own analysis of Mary Ann Shadd Cary. Attention to black travel writing acknowledges black contributions to the travel genre and widens our understandings of larger black literary traditions, complicating critical approaches that exclusively figure slave narratives as the primary form of African-American nineteenth-century cultural expression.[8]

Even as black travel writing challenges our understandings of nineteenth-century black experience, free blackness presents a representational and experiential problem for black travelers and travel writers. Critic Cheryl Fish's formulation of the "unofficial criminal status of free blackness" illuminates the disapproval and out-of-placeness that free black women travelers experienced even before they started on their journeys. Although they were never enslaved, free black women were classified with slaves due to the evidence written on their skin and were subject not only to racism but also to the threat of being captured and sold into slavery.[9]

Nancy Prince's experience of returning by ship from Jamaica to New England (discussed in chapter 1) provides a compelling example of the extreme danger facing black women travelers. While her ship docks unexpectedly at New Orleans for repairs, Prince is threatened, taunted, and forced to remain on board because a crowd of white Southerners promises to take her to jail and then to the auction block should she step onto slave territory. Danger does not lie in wait only on the pier, however. Prince later discovers that her fellow passengers, in particular a white couple from Massachusetts, have conspired to capture and beat her. Although Prince uses a number of successful strategies in response to these incidents in both her life and her text, her story nonetheless demonstrates the extremity of the threat black women travelers face whether they travel through slave territory or through the "free North."[10]

Heightened scrutiny and threat could attend black women traveling; however, *Traveling Economies* interrogates black and white women's travel experiences by asking, could black women's lower status also have facilitated travel? Are there parallels between the scrutiny that "colored tourists" underwent and the social control experienced by white women who violated expectations of feminine behavior? How are formulations of women's autonomy and independence based solely on white women's experience complicated by studying black women travelers' negotiation of racism as well as sexism?

Economies of Class:
Women on the Ragged Edge of Middle-Class Status

While these women travelers found opportunities to negotiate the cultural terms of gender and race on their travels and in their texts, issues of class and economics proved less flexible. Travel and tourism in nineteenth-century America were primarily the province of wealthy white men and, by extension, their wives and daughters. By midcentury a new industry was developing to safely chaperone elite women and their marriageable daughters to exotic locations chosen to entertain and to provide the finishing touches to a girl's qualifications as a would-be society wife. Critic Mary Suzanne Schriber documents the astronomic rise in popularity of touring companies designed to allow young women to travel without compromising their marriageability (read their sexual purity). Schriber's excellent scholarship explains how the practice of travel and travel writing by elite white women reveals the ideological and economic institutions that dominated American travel in the second half of the century and the various ways that women interacted with those social constructs and with the travel genre to tell their stories.[11]

The women presented here, however, did not have consistent access to the social and economic resources or to the widespread convenience of the postbellum tourist industry available to many of the elite women Schriber analyzes. For women like Anne Royall, Amy Morris Bradley, or

Nancy Prince, class is a source of tension and anxiety on their journeys and in their travel writing. While elite women were able to cushion the dangers and inconveniences of travel through the privileges that accompanied higher social standing and wealth—private sleeping berths, porters, chaperones, and guides—women without privileges and resources struggled to support and protect themselves. By representing that struggle, the authors featured in *Traveling Economies* protest the economic and social injustice they experience. If the later institution of tourism is a celebration of middle-class values and wealth and, therefore, middle-class power, earlier narratives of women working and traveling threaten to spoil the party. However, tourism effectively contained the protest and resistance of nonelite women's travel writing by redefining travel as the exclusive province of the wealthy and deluging the reading public with boring, repetitive travel books describing essentially the same trip.[12] The cumulative effect buried the narratives and biographies of working traveling women under a mountain of tourist writing and erased earlier women travelers from the cultural imagination.

Class is of course not reducible to wealth. Rather, class status depends on a range of factors, including education, respectability, family standing, marriage, access to leisure, and also the particularities of specific communities and locations, local social mores, and urban versus rural locations, among other factors. Ragged-edge women travelers attempt to compensate for their lack of wealth by stressing their other middle-class virtues, be they education, relations to genteel if impoverished families, or appropriately feminine comportment (even though they are traveling, they dress in long skirts, are polite and unassuming, and/or do not converse with strange men). Even as white and black women travelers try to deploy class in these ways, their narratives reveal the precariousness of their social position, which is highlighted by frequent experiences of sudden downward social mobility or sustained battles for the mere rudiments of economic security. Discussions of strategies to get bargain rates at inns or on stagecoaches, of being relegated to the steerage section of ships, and of the favorable economic prospects for blacks emigrating to Canada all point to these travelers' negotiations of class and economics on their journeys and in their narratives. Further, ragged-edge authors emphasize the economic barriers operating against women's full social participation at home and propose travel, as opposed to the more-traditional economic solution of marriage, as a possible alternative.[13]

Women travel writers do not represent class and economics as factors encountered solely in their interactions with the marketplace and public sphere, however. As critic Amy Schrager Lang points out in her interrogation of the nineteenth-century syntax of class, the emblem of middle-class experience and values is the properly managed home, attended by the properly feminine woman. Lang further argues that in domestic fiction the middle-class home is a "place in which the effects of class are so thoroughly mediated by an alternative paradigm of gender, the object of which is to produce a condition of classlessness, as to disappear from view."[14] Women travel writers, rather than obscuring the class ramifications of middle-class domesticity, often represent their own economic dispossession in terms of lack of access to safe, secure domestic space. Contesting what I term "exclusive domesticity," women travel authors argue that their exclusion from hearths and homes of their own is not the result of their deficient femininity, but of the increasingly rigid requirements of middle-class status that single women cannot meet in the few occupations open to them, and that virtually require white skin and a wealthy husband. Thus, women's travel writing offers an important counter to representations found in domestic fiction, as their texts highlight the operations of class and economics in the production of "home" rather than obscuring class behind gender.

The private diary of Amy Morris Bradley (analyzed in chapter 1) vividly illustrates these economic and social pressures facing unmarried women, and the potential solution that travel offered to women struggling to support themselves. After working for ten years as a schoolteacher, Bradley has one dollar to her name, along with impaired and worsening health. In a last desperate effort to avoid relying on her friends and family for economic support, she decides to travel to Costa Rica as a governess for a wealthy family. Despite her dismal financial situation, Bradley considers herself a proper middle-class woman, and when her employers treat her "like a servant," she quits and strikes out on her own in Costa Rica without friends, family, or a working knowledge of Spanish. Bradley's story certainly highlights her bravery and initiative, but, more important, her diary showcases the impact of gender and class expectations on individual nonelite women. Bradley explores fully the limited job opportunities open to unmarried middle-class white women—from teaching to piecework sewing and serving as a housekeeper for her father and brother. None of these options, though, provides her with economic security; travel, on the other hand, provides possibilities beyond rigidly prescribed appropriate work for women.

However, as her story suggests, the possibilities accessed through travel also carry significant risks to her health, safety, and social status.[15]

Numerous scholars discussing women's travel texts argue that a gendered division of labor exists in travel writing and that analysis erases the particularity and specificity of texts like Bradley's. Contrasting women authors' concerns with fashion, domestic arrangements, social events, and other personal aspects of travel with the political focus of many travel texts written by wealthy white men, critic Marion Tinling, in her study *Women into the Unknown* (1989), characterizes women's travel texts as primarily interested in "the rhythm of daily life—birth, marriage, child-rearing, death, and household economy. These matters, so much a part of everywoman's life, are basic and universal, enduring through all political changes." Catherine Stevenson in *Victorian Women Travel Writers in Africa* (1982) and Jane Robinson in her survey, *Wayward Women: A Guide to Women Travelers* (1990), similarly argue that women travel writers eschew the political discourse found in men's texts in favor of focusing on the personal and relational aspects of travel. *Traveling Economies* instead examines how women contest and are excluded from the domestic prerogatives that Tinling claims for "everywoman."[16]

Ragged-edge women find themselves excluded from the comforts of both domesticity and tourism. Schriber's *Writing Home* focuses on the operations of capitalism in the development of sanctioned women's tourism; however, that sanction is reserved for women firmly ensconced in the privileges of the middle and upper classes. Mary Louise Pratt's *Imperial Eyes* examines how the economics and scientific discourse of colonialism authorize travel by white male explorers and select elite women, but her focus does not extend beyond women travelers who "occupy a world of servants and servitude where their class and race privilege [is] presupposed, and meals, baths, blankets, and lamps appear from nowhere." Karen Kilcup's recent study of the travel diary of Lorenza Stevens Berbineau, a servant woman traveling with her wealthy employers, addresses issues of class embedded in traveling. Kilcup's focus on a working-class travel author importantly broadens formulations of who was traveling and producing travel texts (whether public or private) in the nineteenth century. But instead of delineating class in terms of rich and poor, wealthy tourists and the servants who accompanied them, as Kilcup does, *Traveling Economies* focuses on an even wider range of class experiences, highlighting the complexity and multiplicity of class experiences had by American women and the variety of strategies they use to represent those experiences. Criticism of black travel writing by authors such as Cheryl Fish and Sandra Gunning offers a compelling analysis of the economic factors operating in some black women's decisions to travel and to produce travel texts; my analysis of the relationship between travel and the black middle class builds upon their discussions and offers a comparative view of nonelite white and black women's texts and lives.[17]

Economies of Publication:
Diverse Authors, Diverse Audiences

Just as the act of traveling could contest the maintenance of class hierarchies for ragged-edge travelers, so too could their travel publications make space in the literary marketplace and expand the travel genre beyond its traditional parameters. Travel writing in its most traditional form was a published book-length description of the journey of a white wealthy male either abroad to a foreign country (or series of foreign locations) or to the unexplored frontier of his own country. Eric J. Leed's *The Mind of the Traveller* (1991) highlights the continuing view of travel and travel writing as a masculine enterprise, which he contends constitutes "a method of extending the male persona in time and space, as conqueror, crusader, explorer, merchant-adventurer, naturalist, anthropologist." "Travel," he maintains, "has been the medium of traditional male immortalities." Male travelers, be they conquerors or merchant-adventurers, record "this feat in bricks, books, and stories," claiming not only the prerogative of travel but also the authority of travel writer, according to Leed.[18]

Not merely male-produced, but claiming a kind of masculine rationality and objectivity, travel writing often presents factual information on terrain, population, agriculture, natural resources, and government, as well as technological information on modes and means of transportation (evaluating, for instance, new rail routes or new steamship lines). However, this fact-oriented reporting is interspersed with personal reflection: meditations in response to scenery, anecdotes collected from fellow travelers, or reflections on interactions with local residents and their alien culture, food, or habits. The result is finally a mixture of genres—autobiography, journalism, short fiction, essay—that allows travel authors a tremendous amount of freedom in both subject matter and style. It is travel writing's quality of being a "literary carpetbag," Schriber claims, that facilitated the mass entry of women authors into the genre in the mid-nineteenth century as they marketed their feminine focus on the domestic aspects of other cultures (in contrast to the politically oriented content of men's narratives) that nonetheless could fit within the wide-ranging expectations audiences brought to travel writing.[19]

The women studied in *Traveling Economies* both fit within the parameters of travel writing—by describing their trips on steamships, stagecoaches, and even on foot; by including detailed information on geography, government, and natural resources and on the "feminine" concerns of fashion, culture, and society; and by claiming that their opinions on all these matters are worth reading—and exceed those expectations in form and content. While some of these authors did publish book-length (and even serial book-length) travel narratives, *Traveling Economies* argues that we gain a fuller understanding of ragged-edge women's participation in the genre when we recognize self-published emigrant's guides, serially published travel letters and travel editorials appearing in newspapers, and private travel writing in diaries and personal letters as contributions to the genre. Including a wide array of travel-writing formats shows the cultural obsession with travel writing and the ways women accessed the popular genre without necessarily having financial or cultural capital to enter the formal literary marketplace. The content of their narratives—stories of unconventional and unexpected women travelers—is not the only source of innovation in their texts. These women in fact changed the travel genre to make it fit their stories and their strategies of representing themselves.

For instance, Julia Archibald Holmes's account of her journey to the top of Pikes Peak in 1858 (discussed in chapter 5) demonstrates ragged-edge travel writers' generic innovations and the interesting and complex contexts of publication that were involved in linking women travel writers with their reading audiences. Acknowledged as the first woman to reach the summit of Pikes Peak, Holmes made her journey wearing bloomers as a protest of conventional women's fashions and wrote about her adventures for an early feminist dress-reform periodical, the *Sibyl*. Revising travel-genre formulations, Holmes uses travel writing to promote an explicitly feminist agenda and to represent herself as a dedicated Woman's Rights and dress-reform activist. She replaces the male adventurer with not just a female traveler but a radically feminist traveler who uses her text to promote her political agenda. While

Holmes includes descriptions of scenery, she also includes a detailed account of her plan for women's physical fitness that will make them better travelers and, ultimately, better citizens. She includes, instead of anecdotes shared by fellow travelers, an account of her spirited debate about the merits of dress reform with the only other woman member of the wagon train. The *Sibyl* published Holmes's travel writing as an important supporting plank of their feminist agenda linking dress reform to increased autonomy and mobility for women and eventually to the legislated guarantee of Woman's Rights and suffrage. Holmes and the *Sibyl* established a mutually beneficial relationship; Holmes gained an audience of like-minded women reformers through the circulation of the *Sibyl*, and the *Sibyl* gained an exemplar of what women who put the magazine's feminist theories into practice could accomplish. By looking at travel writing published in periodicals like the *Sibyl*, we can gain insight into the unexpectedly wide and varied readership for women's travel writing in the early nineteenth century, and thus into the spread of alternative models of femininity and travel writing circulating in the popular imagination.[20]

Economies of Nation

As the example of Holmes's feminist travel writing suggests, the women travel writers in this study were actively engaged with the hot-button issues and debates of antebellum America. Unlike later-century women travel writers who touch only tangentially on political issues, the women in this study foreground discussions of politics and social reform, showing how public debates intersect with the lives of women both individually and collectively. Critic Mary Mason, for example, argues that travel texts by black women "establish a radical and political tradition for Afro-American women's autobiography" that claims space "at the center of public discourse." Mason's groundbreaking work on black women's travel writing can also be extended to the nonelite white women included in this study to suggest black and white women's insistence on using travel and travel writing to gain authority in public and political policy making.[21] Ultimately, ragged-edge travelers practice an unconventional form of nation-building that insists on critiquing the practice of the nation and exposing its limitations and contradictions rather than uncritically advocating expansion.

As Amy Kaplan has demonstrated, conservative discourses of

domesticity and femininity promoted by women like Catherine Beecher and Sarah Josepha Hale, rather than following their own logic and remaining solidly within the domestic sphere, in fact engage, promote, and reflect the contradictions and conflicts of U.S. empire.[22] The ragged-edge travelers studied here advance nation-building (and even U.S. empire) in a very different way, eschewing the focus on the appropriately feminine domestic sphere and instead claiming authority (usually by virtue of their wide-ranging travels) to criticize the political, social, and economic policies and practices of the nation. Their support of the United States is contingent upon their ability and authority to make and publish their criticisms; only then do they endorse the spread of a reformed and truly democratic nation.

Anne Royall (discussed in chapter 2) uses the authority she gains as a traveler to compare and criticize developing social service programs in cities throughout the urban Northeast and Mid-Atlantic in the pages of her *Sketches of History, Life, and Manners in the United States* (1826).[23] Her tours evaluate the practice of government on the local level, which she takes as ultimately reflecting the goals, practices, and administration of the larger nation. Her investigation focuses on the central question, how will the nation treat its most vulnerable citizens—women and the poor? Since she moved from her impoverished childhood on the Alabama frontier to Eastern cities and eventually settled in Washington DC, Royall's travels reverse the course of manifest destiny, moving from the frontier back to the foundations of national government to call her readers and her nation to return to the principles on which the country was founded. She advocates a careful reassessment of the nation before it claims new territory and moves still further from its democratic goals. Opinions like Royall's were most often unwelcome; her subsequent trial as a common scold was a thinly veiled attempt to censor her, and the threatened punishment of the ducking stool is blatant evidence of the violent consequences ragged-edge women faced for their constructive criticism of the nation.

As they cross borders and expand current transnational theories that focus predominantly on male and immigrant populations, ragged-edge travelers invite us to think of the U.S. in global as well as national terms. Nancy Prince, who traveled to Russia in search of employment when racism kept her from practicing a skilled trade as a seamstress and on her return gave travel lectures and published a travel account, is a case in point. Ragged-edge travelers like Prince crossed borders in search of new global markets for their labor and then turned a double profit on that labor by producing texts of their travels and entering yet another marketplace (this time, literary). Foregrounding women's participation in the global marketplace and their attempted control of both their labor and their bodies follows Mae M. Ngai's recent call for a transnational approach to American Studies that emphasizes action, agency, and mobility in those previously perceived only as pawns of transnational capital: "A focus on the transnational, with its emphasis on multiple sites and exchange, can potentially transform the figure of the 'other' from a representational construct to a social actor." Ngai highlights both movement (between multiple locations or nations) and the notion of exchange, including "contact, translation, exchange, negotiation, conflict and other dynamics," as opposed to the one-way extraction of labor, as potential sources of agency.[24] *Traveling Economies* applies Ngai's insight to illuminate the possibilities travel offers for self-determination and self-assertion. Potential agency certainly lured ragged-edge women to travel; often the transnational practice of border crossing allowed them to operate as American citizens abroad in ways that they were not allowed at home.

These women authors did not just cross borders, but they pushed them outward, inviting us to reconsider the early-nineteenth-century United States in hemispheric terms. Mary Ann Shadd Cary advocates for Canadian emigration for African-Americans because of Canada's geographical proximity to the U.S. and because she views it as following the model of U.S. democracy. But whereas in Shadd Cary's view the U.S. denied promised civil rights, Canada instead delivered on those same rights. Prince explores the possibilities of black emigration to Jamaica, similarly searching for a New World home for African-Americans. Holmes with her Western journey pushes the United States across the continent and toward a vision of manifest destiny as the spread of radical feminism. Perhaps the most salient example, however, is Mary Seacole, a self-described Jamaican-born mulatta and author of *Wonderful Adventures of Mrs. Seacole in Many Lands* (1857), who serves as a transnational touchstone throughout *Traveling Economies* (analysis of her narrative appears in multiple chapters).[25] Her description of traveling in the anglophone Caribbean and in Central America highlights her position of compromised citizenship as a black colonial subject and her aggressive attempts to distance herself from the American slaves she encounters (her narrative illuminates the practice of fugitive slaves escaping south into Central America to enjoy some success and even high social standing). Ultimately traveling to the Crimean and becoming a nurse and "heroine" to the British troops there, Seacole uses her global mobility to assert agency and identity. For all these women, a broader conception of America as linked to its neighbors in the hemisphere puts the national issues they address in a larger frame and foregrounds their self-conscious entry onto a world stage.

A global frame for African-Americans involves addressing the continuing effects of diaspora, and the black ragged-edge travelers discussed in *Traveling Economies* negotiate black identity and black nationalism in their lives and texts. In their recent essay, "Unfinished Migrations: Reflections on the African Diaspora and the Making of the Modern World," Tiffany Ruby Patterson and Robin D. G. Kelley argue for an understanding of diaspora as "a process," the notion of process highlighting mobility and cultural construction: "As a process it is constantly being remade through movement, migration, and travel, as well as imagined through thought, cultural production, and political struggle" (20).[26] *Traveling Economies* argues that black travel writing provides exceptionally fertile ground for the study of diaspora as process by enacting mobility and imagining what that mobility means through the cultural production of texts.

Mary Ann Shadd Cary's black travel writing (discussed in chapter 3) can be read in terms of diaspora as process.[27] Traveling to Canada to evaluate the possibilities for black emigration in the wake of the Fugitive Slave Law, Shadd Cary uses her firsthand knowledge to claim authority in the high-stakes national and international debates on the future of African-Americans. Touring black Canadian settlements and evaluating them in the pages of the newspaper she founds and edits, the *Provincial Freeman,* Shadd Cary promotes emigration and discusses the specific threats and problems facing existing Canadian black communities. Her travel writing illustrates the complicated process of finding a national home for African-Americans and insists on building communities despite the risks. The result is not only a new practice of travel writing but also a new version of black nationalism focused on the creation and maintenance of local black communities.

Traveling Economies focuses on the period 1820–1860, not because this marks the start of American women's travel writing (important predecessors such as Sarah Kemble Knight and Elizabeth Ashbridge were writing significantly earlier), but because this era marks the entrance of women into major public reform movements, best-selling literary success, and significant participation in travel and tourism. The 1820s and 1830s produced women activists and public speakers such as the

Grimke sisters, Maria Stewart, and Frances Wright (discussed in chapter 4), while the 1840s saw the marked rise in women's abolition and feminist activism. The passage of the Fugitive Slave Law in 1850 legislatively curtailed the mobility of free blacks, even while the decade began the rise of white, middle-class women's unprecedented access to and participation in tourism. The Civil War provides a logical endpoint to the investigation of *Traveling Economies*, as it briefly slowed both the practice of women's travel and the production of travel texts, which rebounded and proliferated in the postbellum era.

Making sense of the upheaval of industrialization, urbanization, Woman's Rights, and abolition, women's early-nineteenth-century travel writing provided readers with a means to understand their rapidly changing world. As these women's bodies and their texts circulated through antebellum culture, they performed what critic Paul Lauter terms "cultural work," a process through which texts "construct the frameworks, fashion the metaphors, create the very language by which people comprehend their experiences and think about their world."[28] The female traveler and her travel text constituted just such frameworks and metaphors, which made and challenged the epistemologies of early-nineteenth-century America. The alternative visions of gender, race, and class found in these women's narratives suggest the wide scope of and diverse participation in public and private debates about national identity and citizenship. The figure of the female traveler, emerging as she does so early in the century, suggests a competing vision of women's possibilities beyond hearth and home significantly predating the formal Woman's Rights movement. Whether challenging or reinforcing the status quo of middle-class wealth and power, the proliferation and popularity of women's travel texts invite us to rethink twenty-first-century formulations of how nineteenth-century Americans thought about their world.[29]

· *One* ·

Ragged-Edge Travelers
Amy Morris Bradley and Nancy Prince
Evaluate the Economies of Travel

The first [motive], my dependence upon my friends. For with the health that
had been mine for more than two years before I left, it was impossible for me
to labor enough to earn my board, and it was very painful to me to see those
around me working without being able to render them any assistance. This
was the first and principal reason of my leaving.
  —Amy Morris Bradley journal entry, 2 January 1856[1]

After seven years of anxiety and toil, I made up my mind to leave my country.
  —Nancy Prince, *A Narrative of the Life and Travels of Mrs. Nancy Prince*,
    Written by Herself, Second Edition, 1853[2]

If one is possessed of sufficient courage to buy a ticket, hire a porter or cab-
man or pay a hotel bill, one has enough to last one around the world.
  —Lilian Leland, *Traveling Alone: A Woman's Journey Around the World*, 1890[3]

       *T*he unlikely heroines of their own travel narratives, Amy
Morris Bradley and Nancy Prince recount long and difficult
journeys across the Atlantic and through the Caribbean, riding mules
and falling into sinkholes, suffering seasickness and evading kidnap-
pers. Bradley travels from Maine to San Juan, Costa Rica, in 1853,
remaining in the city for four years before returning to the States. Her
unpublished travel diary records the steamship journey that leaves her
prostrate with seasickness, her dizzying ride on mule back along the
treacherous cliffs of the overland route across the Isthmus of Panama,
and her ingenuity in starting a life and business after the governess
position she has come for leaves her dissatisfied and without the money
to return home. Prince's *Narrative of the Life of Mrs. Nancy Prince*, first
published in 1850, documents the unprecedented extensive travel of
a free black woman, chronicling her trip from New England to St.
Petersburg, Russia, in 1824, her nine-year residence as the new wife of

a member of the Russian court, her struggles after her husband's death and return to the United States, and her subsequent missionary travels to newly emancipated Jamaica in the 1840s.

Lilian Leland's world travels (1884–86) begin sixty years after Prince embarks for St. Petersburg and demonstrate the seismic shift in women's access to and participation in travel that occurs over the course of the century. Comparing Leland's journey and writing with Bradley's and Prince's dramatizes the difference between travel undertaken from economic or social necessity and the privileged experience of tourism, as well as between travel writing that protests social and economic injustice and travelogues that catalog the benefits of wealth. The scope of Leland's travels are impressive, as the preface to her travel text summarizes, "a journey which carried her around the world, to many lands and on many seas, from Cape Horn to the North Cape and from the Rocky Mountains to the Himalayas; but little less than sixty thousand miles in distance and covering a period of about two years" (vii). However, as the epigraph above suggests, travel, even an adventurous journey undertaken by a young woman "without escort or protection" (vii), was a commodity purchased with middle-class wealth rather than with "courage."

Women gained more and more access to tourism as technological advances in travel—particularly steamships, railroads, and highways—became available early in the 1820s and developed in speed, luxury, and safety as the century progressed. Leland goes so far as to lament the increased ease and convenience of travel, longing instead for discomfort, adventure, and camel rides:

> To-day we traverse a continent in a few days, sitting comfortably in luxuriously fitted cars, where she [Ida Pfeiffer, Leland's traveling female forebear and role model] spent tedious weeks plodding wearisomely across burning plains and over snowy ranges. Drawn by the deliberate water buffalo, borne by the opinionated donkey, the positive mule, the stately camel, or in palanquin by human hands, she traversed deserts and climbed mountains. The tent and the rude hut of the native sheltered her more often than the hotel. Instead of the record breaking steamer, a floating palace in appointments and size, pursuing a given course in a given time, with little or no reference to wind and wave, she crossed the oceans in sailing vessels, tossed and buffeted by the furious gales of Cape Horn and delayed by the burning calms of the equatorial seas.

America leads the world in the speed, comfort and luxury of her railroad service, and there is now an unbroken connection of comfortable steamer and comfortable car right around the globe, with European or American hotels at every junction. (358)

Here we see that the romance of saddle sores, seasickness, and unforeseen yet inevitable and interminable delays has been replaced by speed, comfort, and ease, all available for the price of a ticket, porter, and hotel room.[4]

Regretting that "civilization is spreading over every part of the world," and that "'hairbreadth 'scapes' and dangerous adventures with cannibal and savage" (357) are so much harder to come by, Leland hints at the systems designed to control and commodify women's travel, which are already firmly in place by the time she embarks. Chaperoned, packaged tours such as those provided by Thomas Cook flourished by the mid-1860s, and increasingly catered to women clients, as critic James Buzard documents in his study, *Off the Beaten Track.* Focusing on the popularity of tourism among American women during the second half of the nineteenth century, critic Mary Suzanne Schriber describes the extent of the commercialization of women's travel:

Burgeoning numbers of female travelers, consuming the paraphernalia of travel as well as the thing itself, created healthy markets beyond those of transportation, touring companies, and accommodations. Artifacts such as steamer trunks, clothing, farewell gifts, stationery, travel books, and travel guides were profitable . . . Once women traveled in numbers sufficient to constitute a substantial market, female-specific subindustries flourished. (24–25)

Women tourists traveled to solidify their social position—showing off wealth by consuming chaperoned tours, the latest guidebooks, matching luggage and a travel wardrobe to fill it; obtaining the polish of travel to complete their education as proper young ladies and future wives; and escaping the monotony of their domestic routine to return refreshed and convinced of the superiority of home (in both the local and national senses).[5] In fact, tourism worked so well to reinforce the privileges and prerogatives of the comfortable middle class that by the end of the century the figure of the touring woman became a stock character and laughable symbol of middle-class pretension, provincialism, and consumerism. Thus, although it would seem that travel would have disrupted women's confinement to hearth and home, tourism instead successfully co-opted women's travel to reinforce gender roles and the middle-class power structures that gender roles supported.[6]

Hordes of female tourists did not spring up overnight, but were preceded by travelers like Bradley and Prince who journeyed in search of employment. Insisting on their respectability and femininity despite the fact that they leave the female sphere of home, these women travelers and their texts test the boundaries of gender roles and present their readers with the possibility of mobile, autonomous, and yet appropriately feminine women. Other than the fact that they traveled, Prince and Bradley would seem to have little in common in their narratives—one a schoolteacher in rural Maine, the other a free black woman in Boston; one a private diary, the other a fairly successful book reprinted in three editions. Comparing the two makes sense, however, when we put them in the context of nineteenth-century American women's travel. An analysis of Prince and Bradley should focus on travel between the extremes of wealthy tourism and forced relocation in order to examine an often-overlooked mode of travel—the elected journeys of single women who travel for work. "Ragged-edge travel" is my designation for these work-motivated trips that capitalized on new, inexpensive mass transit and that risked inconvenience or even danger without the benefits of chaperones, first-class accommodations, or guided tours. In contrast to wealthy women tourists, Bradley and Prince did not have middle-class domesticity as their journeys' point of departure and ultimate destination. Both women traveled in search of economic and social opportunities, using travel to locate alternative markets for the labor and talent that were devalued at home, having found comfort and security the exclusive province of wealthier Americans. Travel for both women represents risk and possibility, and ultimately a loud protest against their uncertain status on the ragged edges of middle-class prosperity.

Analyzing what I term the "Economies of Travel" for all three women (Leland serves as an illustrative tourist counterpart to Prince and Bradley's ragged-edge travel)—their own evaluation of the risks and rewards of travel, the subsequent freedom and danger they experience, and finally the strategies of writing and publication they employ—highlights the widely varying material conditions of ragged-edge and tourist travel, as well as the generic innovations ragged-edge travelers make in standard travel-writing formats to tell their stories. Extended discussions of their economic motivations for traveling, passages in which they become the observed as well as traveling observer, and their use of travel publications to turn a double profit on their transnational traveling labor or to leave a roadmap for future ragged-edge travelers constitute significant departures from traditional travel writing and invite us to reassess the changing meaning of women's mobility across the nineteenth century.[7]

"How I Came to Go"

Under the heading "How I Came to Go," Leland presents her decision to travel as one that is made for her, when the unnamed "head of [her] house" offers to buy her a ticket on the steamer *Santa Rosa* headed to San Francisco via Cape Horn (1). Despite her "horror" of the "fatigue and deprivations of travel—the attention to baggage, tickets, changes, et cetera, required in traveling alone," Leland stubbornly commits herself to the journey, admitting that she has talked of traveling for years without really intending to go (1). Leland's denial of responsibility in her own traveling links her more closely with working-class women travelers than with Bradley and Prince. For instance, Lorenza Stevens Berbineau's diary (recently edited by Karen Kilcup) of her 1851 trip to Europe as a servant to a wealthy Boston family begins aboard the ship with no prior discussion of whether or why to go, emphasizing her lack of power over her mobility.[8] While Berbineau's trip is certainly not the fulfillment of an expressed (if not truly desired) whim, as is the case with Leland, nonetheless others, in this case her employers, control the opportunity and means of travel.

In contrast, the decision to travel is a much more complicated business for Bradley and Prince, since their position between the wealth of Leland and the servitude of Berbineau presents special economic and social obstacles. In their discussions of the risks and rewards of traveling and the experiences that encourage or force them to leave, the question of whether to travel centers on their experiences of home. Nineteenth-century notions of femininity focus on middle-class white women happily and properly managing homes that are comfortable havens from the public world of men, markets, politics, and travel. Appropriately feminine women occupy appropriate domestic space, and although critics including Amy Kaplan, Linda Kerber, and Gillian

Brown have demonstrated the limits and inadequacy of separate-spheres formulations of women's experience, instead arguing for more-complex understandings of the ways in which women participated in public life, the doctrine of separate spheres nevertheless operated powerfully on ideological, if not always practical, levels.[9] These formulations of femininity and domesticity were predicated on class privilege in ways that have not been fully interrogated; the texts of Bradley and Prince offer data on how less-privileged women interacted with their society's definitions of womanhood. Ragged-edge women travelers effectively uncouple domesticity and femininity and lay bare the economic and class underpinnings of hearth and home. Rather than merely recording their longing for access to domesticity, they interrogate domesticity and question the terms on which they can and cannot gain access to "homes in the better sense," critic Amy Lang's term for the ideal middle-class domestic setting.[10] In other words, Bradley and Prince very clearly articulate the gap between the performance of appropriate femininity that is supposed to result in a safe and comfortable domestic space and the rigid class boundaries based on wealth and power that exclude many women not merely from the luxuries of the middle-class home, but from its basic economic security as well. Ragged-edge travelers' open discussions of finances and their use of travel as a means to secure employment in order to eventually purchase domestic comfort challenge what I term "exclusive domesticity" and highlight the ways in which domesticity and travel are, rather than diametrically opposed, interdependent and in constant tension for both women.

In the texts of both Bradley and Prince lengthy discussions of their economic and social struggles in the northeastern United States preface descriptions of their adventures abroad. Despite evidence of their respectability, education, and industriousness, both Bradley (by dint of her genteel poverty) and Prince (by dint of being a free black woman in the racist Northeast) are effectively excluded from the privileges and prerogatives of domesticity. For the unmarried Bradley, domesticity does not offer security, but instead results in frustration with her limited role and persistent financial insolvency. As a black woman, Prince can gain access to domesticity only as a servant, a position of more-severe insecurity that depends on the goodwill of her employers and the performance of backbreaking labor. Their narratives emphasize the crucial distinction between places where you live and the middle-class ideal of home. Bradley's use of a birdcage image to represent her life before traveling and Prince's description of her life as a servant and struggling seamstress tell us why they decide travel is worth the risk.

Amy Morris Bradley traveled from East Vasselboro, Maine, to San Juan, Costa Rica, in 1852 and recorded in her private diary and letter book (her diary contains copies of letters she sent and received) the reasons she decided to travel and the events of what becomes a four-year residence in Costa Rica. The unmarried, educated daughter of a respectable family, Bradley struggled to support herself—eventually trying virtually all of the occupations open to middle-class women: teaching, sewing, and housekeeping for her father and brother. Although Bradley worked, she would not have identified herself as belonging to the working class; if she had been married, her economic picture would likely have been rosier (although her family's finances suggest the limits of that prospect). Her laments about suitable employment suggest the "problem" that single women posed to society's ideas about women as exclusively wives and mothers. In the epigraph at the start of this chapter, Bradley cites her "dependence" upon her friends as the primary motive for traveling. Here she recasts the gendered notion of dependence in economic terms; she is not a clinging vine of appropriately feminine frailty, but a would-be worker anxious "to labor enough to earn [her] board," who is financially rather than emotionally "dependent." Her emphasis on her economic motivations and her representation of herself as both feminine and poor use the travel genre to redraw the boundaries of femininity and domesticity.

Struggling with her own desire for autonomy and with the gendered expectations of middle-class women's domesticity and submissiveness, Bradley expresses her frustration through her birdcage image: "The inward stirring, the aimless restlessness of spirit . . . O this spirit longs to be free! But with each effort like a caged bird its means are lessened by the tenement in which it is enclosed."[11] Bradley reverses common thinking on domesticity with this image—home is not a safe haven, but a miserable cage.

However, she is not only protesting middle-class white women's limited access to the public world of work, politics, and travel. Bradley underscores the class dimensions of domesticity with her birdcage image. Domesticity is not, for her, a gilded cage of comfort and ease, albeit with necessarily curtailed freedoms. Instead, Bradley's use of the word "tenement" signals her distance from the ideal of "home in the better sense." Here she borrows from midcentury formulations in which, according to Lang, "'home' was the antithesis of the over-crowded, disorderly, inharmonious tenement inhabited by the unruly poor." Bradley's version of domesticity is as far from the middle-class ideal as a tenement is from a proper home. For women on the ragged edges of middle-class privilege, the performance of domesticity and femininity does not guarantee comfort or security. Stripped of the gilding of at least a certain level of wealth, femininity and domesticity offer only confinement and dependence without the rewards of stability and security. Travel, which would seem to jeopardize any ties to home and appropriate femininity, thus becomes a viable option for Bradley.[12]

What circumstances have brought Bradley to this point? As a teacher for nearly a decade, she is not able to secure financial independence, lamenting her situation: "I little thought when I commenced teaching ten years ago at this time, I should be found with a pocket empty as it then was. O No! But those were my days of romance. The later years have been of stern reality changing my ideas of life almost entirely." Again, we have the marked discrepancy between the domestic ideal and the "stern reality"—this time framed in sentimental terms. The narrative of her life would be not a romance but a gritty story of poverty and disappointment. Her "ideas of life" come from sentimental fiction and the larger culture's celebration of domesticity. In rejecting the genre, she protests its message. Reality for Bradley is stern indeed, as shown by the sad state of her savings: "I send you the two dollars you so much desire, which is all the money I have, (excepting a gold dollar my cousin gave me a year last Christmas), else I would send you more."[13] She eventually trades sentiment for the travel genre, risking the unsatisfying life she knows for the promise and possibility of travel.

The paltry return on her ten years of teaching encouraged Bradley, who was suffering from failing health, to retreat to the domestic sphere of her family, where she served as housekeeper for her father and brother before she finally decided to travel. Her description of her brief interlude as a housekeeper highlights the inhospitable nature of "home." Announcing her new occupation, Bradley writes: "I am keeping house for my eldest brother, Asa. I have four in my family—My Father, Brother, apprentice boy, and myself. I do all the work myself except the washing and ironing." She emphasizes the labor involved in housekeeping because she does not have the servants that wealthier women would have, except for the most arduous tasks, such as laundry. Bradley is initially enthusiastic about her housekeeping efforts, declaring to Jones, "I wish you could see how nice I live—what a fine housekeeper I make!" In fact, Bradley's stint as the mistress of her brother's house ends in a few months. By November Bradley writes, "I am not keeping house. Are you surprised? You would not be, if you knew how my brother treated me!!" Not a picture of domestic bliss, or even of a gilded cage, Bradley's emphatic rejection of housekeeping hints at patriarchal control and domination. Thus, even in the supposedly female-centered and controlled space of the home, Bradley does not have the autonomy that she craves, and the supposed refuge of hearth and home turns out to be a fraught and conflicted place.[14]

Bradley responds to her unhappy domestic situation by turning her thoughts to travel. In a letter to a friend who has recently relocated to San Francisco, Bradley writes at length about planning her own California emigration. Her inquiry is clearly preliminary; she is not even familiar with the route or the conveyances she will use on the journey to California. Rather than an actual journey, the trip to California remains in the realm of fantasy, a dreamed-of escape from her domestic duties and her family. Stern financial reality, it appears, intrudes again into Bradley's fantasy of escape—a third-class ticket to California cost $185 in 1850.[15]

Bradley frames her fantasy in concrete economic terms, even though she cannot afford to actually go. She speculates that in California social and economic possibilities will be open to women of talent and industry:

> I can teach, make dresses, & shirts, etc. Am a pattern of a housekeeper. If ladies were allowed—could make a tolerable clerk or bookkeeper—or I might keep a boarding house . . . I can stitch boots—as for shoeing horses, I can not do that—but might possibly learn. What wages could such a prodigy demand, think you?[16]

Among her marketable abilities Bradley lists both traditionally feminine skills (teaching, dressmaking, housekeeping) and traditionally masculine ones (clerking, bookkeeping, shoeing horses). Most of the skills she lists are ones that she already possesses, but that at home in Maine are currently undervalued or limited only to men.

Portraying herself as a laboring "prodigy," Bradley draws attention to the labor and skill that are usually masked by domesticity and femininity. Writing to a male friend, William Fuller, who has spent time in California, Bradley is at pains to show the marketable value of her feminine work experience, stressing on her pseudorésumé the invisible labor of housekeeping and the underpaid, underrecognized feminine field of teaching. The frontier of California, where a scarcity of women translates into a better market for traditional women's work and more possibilities for entering traditionally masculine fields, revalues the work ragged-edge women do. Travel, then, can translate into "wages," as Bradley imagines the benefits of locating new markets for her labor. Free black women more often employed geographic mobility in their searches for employment (as we will see with Prince); however, Bradley's diary invites us to consider whether other ragged-edge (but nonetheless middle-class) white women considered travel a viable alternative or actually undertook travel for the purposes of securing better-paying work. Bradley's speculation sets the stage for her actual journey to Costa Rica, a trip on which she embarked with only two weeks' notice because she has already fantasized about the economic and social autonomy travel might offer.

Travel shifts from fantasy to reality when Bradley is offered a job as a governess for a wealthy Costa Rican family, the Medinas. Bradley's friend and fellow teacher, Stacy Baxter, has been boarding the Medina boys as his students and suggests Bradley for the position. The difficulties of funding travel are overcome by the promise of Mr. Medina, who "will pay all [Bradley's] expenses there and back again . . . and pay [her] ten dollars a month and perhaps more." With her teaching experience, Bradley is more than qualified for the position, and the job falls within the narrow range of acceptable occupations for unmarried middle-class women. Governesses usually occupied a social level above household domestic servants, and teaching required a level of education not needed for working-class employees such as servants or factory workers. There was certainly the contradiction that "proper" middle-class women were not supposed to work or travel; Bradley's position on the margins of the more-secure middle class allows her some leeway in gendered expectations about work. In fact, Bradley's status as an unmarried, impoverished, but nonetheless middle-class woman suited her well for the job. Mr. Medina "wants to take a lady with him," and Bradley had the necessary gentility as well as the financial motivation to leave home in search of work. Her skilled labor and class position had a much higher value when transported across national borders to Costa Rica. Thus, Bradley found new markets and endeavors to capitalize on herself as a global commodity.[17]

The opportunity to support herself respectably and see the world convinces Bradley to set sail for Central America from New York on 17

November 1853. Baxter notes that the trip "will require some go ahead on [Bradley's] part" as it is a "formidable undertaking," but he credits her with the courage to succeed: "Yours is a brave heart Amy—Listen to its teachings and what it saith *do*—and do quickly." Despite Baxter's assurances ("I have no doubt but Mr. Medina will do well by you"), the prospect of journeying so far with a strange man over dangerous oceans and the Isthmus of Central America does indeed prove to be "formidable."[18] But in Bradley's calculation of the economies of travel, the risks are far outweighed by the rewards travel promises.

By fully representing how her poverty and alienation from domesticity fuel her decision to travel, Bradley exceeds the parameters of the travel genre by focusing as much attention on why she goes as on what happens when she gets to her destination. The result is a cogent critique of the exclusive nature of domesticity and, by extension, the workings of class and gender in American society. Nancy Prince's similar focus on her motivation for traveling voices even sharper criticism of the racism and sexism that plagued the urban centers of the "free" North.

Prince's experience as a free black woman in New England is even more alienated from the privilege and comfort of "home in the better sense" than Bradley's. Because Prince is a prominent member of the black middle class by the time she writes her narrative—she is an uplift worker and abolitionist who moves in the circles of Boston's well-known black and white abolitionists—her simultaneous poverty underlines the second-class status of free blacks and of Prince herself. Domesticity required the invisible and underpaid labor of women like Prince. Her black skin, then, is read not only as a sign of racial difference (and inferiority) but also as a sign of servility. Her access to domestic space was limited to work as a servant. Travel represents risk and possibility for Prince, as demonstrated by stories she includes in her narrative's opening pages of her family's escapes from both slavery and indentured servitude. Although she starts with what is in effect a mini–slave narrative, Prince is at pains, as critic Cheryl Fish argues, to "shift the focus from forced to chosen mobility," from the trauma of the middle passage to the potential liberation of her own chosen journeys. Including descriptions of her brother's work as a merchant seaman as well as her own transatlantic journey, Prince further highlights elective and working travel and presents "the circulation of ideas and activists as well as the movement of key cultural and political artifacts" such as tracts and books that critic Paul Gilroy identifies as central to the "Black Atlantic," his term for the transnational cultural exchange that results from the movement of black people around the globe, but particularly across the Atlantic, during and after the slave trade. As significant as her transatlantic mobility is to an understanding of the Black Atlantic, Prince spends a considerable portion of her narrative documenting how her decision to go resulted from her experience of racism and discrimination at home. Her journeys abroad, first to St. Petersburg, Russia, and then two times to post-Emancipation Jamaica, are made in search of the safe domestic space that she cannot find in the racist northeastern United States.[19]

Although Prince's epigraph at the start of this chapter declares that she leaves the United States after seven years of unsuccessful "toil," she has in fact been struggling from the age of eight to support herself and her family, making the true time of "toil" seventeen years by the time she embarks at age twenty-five. Thirteen pages of Prince's eighty-nine-page narrative describe her unceasing efforts to hold her family together after her mother is widowed twice, remarries a useless man, and has eight children. Prince represents her only legitimate access to middle-class domesticity—as an overworked servant—early in her narrative, when she describes the grueling and unending labor expected of household servants:

> There were seven in the family, one sick with a fever, and another in a consumption; and of course, the work must have been very severe, especially the washings. Sabbath evening I had to prepare for the wash; soap the clothes and put them into the steamer, set the kettle of water to boiling, and then close in the steam, and let the pipe from the boiler into the steam box that held the clothes. At two o'clock, on the morning of Monday, the bell was rung for me to get up; but, that was not all, they said I was too slow, and the washing was not done well; I had to leave the tub to tend the door and wait on the family, and was not spoken kind to, at that. (11)

The physical demands of wash day, coupled with duties as a housemaid and nursemaid, do not even allow time for sleep. Despite Prince's hard work, she is roundly abused by the family, a sign of her inferior status and her alienation from the comforts and privileges of "home in the better sense" even while she lives there. Her account emphasizes the unrelenting labor involved in maintaining domesticity, and highlights the dependence of domesticity on the low-paid labor of servants like

Prince. Besides working as a servant herself, Prince also finds employment for her numerous brothers and sisters. Fish labels Prince's caretaking role as an alternative form of the domestic and maternal, which she calls "othermothering," but farming her brothers and sisters out as servants to experience the kind of abuse and overwork that she does in the scene above instead confirms her exclusion from domesticity.[20]

Her efforts to realize the "promise of comfort and respectability" continue to be made in vain while she remains in the United States (18). One of several lengthy passages describing her efforts captures Prince's frustration and desperation:

> When winter came, poor mother's health was declining. Little Samuel could do but little; my father-in-law [actually Prince's stepfather] was very cross, his disappointment was very great, for he expected to be supported by my brother George and myself. I could not see my mother suffer, therefore I left my place and went to Salem to watch over her and Samuel, and lived in the Rev. Dr. Bolle's family. In the Spring, I returned to Boston, and took my brother Samuel with me; soon after, my sister Lucy left her place and went to her mother, but was not permitted to stay; my mother wrote to me, requesting me to take care of her. I then determined, in my mind, to bring her to Boston, and if possible, procure a place for her; I then had Samuel and John on my hands; Lucy was not nine, and very small of her age, I could not easily get her a place, but fortunately obtained board for her and Samuel for one dollar a week. My brother John, whom I had boarded, at last got a place where he had wages. Soon the Lord opened the way for little Samuel; Dr. Phelps took him to bring up: so that I was left with one only to sustain; soon my hopes were blasted. John left his place, and was several months on my hands again; finally, he made up his mind to go to sea; I was so thankful that he had concluded to do something, that I took two months' wages in advance to fit him out for Liverpool, in five months he returned without a single thing but the clothes he had on. (18–19)

Swinging from hope to despair with each sentence, Prince conveys the extremity of her family's financial insecurity; each family member must work, whether or not they are small children or teenagers. Without a family home, the children must pay to board, be sent into service, or be raised by other families. The risks to the children's safety and morality are vividly illustrated in Prince's earlier account of a sister being "deluded away" into a brothel (12–13). Unlike in Bradley's diary, travel is not here presented as a longed-for escape. Instead, for Prince the effort to realize the "promise of comfort and respectability" is all consuming. Prince does not have time to fantasize about travel and instead demonstrates her appropriately feminine concern for her family's lack of "home in the better sense," which she blames not on racial inferiority but on a marketplace that devalues black labor and limits free blacks to menial service jobs. Her attempts to break this cycle by apprenticing in trade fail, and it is only when this last recourse is exhausted that she abruptly announces her decision "to leave my country" (20). She too will take her undervalued labor to new markets through travel, crossing borders and oceans in search of recognition and payment for her skill and hard work.

Prince does finally experience domestic and financial security in Russia, which I will discuss in the following pages; however, her eventual return to Boston is a return to the same discomfort and insecurity she left nine years before. Her unexpected tumble down a coal chute in the home of a sympathetic white abolitionist underscores the exclusive nature of domesticity for free black women. Offered as an explanation of her subsequent ill health, which inspires and necessitates her turn to writing for a means of financial support, the fall is described by Prince in this fashion:

> I was invited to Mrs. Ingraham's . . . to spend a week. There I met with much encouragement to labor in the cause . . . Saturday evening I went to the bath room, where I left my neck ribbon: returning after it, I had the misfortune to fall through an open trap door, down fifteen feet, on hard coal. I had no light with me. I dislocated my left shoulder, and was generally very much bruised; my screams brought the girl to my assistance. (55–56)

Prince's fall emphasizes her trespass into middle-class domestic space—a place of comfort and security reserved for whites only. Even in the sympathetic proabolition space of Mrs. Ingraham's "home in the better sense," surprising dangers exist for Prince. Her narrative demonstrates that black women are excluded from domesticity not because they are not feminine but because they are not white. In fact, she repeatedly insists on her proper femininity, a strategy Frances Smith

Foster notes in her analysis of other passages in Prince's narrative.[21] In this scene, the neck ribbon reminds her readers of her careful attention to her feminine appearance, a signal of her appropriate femininity. We see this care repeated in other women's travel writing—emphasizing appropriate femininity through dress to counteract their transgressive mobility. For a black woman such as Prince, however, the performance of femininity is not sufficient to guarantee the protections and comforts of middle-class womanhood, and domestic space remains dangerous and fraught.

She eventually returns to the free black community in Boston with the hope of finding a home in the city and the black community. Instead, class and race work to deny her security even within the marginalized free black community:

> The first twenty months after my arrival in the city, notwithstanding my often infirmities, I labored with much success, until I hired with and from those with whom I mostly sympathized, and shared in common the disadvantages and stigma that is heaped upon us, in this our professed Christian land. But my lot was like the man that went down from Jerusalem, and fell among thieves, which stripped him of his raiment, and wounding him, departed, leaving him half dead. What I did not lose, when cast away, has been taken from my room where I hired. Three times I had been broken up in business, embarrassed and obliged to move, when not able to wait on myself. (84–85)

When she throws her lot in with her fellow blacks, she not only "share[s] in common [their] disadvantages and stigma[ta]," but also experiences betrayal and even theft of her belongings. Economic strife breaks apart the black community as its members turn on each other. There is no hope for domestic space, even if that space is communal. The forces of economics intrude on race solidarity and encourage neighbors to exploit each other.

Given her representations of her continually frustrated attempts to support herself and her family, readers are often astounded by Prince's travel to such a distant and unexpected location—St. Petersburg, Russia. For the most part, we expect accounts of black life in the nineteenth century to focus on slavery, with travel and mobility associated only with escaping fugitive slaves. Prince's experiences of racism and poverty illustrate her own time's difficulty with the concept of free blacks, even in the proabolition hotbed of Massachusetts. Prince's marriage to Nero Prince makes her unlikely travel to Russia possible. Blacks were introduced into the Russian court by Peter the Great as a source of novelty and exoticism. Nero's position as a porter in the emperor's court follows this tradition.[22] Prince's narrative offers important insight into the experiences of blacks in Russia (an admittedly very small group) in the early 1800s, and scholars of Russian history use her text as one of only a few primary sources on the subject. As will be discussed later in this chapter, Prince was able to capitalize on her Russian travels by offering public lectures.

But before Prince could become an authority on blacks living in the Russian court, she needed to get there, and her marriage provided a relief from her crushing economic hardships and a ticket to St. Petersburg. Interestingly, in her narrative Prince frames the marriage without romantic conventions, as if it is primarily a means to the end of travel:

> And after seven years of anxiety and toil, I made up my mind to leave my country. September 1st, 1823, Mr. Prince arrived from Russia. February 15th, 1824, we were married. April 14th, we embarked on board the Romulus, Captain Epes Sargent commander, bound for Russia. (20–21)

The silence surrounding Prince's marriage (there are only a few other references to her husband, one of which announces his death) may be a self-protective strategy that restricts readers' access to the most private and intimate details of her life. Alternatively, Fish argues that Prince's emphasis on her decision to travel rather than on her marriage reveals "the significance of geographical mobility and spiritual empowerment for the black woman's sense of freedom, agency, and necessary risk."[23] Practically speaking, Prince's marriage secures her the means and status she needs to escape the oppressive Northeast. Her exclusion from the comforts and security of domesticity makes the decision to travel a relatively easy one, as was the case with Bradley. The added burden of race makes Prince's departure perhaps less expected, given her even more limited financial resources, but all the more urgent as she has no family or friends on whom she can be dependent (as Bradley complains of being). The first third of Prince's narrative does not mention travel, invoking instead the slave-narrative genre (even though she is never enslaved). Her switch to the travel genre is crucial as it offers her a way to reimagine black womanhood in order to highlight autonomy and self-control and claim femininity at the same time that she pushes the boundaries of gender and race.

What Happens When They Go

The prospect of traveling alone across oceans to unfamiliar territories involves dangers that Bradley and Prince weigh in their decisions, and risks they do not even imagine. If, however, they shared Leland's privileged position, there would be no reason to hesitate:

> It is a question in my mind whether after all the advantages are not in favor of the woman who travels alone. To travel, strictly speaking, alone, is impossible, unless one goes afoot or by canoe. The traveler by train or steamer must perforce move along with a crowd. The woman who travels with husband, father or brother may be supposed to have one man dedicated to her especial protection, but as the woman who is alone appeals naturally to the heart of every brave and honest man, she becomes the charge of the officials and her fellow passengers as well, and her unprotected condition secures the kindest attention and most considerate care of those who are best able to assist and protect her.
>
> In the event of an accident at sea the officers of a vessel take particular care of the lone woman, holding themselves in a measure responsible for her safety. Under ordinary circumstances they will endeavor to entertain her, advise and direct her, and when she passes beyond their own jurisdiction they will bespeak for her the special care of their most trusted friends and strive in every way to secure the future comfort, safety and pleasure of their transient charge.
>
> Of all the pleasant memories of a voyage around the world the most pleasant are of kindnesses received and the most gratifying knowledge acquired is the knowledge of the unselfish kindliness of the heart of man. (358)

Leland's happy experience of deference and protection was, unfortunately, not shared by ragged-edge travelers. Instead, the "crowd" which buoyed Leland along scrutinized, questioned, and even threatened Bradley and Prince. Fellow passengers stood in for society at large, registering at best surprise and at worst violent disapproval of women's social and geographical mobility, rather than "kind attention" and "particular care." Leland's wealth and the firmly established institution of tourism mediated her experience. Both ragged-edge narratives, in contrast, feature descriptions of the scrutiny their authors endured, the continuing efforts of those authors to work abroad, and the physical danger they experienced both from the process of travel (mule rides along cliffs) and from fellow passengers and residents of the places they visit (Southern slave holders threatening violence and enslavement). Once they depart, the economies of travel that they calculated are out of their control; the risks to both their social standing and their physical bodies were often much greater than they anticipated. Even as their travel writing pays special attention to these new and extreme risks, ultimately their extraordinary stories place the endurance, resourcefulness, and accomplishment of their unlikely heroines center stage.

These conflicts and confrontations with fellow passengers and surprised local residents demonstrate the ways in which bodies functioned as social texts in nineteenth-century America (and today, for that matter). Even as they traveled abroad, women travelers continued to be "read" as out of place and even dangerous themselves. Nineteenth-century American culture came to rely on visual cues of identity and status more and more heavily as urbanization and industrialization disrupted small-town networks of kinship and friendship. Even as mobility became a central element of American life, particularly for nonelite men and women who often left hometowns and established social networks of family and friends in search of economic opportunities in cities or on the frontier, women were expected only to accompany husbands and families, not to travel alone themselves. As we will see with Bradley, leaving behind family and friends could also mean jeopardizing class status, especially for women who relied on factors other than wealth to establish their social status. Reactions to Prince's skin color reinforced what Fish terms "the unofficial criminal status of free blackness" by automatically equating blackness with slavery. Bodies became texts on which markers of conformity and difference were read. Onlookers may have read a woman's modest dress neckline, crinoline, and shopping basket as signs of appropriate middle-class femininity; add a suitcase or, more shockingly, black skin, and that body was suddenly troublesome.[24]

Extending our discussion of nineteenth-century bodies as social texts, Jennifer Terry and Jacqueline Urla's formulation of "embodied deviance" suggests that the social gaze did not just register difference, but assigned value to deviation. Believing that deviance, which can range from being poor or black to being an actual criminal or exhibiting antisocial behavior, registered on a person's body as a mark that could be perceived, society could then maintain and enforce social hierarchies by limiting or granting access to power and privilege (or, more practically speaking, jobs or social services). For women and African-Americans, their bodies (with markers like breasts and dark skin tone) were always figured in relation to their deviance from white male bodies and found inferior and, therefore, subordinate. Behavior that challenged or undermined women's and blacks' inferiority and dependence elicited a social response that punished the individual in question and reinforced the rules for other would-be transgressors. Applied to travel and travel writing, women learned that travel was dangerous to their reputations as well as their bodies through a cultural "rhetoric of peril," according to critic Kristi Siegel, that taught women to stay at home or at least to travel only on a "safe" chaperoned tour. Women who traveled on their own got what was coming to them, whether that was injury on their trips or social ostracism when they returned home.[25]

The chivalry accorded to white women travelers cushioned their experience of this peril and inconvenience of travel; Leland, for instance, is comfortably sure that "in the event of an accident at sea the officers of a vessel take particular care of the lone woman," a benefit that is directly tied to her white skin and full pocketbook. Forced to take a very different approach to shipboard safety, another black female traveler, Jamaican Mary Seacole, includes this telling detail in her travel account: "During the time when the contest between fire and water was doubtful [her steamship from Jamaica to Central America catches fire], I entered into an amicable arrangement with the ship's cook, whereby, in consideration of two pounds—which I was not, however, to pay until the crisis arrived—he agreed to lash me on a large hen-coop."[26] Seacole must manage her limited financial resources (she is careful not to prematurely squander the considerable sum of two pounds) and her marginal position as a traveling black woman. She must protect herself because she cannot expect the white crew to make her the object of their chivalrous concern. Neither can Seacole expect her white readership to approve of her unorthodox travels. While Leland can, to a large extent, comfort her readers with her repeated references to the chivalrous care she receives, Seacole must carefully address her audience's response to the surprising and unwelcome figure of the black female traveler.

Before we return to Bradley and Prince, a brief further look at Seacole and her white contemporary, Mrs. D. B. Bates, will demonstrate how comparing black and white women's travel texts reveals not only the differences in the material conditions of their travel, but also the different strategies they use to present themselves to their readers. Seacole chronicles her travels through Central America and Panama and to the battlefront of the Crimean War in *Wonderful Adventures of Mrs. Seacole in Many Lands*, published in 1857. Subjected to inspection, Seacole negotiates her racial difference and reactions to it by carefully shifting the reader's gaze away from her body and onto her clothes. Despite her race and her mobility, Seacole insists on presenting herself as a respectable, feminine woman and supports this performance by dressing the part, no matter the setting in which she places herself. For example, she insists on dressing up while she travels on the Panama route to California, a location referred to as "the pesthole of the world" by American newspapers at the time.[27] On her journey, Seacole encounters a "steep slippery bank" of "Gatun clay" that seriously undermines her "due regard to personal appearance" (12–13). Describing her carefully chosen outfit, "a delicate light blue dress, a white bonnet prettily trimmed, and an equally chaste shawl," Seacole invites her readers to "sympathize with [her] distress" as she "flounder[s] about terribly, more than once losing [her] footing altogether" (13). Despite the mud and her inconvenient stays and skirts, Seacole conquers the dangerous hill, although her dress does not fare so well: "My pretty dress, from its contact with the Gatun clay, looked as red as if, in the pursuit of science, I had passed it through a strong solution of muriatic acid" (13). Her insistence on dressing up without regard for the danger or dirt of the journey casts her as hyperfeminine, respecting the dictates of the ideology of femininity no matter the cost, and therefore deserving of sympathy from both her readers and her fellow travelers.

While Seacole goes to great lengths both sartorially and textually to mediate the response to her unexpected traveling black female body, the published account of a European-American woman, Mrs. D. B. Bates, shows how class and race privilege can operate to shield the experience of women travelers, much in the way that Leland describes. Bates, originally from Boston and the wife of a steamship captain, published an account of her journey through the same area of Panama, *Incidents on*

Land and Water, or Four Years on the Pacific Coast, in 1858, one year after Seacole published her narrative.[28] Bates acknowledges that seasoned travelers "advised all the ladies to dispense with the side-saddle all together, as it would be utterly impossible for them to retain their seats" (291). In addition to a "gentleman's Spanish saddle," the women are outfitted with "India-rubber boots, and pants, and a large sombrero, as a protection for [their] heads" (291–92). The dangerous overland route across Panama is no place to stand on ceremony or insist on wearing silk or ribbons; one of Bates's fellow female travelers almost dies en route (306). Bates's account emphasizes the practicality of masculine modes of riding and dress; however, her sensible outfit does not protect her from ridiculousness. Like Seacole, she also falls victim to the Panamanian mud, despite her more-practical attire: "After remaining a few moments in the mud, I made an attempt to walk. I would go a few steps and then fall; pick myself up again, take a few more steps, and then tumble the other way" (306). This incident in Bates's narrative very closely mirrors Seacole's struggle up the muddy hill, although Bates has no silk dress to worry about ruining. Unlike Seacole, Bates is rescued by a "gentleman" who "came along, picked [her] up, and carried [her] to the desired haven" (306). She is recognized as a white, middle-class woman in need of rescue, despite her choice of pants instead of skirts. As we will see with Bradley, whiteness offered a level of protection even for traveling women breaking the rules of middle-class femininity. For black women like Prince and Seacole, the risks of mobility and autonomy were much more dangerous. Comparing their travel texts illuminates how race impacted the experience, representations, and ideologies of travel.

To return to Bradley, we see that on her sea journey to Costa Rica she arouses suspicion, and her decision to travel becomes a public issue. Quizzed about her identity and motives for traveling, Bradley is clearly conspicuousness as a lone female traveler. After spending four days seasick in her cabin, she describes the scene in which she emerges to find herself the object of general curiosity and interest:

> I slowly ascended the stairs which led to the deck hoping that the fresh air would strengthen my poor feeble system, but I had scarcely reached the top stair when my strength failed, and I was obliged to sit down on the floor of the deck and lean my head against the ceiling. Kind hearts were moved by my ghastly countenance, and every assistance was rendered to restore me, I soon recovered sufficiently to walk a little way where they gave me a comfortable seat, and then

> came the questions. Where is your husband, or with whom are you
> traveling Where are you going? [W]hen I told them I was going to
> Costa Rica, as governess in the family of the gentleman who was then
> somewhere on board . . . they shook their heads and seemed to feel
> much sympathy for me.

Bradley's weakness after her illness serves as a pretext for this outpour-
ing of social concern, but care and concern expressed for a single woman
traveling alone also suggests social disapproval of her traveling.[29]

By asking, where is your husband? the group seeks to identify her
marital status and supply the protection a husband or guardian normally would. The question suggests the inappropriateness of a woman
traveling without male supervision. While Leland finds fellow passengers and the ship's crew ready and willing to supply the place of her
male escort and protector, Bradley is traveling before women's tourism
becomes commonplace, and her berth in steerage does not purchase
the attentive service of the ship's staff. Considered inappropriate and
at risk, Bradley is obligated to supply the details of her travel arrangements and companions to satisfy her fellow passengers' curiosity. The
questioning reveals the not-so-hidden ideologies that reduce all women
to sexual objects (inherently weak and vulnerable and therefore available for male consumption through marriage or violence), which effectively undercut female autonomy. By traveling alone, Bradley makes a
spectacle of herself, and her fellow travelers assume the right to interrogate her about her identity and her journey. The fact that her travel is
not merely a personal decision, but instead a matter of public interest
and potential sanction, signals the cultural anxiety that ragged-edge
women's mobility provoked.

Bradley's experience of work while traveling forces her to confront
still more unexpected social repercussions of her decision to travel.
Although the governess position seems to provide Bradley with the
perfect solution to her economic problems, she quickly discovers that
her employers do not consider her a "lady," treating her instead as
hired help. The swift change in status shocks Bradley, but her position on the margins of the middle class makes her particularly vulnerable, especially once she leaves the support of friends and family back
home. Without the social circle in which she has already established
herself and without wealth and the respectability it brings, Bradley
finds herself in a precarious social position. Biographer Diane Cashman
describes the clashing expectations of the Medina family and their new

governess: "[Bradley] expected to be treated as an equal, who would be offered sympathy and protection throughout the harrowing journey. Instead, her employer chose to distance himself socially from his daughter's governess and retreated to his stateroom to leave Amy to fend for herself in steerage."[30] Bradley's marginal class position allows her to slip in status from gentility to servant very quickly.

She does not quietly accept her lowered status; on the contrary, she actively resists being treated like hired help. In her journal she notes that the beginning of her journey is also the start of her "tug of war" with the Medina family. Once she arrives in Puntarenas, Costa Rica, Bradley records a series of slights she experiences. Her room is

> excessively uncomfortable—a cot bedstead with a piece of straw matting for a mattress, on a sheet in which I have slept in ever since my arrival, a green baize blanket for my covering. There is no carpet on the floor that looks as if it has not been washed since the house was built—a small table with no paint, except daubs of ink—a miserable washstand with a badly cracked basin.

Three weeks after her arrival, Bradley still cannot get her clothes washed. The family also refuses to introduce her to their visitors, limiting her contact with anyone but servants.[31]

Bradley recognizes the family's attempts to control and demean her: "Do they wish to make a servant of me? It seems so." Despite the fact that she is completely without friends, family, or money, thousands of miles from home, Bradley declares that "they will not do it!" and makes plans to leave the Medina household. Bradley's determination to leave the only people she knows in Costa Rica to strike out on her own is extraordinary. However, her sense of herself as a respectable, middle-class woman is at stake. Although she frequently pushes at the boundaries of proper middle-class femininity (by rejecting housework, traveling, and working) and does not have the requisite financial resources, Bradley nevertheless identifies herself as middle-class and relies on the privilege of that social position. On her eventual and planned-for return home, she will not be living in a "classless" society, but in a stratified society that does not facilitate upward social mobility (despite the rhetoric of rags to riches) and that punishes women whose attempts to move up back-fire. Given the difficulty of maintaining her middle-class standing at home (and its attendant privileges of respectability), she is well aware that any further lowering of status would forever alienate her from middle-class comfort and security. Her story reveals the social risks involved when women travel without the full benefits of white, middle-class wealth and power.[32]

Although the job that originally sparked her decision to travel fails, she continues to focus on her goal of financial independence during her time abroad. By February 1854 Bradley has left the Medinas and records that she is "desirous of obtaining a situation as a teacher or dressmaker."[33] She does not seriously consider returning home, because "the same difficulties, trials and vexations would be [hers], if there, as before." Consequently, rather than facing dependence at home, Bradley strikes out on her own to support herself in a new country. After dressmaking to earn money and studying to improve her Spanish, Bradley establishes "Costa Rica's first English school" in San Jose. Attracting prestigious students like the children of San Jose's governor, Bradley and her school are a success. She even fights off a male teaching rival who threatens to steal her students and bankrupt her school. On 13 October 1856 she notes that she has hired an assistant teacher and that the school has expanded to thirty-three students. Bradley returns to the United States in 1857 with "a $500 nest egg from her Costa Rican school," according to Cashman. After four years abroad, Bradley realizes a significant improvement on her paltry one-dollar gold piece. She successfully locates foreign markets for her labor, but she also trades on her status as an American woman abroad, which allows her to defy the gender expectations of the places she visits. Although her diary includes almost no references to Costa Rican middle-class women, at home in their own culture they probably would not have had the freedom to pursue entrepreneurship the way that Bradley does. Bradley's position as a foreigner may grant her more latitude in her behavior while still allowing her enough respectability to teach the children of wealthy Costa Ricans. Thus, traveling alone and working, which could threaten Bradley's status and position in her own home setting, instead secure her independence when she returns.[34]

That independence comes at a price, though: in addition to the social danger she risks almost becoming a servant, she faces physical danger in her journey to Costa Rica. These scenes of physical danger emerge as a common element of ragged-edge women's travel narratives, performing similar functions and raising similar issues in all the texts presented in *Traveling Economies*. Physical danger focuses attention on the travelers' female bodies while simultaneously challenging the meaning culturally assigned to their female forms. Highlighting the out-of-placeness of their female bodies, these passages signal the travelers' anxiety about their transgression, dramatize the risk to their social standing, and symbolize the vulnerability of their life back home as women excluded from middle-class comfort and security. Chapter 4 will analyze the subversive representations of unfeminine determination, strength, and intelligence, which are also important features of the strategic representation of female bodies in danger.

Bradley's description of her mule ride over treacherous terrain focuses attention on her out-of-place female body and symbolizes the social as well as physical risks she runs by traveling. By representing both the danger and her survival, Bradley questions the narrow limits placed on women's lives by society. Her voyage begins by steamer from New York, continues up the San Juan River in Nicaragua, and finally follows the overland route to her final destination, Puntarenas, Costa Rica. For the overland portion of the journey Bradley rides mules over a rocky and difficult trail. Despite the hardship of the journey, Bradley finds humor in the image of herself astride her trusty mule: "Imagine me dressed in my brown linen with a broad brimmed 'Sombrero' and blue ribbon, my Bay State shawl spread over the saddle [and] sitting very gracefully thereon." However, her journal reveals the arduousness of later stages of the mule ride:

> Next morning, Sunday, we commenced our overland route to Puntar-
> enas. We traveled from 8 o'clock A.M. till evening, up most difficult
> rocky mountains, then down their dangerous sides—one misstep of
> our mules, and we must have been dashed in pieces, in the depths
> below; but the sure-footed beasts carried us safely o'er, and to the
> Father I offered my prayer.

Bradley leaves home to escape from domesticity and financial dependence—as we see in this scene she literally risks her life for freedom from those social and economic constraints. She risks her life in another sense as well. After traveling alone she may no longer be considered a marriageable woman, or she may succeed in finding a satisfying alternative to becoming a wife and mother. Either way, her life will no longer follow conventional, middle-class social scripts, and she may be risking forever any access to the goal of comfort, security, and respectability.[35]

Prince's experiences of scrutiny and danger are much more severe than the discomfort Bradley endures; as a free black woman her presence does not merely surprise her fellow passengers, but provokes

violent threats and even plots to kidnap and beat her. The intensity
of the reaction to Prince results from cultural anxiety about how free
blacks fit into American society. Seen as competition for scarce jobs in
the Northeast, or as subhuman property in the slaveholding South, in
all parts of the nation a mobile free black population threatened white
economic and social superiority. Recording the scrutiny and danger in
her travel narrative, Prince warns other would-be black female travelers and celebrates her persistence, intelligence, and endurance. Clearly
her account is completely different from the sheltered tourism of later
women like Leland, since it emphasizes the impact of her race on her
experience of travel and also points out her continuing concern with
work and finances on her journey.[36] Whether that work is sewing in
Russia or missionary activity in Jamaica, Prince travels in search of the
economic and social benefits denied African-Americans at home, even
as trials and danger on her trip remind her of what she thought she left
behind. Not only the material conditions of her traveling but her travel
narrative itself is shaped by her experiences of race and class, as Prince
cogently critiques racism and sexism, a very different project from
Leland's celebration of her own enjoyment of middle-class privilege.

Once in St. Petersburg, Prince pursues the entrepreneurial ventures
that were thwarted in the United States. Her first venture, taking children to board, commences just three weeks after she sets up housekeeping in her new country (39). Prince then realizes that "baby linen
making and childrens' [sic] garments were in great demand" and starts
her own business (39). Her enterprise quickly expands and she hires
a "journeywoman and apprentices" and even attracts the empress as
a customer (39). Critic Sandra Gunning interprets Prince's two busi-
nesses as manifestations of Prince's "new vision of herself as a respected
maternal figure," a position that "could only come to fruition beyond
the circumscribed circle of black American life." Combined with the
story of her entrepreneurial success, Prince's discussion of herself as a
"respected maternal figure" in Russia emphasizes the economic underpinnings of the maternal and domestic back home.[37]

The support of the empress emphasizes the difference between
attitudes toward black economic activity in the United States and in
Russia. While Prince's efforts in the States failed consistently, Russia
offers favorable conditions for her entrepreneurial efforts. The empress
takes an active interest in Prince, who is considered a member of the
court despite her skin color: "The present Empress is a very active one,

and inquired of me respecting my business" (39). This initial interest becomes tangible (and for Prince, profitable) support for her enterprise, as the Empress both buys and advertises Prince's wares: "[The empress] gave me much encouragement by purchasing of me garments for herself and children, handsomely wrought in French and English styles, and many of the nobility also followed her example" (39). Emphasizing the high quality and style of the goods she produces, as well as her famous customer, Prince challenges stereotypes of African-American inferiority by presenting her own success story. Thus, her business achievement in Russia implicates American prejudice in her previous failures back home.

The empress's patronage emphasizes that Prince was not only economically successful but also socially accepted within czarist society. Skill and ability paired with business relationships with influential and elite community leaders constitute Prince's revision of middle-class identity, a revision based on the theory of a democratic meritocracy rather than the reality of America's highly stratified and segregated society. Hence, according to Gunning, even as she describes czarist court life, Prince presents "Russia as a site of displaced engagement with the social conditions of her native land." However, Gunning's comparison of Prince's text to James Buzard's formulation of wealthy white Americans' "temporary, revivifying departure from compromised social existence" while touring Europe fails to fully appreciate Prince's revision of the travel genre. Prince crafts a wide-ranging critique of American society that questions her exclusion from the benefits and privileges of both full citizenship and middle-class status, and, by extension, the exclusion of the free black community from those benefits and privileges. Her unexpected participation in both travel and travel writing challenges notions (then and now) about who traveled in nineteenth-century America; her text raises related questions about how travel writing by marginalized authors can effectively protest sources of social injustice back home. Even as Prince compellingly portrays the economic and social conditions that make travel an attractive or even desperate option, her travel is not an escape, temporary or otherwise. She remains engaged with the both the ideals and the realities of the United States, traveling and writing to call attention to the gap between the theory and practice of the emerging nation.[38]

Prince's representation of czarist court life contrasts the court's racial tolerance with her earlier account of racism and economic discrimination in the United States. Her lengthy description of her court reception highlights her position in a society that, while stratified, is not organized along race lines:

> As we passed through the beautiful hall, a door was opened by two colored men in official dress. The Emperor Alexander, stood on his throne, in his royal apparel . . . as I entered, the Emperor stepped forward with great politeness and condescension, and welcomed me, and asked several questions; he then accompanied us to the Empress Elizabeth; she stood in her dignity, and received me in the same manner the Emperor had. They presented me with a watch, &c. It was customary in those days, when any one married, belonging to the court, to present them with gifts, according to their standard; there was no prejudice against color; there were there all casts [*sic*], and the people of all nations, each in their place. (23)

Prince notes the presence of the black porters, pointing to the participation of blacks in court, their "official dress" signaling their status. Prince's husband holds a position as a porter, and Prince is honored because of her marriage to a member of the court. Her reception by Russian heads of state is a dramatic shift from the narrative's earlier descriptions of her life of struggle in America. As a poor black woman, Prince was assigned a position of powerlessness within larger American society. The visible markers of her gender and race translated into a corresponding marginal social position that limited her access to economic opportunity. In Russia, however, Prince assumes social standing and public acknowledgment of her new status.

Her ringing endorsement of her new home as free from "prejudice against color" may be overly optimistic, but her presentation is strategic. Russia becomes a utopia in the context of Prince's narrative—a racially tolerant alternative to the injustice of her home country. However, the racial tolerance that Prince experiences does not negate the severe oppression enacted simultaneously through the Russian system of serfdom. The omission of an extended discussion of serfdom from her account reveals her narrative's primary concern with social injustice at home in the United States, as opposed to the exploitation she witnesses abroad. As historian Peter Kolchin argues, parallels existed between the treatment of Russian serfs and American slaves: "Serfs could be bought and sold, traded, won and lost at cards. They were, in short, personal property . . . The control also extended to the bodies of the serfs, who could be corporally punished as an owner saw fit, removed from their loved ones at his whim, and denied his permission to marry."[39]

Prince does briefly make her own comparison between slavery and serfdom: "The village houses are built of logs corked with oakum, where the peasants reside. This class of people till the land, most of them are slaves and are very degraded. The rich own the poor, but they are not suffered to separate families or sell them off the soil. All are subject to the Emperor" (38). In her mention of serfs, Prince highlights the distinction between their situation and what she perceives as the worst aspect of American slavery, namely, the separation of family members. Her criticism of slavery also has class dimensions, since the breakup of families in slavery signals blacks' exclusion from the privileges and prerogatives of white, middle-class domesticity. Social and kin networks that can establish class standing and respectability even without wealth are also disrupted when families are torn apart. Arguing that all Russians of all social positions are ultimately "subject to the Emperor," Prince implicates the use and abuse of privilege by members of the American middle class and the lack of recourse for African-Americans (as opposed to Russians, who all have at least limited access to protection and citizenship). Rather than criticizing Russia as another society built on forced labor, Prince focuses on the economic opportunities open to her as a black woman in Russian society. Her description of the serfs is immediately followed by her account of her successful business venture as a seamstress.

Prince uses her description of social institutions and conventions in a foreign country, the accepted content of travel writing, to criticize the operation of society in her home nation. Comparing Russian serfdom and American slavery, she identifies race prejudice, the inevitable outcome of chattel slavery, as the paramount social injustice. Comparing Russian serfdom to American slavery is less compelling for Prince than comparing the experience of living as a black woman in the two countries. Her success in Russia belies the stereotypes about black inferiority that fueled the prejudice she encountered in the hypocritical North. What is different between the two places is not Prince herself—she carries her skill and intelligence with her on her travels—but social attitudes toward the possibilities open to black women.

Prince returns from Russia due to ill health in 1833, "having been absent about nine years and six months" (40). Her husband, who remained in Russia to earn money before returning to the United States, dies unexpectedly and leaves Prince a widow. She resides in Boston until her next journey, this time to post-Emancipation Jamaica, and works in "different occupations," participating in William Lloyd Garrison's Anti-Slavery Society (42).[40] Her narrative omits a detailed account of this period of her life; her subsequent decision to travel again suggests that the same difficulties with employment probably recurred and that travel once again provided a potential solution. Her second and third journeys take her to Jamaica, where she evaluates the possibilities for black emigration to the island and investigates prospects for pursuing uplift work herself among the emancipated Jamaican blacks and American fugitives who have already relocated.[41]

The third chapter's discussion of Mary Ann Shadd Cary will explore how free black women use travel to claim authority and gain voice in national and international debates on citizenship, black nationalism, and racial uplift. However, the remainder of the discussion of Prince will focus on her return journey, when she experiences threats of violence, imprisonment, and enslavement that throw into relief the extreme risk she runs as a black female traveler. Recording the threats in her travel narrative, Prince warns other would-be black female travelers and exposes the race politics of "home" (in this case, in the worst sense).[42]

While elite white women's bodies were hidden behind the rhetoric of domesticity, "the black woman's body was always envisioned as public and exposed," according to critic Carla Peterson. Black slave women's bodies were visually and even physically available on the auction block, and assumptions about blacks being subhuman and black women being unfeminine combined with that visual access to deny black women power in both public and private settings. Traveling contested these formulations of black womanhood, ascribing autonomy and mobility to black women who were supposed to be dehumanized producers of physical and reproductive labor.[43]

Prince's travel narrative vividly depicts the violence that polices black mobility. A storm disables Prince's ship and it must stop for a week in New Orleans to effect repairs. During the layover, Prince is forced to stay on board the ship, unable to disembark because whites on shore threaten to capture, imprison, and enslave her (76). Prince immediately attracts attention; she terms herself "a spectacle for observation" by the white slave owners on the dock (76). Like Bradley, she is subject to interrogation, but the questions pertain to her slave or free status, as opposed to her marital status. Prince describes the inquisition that immediately follows the ship's arrival: "The people were very busy about me; one man asked me who I belonged to, and many other rude questions; he asked me where I was born" (76). This series of "rude questions" begins, of course, with the supposition that Prince is a slave. Her skin color is instantly registered and interpreted as a sign of slave status, the white gaze inscribing Prince within existing social frameworks, in this case those of chattel slavery. While Bradley's fellow passengers judge her actions against standards of acceptable middle-class feminine behavior, the whites in New Orleans perceive Prince's traveling as a violation of race expectations.

As travelers and travel writers, both Prince and Bradley intend to observe foreign locations and people and to record those observations. What each of their narratives demonstrates is that their unexpected presence as female travelers makes them into tourist attractions. The result is that both women become objects for public consumption, a situation that undermines the self-determination they seek through travel. Peterson asserts that black women travelers consistently experienced this objectification and became what she terms "Colored Tourists," observers who found themselves scrutinized by the very people they were intent on studying. According to Peterson, Prince's account "illustrate[s] the stance of the black female social explorer who authorizes herself to gaze at the Other but must in turn, and despite all attempts at self-protection, become a commodity and subject herself to this Other's gaze."[44] The gaze that instantly records Prince's skin color and registers her out-of-placeness as a traveler reinforces the objectification of slavery that ultimately extends to free blacks and excludes them from the middle-class prerogatives of self-possession and privacy. Our previous discussion of Bradley expands Peterson's formulation to include ragged-edge white female travelers. To extend Peterson's argument to Bradley is not to rob it of its crucial specificity, but instead draws attention to the heightened visibility of both white and black women travelers—this, combined with the circulation of their texts, suggests the powerful place they occupied in antebellum America's cultural consciousness, embodying the culture's anxiety over both women's and blacks' self-determination.

Even as they record moments of being scrutinized in their texts, ragged-edge travelers also lay claim to the observer's gaze typically found in conventional travel writing, a move that insists on their autonomy and agency despite the unfavorable response to their unwelcome traveling presence. Immediately before she narrates her experience in New Orleans, for instance, Prince includes a description of slaves she observes from the ship, emphasizing the difference between herself and them: "I was made to forget my own condition, as I looked with pity on the poor slaves, who were laboring and toiling, on either side, as far as could be seen with a glass" (76). Looking through binoculars at slaves working in the fields, Prince signals both her physical distance from the people she observes and her social distance from the status of slave. Her observations lay bare the limited vision of the whites, who mistake her identity and who cannot conceive of a woman both black and free. Although Prince expresses sympathy for the slaves, she primarily uses their bodies to establish her own identity, to contrast their slavery with her freedom, their stasis with her mobility, their objectification with her agency. Hence, Prince's black female traveling body is no longer a blank canvas onto which cultural meaning is written; the project of her travel writing becomes rewriting her own black female body and the meaning it carries.

Discrimination, enslavement, and violence—these are the escalating threats that Prince negotiates as a black female traveler. The degree of race hatred that she portrays in her narrative—the danger she faces whether at home or traveling—illuminates the failure of the United States to provide basic protections, much less the constitutional guarantees of life, liberty, and the pursuit of happiness, to those outside the racial and economic boundaries of the middle class. What is at stake is not just Prince's right to travel or to write, but to live outside slavery and to live at all. The final scene I will discuss in this section illustrates the severity of the physical and social risk run by black female travelers.

Once Prince is finally homeward bound to New England from her second trip to Jamaica, she includes a conversation with the ship's captain, which reveals the extent of the danger she faces on her journey. The captain congratulates Prince on her wisdom in remaining on the ship while it was docked in the Southern ports and tells her about a plot engineered by Prince's white fellow passengers:

The Captain asked me why I did not go ashore when there in the

Comet; "had you," said he, "they intended to beat you. John and Lucy Davenport, of Salem, laid down the first ten dollars towards a hundred for that person who should get you there." (81)

The captain's casual tone belies the violence of the plot against Prince. If she had been lured or taken from the relative safety of the ship, Prince would have been at the mercy of "respectable" white people like the Davenports. Prince's presence as a free black woman traveler and outspoken abolitionist so offends her white fellow passengers that they raise money to pay her would-be attackers. Apparently headed for Salem, Massachusetts, the Davenports are Northerners, showing that this kind of violent threat is not solely the province of Southern slaveholders.

The resistance in this scene is found in Prince's survival. Cheryl Fish has drawn attention to Prince's defiant "back talk" during her response to the inquisition on the dock, when she asserts her humanity and condemns both slavery and slaveholders.[45] In the conversation with the captain, Prince does not record her own reaction to his comments. So while she refuses to be silenced on the docks in New Orleans and Key West, she chooses to be silent in her text following the revelation of the violent plot against her. Perhaps the reason for this choice is that the extent of the violence and racism arrayed against her in effect speaks more strongly than even her own words could. Her escape from the threatened beating, as well as from imprisonment or enslavement, testifies to her strength of will, her quick-thinking intelligence, and her spirit, as well as to some measure of luck. While existence on the margins of society secures a measure of freedom for some black women travelers, this scene reveals the vulnerability and pain that also mark that existence. As Peterson notes, "Indeed, margins are often uncomfortable places; as the lives of African-American women, past and present, exemplify, they can be sources of horrifying pain, generators of unspeakable terrors, particularly in their exploitation of the black female body."[46] Prince's very survival in a world so hostile to her existence defies the systems and ideologies that perpetuate that hostility. Travel is an important strategy for resistance, but the scrutiny and danger that Prince experiences attempt to curtail her troubling mobility and autonomy. Her limited success battling danger and discrimination is, of course, worlds away from the experience of later tourists like Leland. However, that success does suggest the need for better and more-effective controls on women's, and particularly black women's, travel that the institution of tourism eventually fills when chaperoned tours conveniently exclude black women through high prices and racial segregation.

Circulating Bodies, Circulating Texts: Who Was Reading Women's Travel?

Contemporary reviews of Leland's travel narrative rank her accomplishment alongside that of the most famous traveling women of the late nineteenth century. *Overland Monthly and Out West Magazine* (one publication) proclaims, "Leland was a forerunner of Nelly Bly and Elizabeth Bisland in circling the world in the character of the unprotected female," while the *New York Daily Tribune* titled its review of her book "A Yankee Ida Pfeiffer, Going Round the World."[47] Even as both publications place Leland on a growing list of women world travelers, the comparison to her more-famous contemporaries reinforces the women's exceptionality rather than acknowledging and sanctioning women's mobility. Leland's success is not the rule, but "the secret of Miss Leland's success as a traveller is, however, an open one. She is plainly a young woman of exceptional self-control and steady good temper" (*NYDT*). Even her sterling character, however, offers scant protection from the dangers surrounding the female traveler. Although the *Tribune* acknowledges that "she was but once in all her extensive journeyings even threatened with insult," both reviews evoke the threat of "insult and harm" (*OMOWM*) to discourage their female readers from following Leland around the globe. Leland circumvents the danger "by her resolute refusal to seem to see anything that is unpleasant," (*OMOWM*) but her good humor and her cultivation of "the traditional 'stony British stare'" (*NYDT*) seem ridiculously little protection against the threats conjured in the pages of the reviews, never mind actually on the road. The review's description of the risk she runs "trusting herself alone with the Arab guides and beggars who swarm" the pyramids uses racist rhetoric to frighten women into staying home, but there are still more dangers to consider (*NYDT*).

Overland Monthly decries Leland's "tastes" as "hopelessly and aggressively philistine," a critique echoed by the *Tribune*: "The young traveller's comments upon men and cities and works of art [in other words, her entire narrative] are decidedly entertaining, and not seldom because of the nave [*sic*] crudity [*sic*] and lack of culture which characterizes them." Luckily for Leland she is blissfully unaware of "her own dense incapacity as a critic" (*NYDT*). The danger here is, of course, publicly revealing stupidity and naïveté, a problem that threatens women in particular, as travel and travel writing are apt, according to these reviews, to reveal the intellectual weaknesses of the so-called weaker sex. It is not just that "a little touch of the common in her way of looking at things" (*OMOWM*) is the problem; it is that the public revelation of her bad taste and uneducated opinions again argue that women are better off at home than out in the world publishing travel books. And ultimately that is the point both reviews are at pains to make:

> The fact that a young and pretty woman can in these days go all around the world with perfect impunity may easily be made to carry too much significance. Miss Leland's triumphant success was, we have no doubt, very largely due to her own reserve and circumspection . . . but it would probably not be wise for even American women [Leland herself is American] to "go and do likewise" on a considerable scale, seeing that temperament is an important factor in the case. (*NYDT*)

Even as both reviews celebrate the magnitude of Leland's accomplishment, they also reduce her text to an occasion to admonish women not to follow in her traveling footsteps.

Both reviews of Leland's text take her narrative seriously, however, even if they do discourage other would-be women world travelers. But Schriber raises the possibility that Leland's text may be a "pseudo-account, a parody of other travel accounts by lone female travelers"; she cites the text's hyperbole, its "'Twainesque' diction," and its excessive repetition of "alone" and "woman alone." Even though she raises her concerns about the authenticity of the text, Schriber ultimately concludes that fake or not, Leland's travel narrative confirms "the lone woman traveler's visibility and the prominence enjoyed by her accounts of travel." While I cannot offer definitive proof that Leland's text was not a parody, these contemporary reviews suggest that her text was not received as such by readers. I agree with Schriber that a parody would only reinforce the figure of the woman traveler in the popular imagination and that familiarity with the subject, in this case the woman traveler, is necessary for successful parody.[48] What *Traveling*

Alone tells us, in either case, is that women travelers and the published version of their adventures continued to be a hot commodity until the end of the nineteenth century. Leland's publication, trading as it did on the popularity of women's travel narratives, invites us to look back on the circumstances under which the accounts of Bradley and Prince were published.

Who read Prince's published travel text? Did friends or relatives read Bradley's diary? How did contemporary readers react to their texts? Did written accounts of their unconventional travels generate the same level of disapproval in readers as they record it generating in their fellow passengers? Questions about the reception of both women's texts lead us to ask whether the figure of the female traveler was an anomaly in the early nineteenth century—or whether the intense reaction Prince and Bradley experienced signaled growing cultural anxiety about increasingly mobile women.

Bradley describes herself as an anomaly, but she nevertheless solicits acceptance and tolerance of her behavior from her audience. Bradley's self-portrait, recorded in a letter to her young female cousins, Betsy and Elizabeth Bradley, highlights her deviance from traditional femininity:

> I am an old maid of 34 years. My eyes are large and gray—forehead high, but freckled, large nose and mouth—but my cousins don't be frightened, I have got a great warm heart to go with these ugly features, so 'tis barely possible, you might love me a little, if I am plain looking.
>
> You need not be surprised when the warm weather comes, to see me at your place. It would be just like me some morning to take a carpetbag, jump into the cars and go. There is no aristocracy about me. I am a true Republican—detest all the false customs of society, etc., etc.

Conventional in neither her appearance nor her actions, Bradley links her unexpected behavior and her desire to travel. An "old maid," she has not followed the traditional path to marriage and domesticity taken by many of her white, middle-class female contemporaries. Travel functions as an escape from these unrealizable domestic expectations, and travel writing serves as an outlet for her critique of the society that produces limiting ideologies of proper femininity and limited options for women who seek to support themselves.[49]

Bradley's journal also indicates a wider audience for her social criti-

cism. Containing copies of letters addressed to her niece and young
female cousins, her journal is semipublic. Intending to influence, to
advise, and "to give to my dear niece the plain, unvarnished history of
the aunt whom she thinks—according to her last kind letter, she some-
what resembles," Bradley intends for her writing to occupy the place
of legacy for her female relatives. Her story offers her niece and cousins
a map of obstacles to female accomplishment and the example of her
own defiant success.[50]

While Bradley's life and travel diary represent resistance on a personal or small-scale level, Prince with her published account of her *Life
and Travels* self-consciously enters into the public debates raging over
issues of abolition and emigration. A review of the pamphlet *The West
Indies, Being a Description of the Islands, Progress of Christianity, Education,
and Liberty Among the Colored Population Generally, By Mrs. Nancy Prince*
(1841), which Prince developed and expanded in her later published
narrative, appears in the *Colored American* and acknowledges Prince as
an "eye-witness" and authority on the question of black emigration to
Jamaica. Praising Prince as "an intelligent colored female," the *Colored
American* congratulates her on proving the correctness of the paper's
stance against emigration.[51] As we will see in the third chapter's discussion of Mary Ann Shadd Cary, traveling and travel writing could authorize black women's entry into political speech and activism within the
black community. While Prince's *Narrative* continued to voice her political opinions on slavery, racism, and emigration, it also was intended
to support her financially. She had already generated income from her
travels; she had given public lectures on her time in Russia and had sold
her Jamaican emigration pamphlet, advertising both in the abolitionist
newspaper *Liberator*.[52] Prince's *Narrative* was reprinted in three editions,
so her text did reach an audience (most likely of the black community
and white abolitionists), but it most likely did not alleviate the desperate financial needs that had inspired her writing:

> My object is not a vain desire to appear before the public; but, by the
> sale, I hope to obtain the means to supply my necessities. There are
> many benevolent societies for the support of Widows, but I am desir-
> ous not to avail myself of them, so long as I can support myself by
> my own endeavors. Infirmities are coming upon me, which induce
> me to solicit the patronage of my friends and the public on the sale of
> this work. Not wishing to throw myself on them, I take this method
> to help myself, as health and strength are gone. (3)

Highlighting "Travels" in the title of her narrative, Prince strategically inserts her text into the growing market for travel writing, which will be discussed in more depth in the following chapter on Anne Royall. Like her lectures, Prince's *Narrative* trades on the cultural fascination with travel and mobility that had apparently, at least momentarily, overcome the suspicion of traveling women and blacks that existed simultaneously in the popular imagination. It may well be that Prince's black and white abolitionist audiences were more tolerant of black autonomy and personhood, and as consumers of slave narratives were more accepting of black mobility, at least in the form of stories of fugitive slaves running to the North. Prince's own experiences of racism in Boston suggest the limits of this possibility, but her text certainly did circulate, at least in the abolitionist center of Boston, and along with this circulation the figure of the black woman traveler entered the cultural imagination.

While Bradley's letters to her nieces and Prince's racial uplift work and published travel narrative extend their voices into their communities and their goals beyond their own personal success, the travel writing of Anne Royall and Mary Ann Shadd Cary focuses on wider public issues of community improvement and, ultimately, nation-building. Concerned with legislative reform, the management of public institutions and finances, and national debates on emigration and abolition, the travel writing of these two women journalists is unorthodox in its content and form. Their journalistic travel writing circulated in the potentially wider circles of subscription book sales for Royall and newspaper-column inches for Shadd Cary, suggesting that representations of female travelers, like their travel texts, were gaining a larger audience and were therefore impacting cultural ideas about women, travel, national identity, and citizenship.

· Two ·

Scolding the Nation
The Political Travel Writing of Anne Royall

"Pray sir," asked Tims. "what is the proper and legal definition of a common scold? When can a scold be said to be common?; for as to being a scold, you know all women are that."
—Newspaper coverage of Anne Royall's "common scold" trial[1]

The tabloid scandal of 1829, the trial of Anne Newport Royall—travel writer, newspaperwoman, muckraker, and political watchdog—filled the courthouse with Washington's elite and the gossip columns with accounts of testimony and speculations on Royall's crimes. Charged with being a "common scold," Royall was accused of violating standards of feminine behavior and decency; testimony described the obscenities she had hurled at her neighbors, members of a neighboring Presbyterian church. While witnesses against her focused on the "torrents of the most coarse, vulgar, and obscene language" Royall had "not ceased to pour out on every one of them," the real issue was not the insults she hurled in the street, but the power of the diatribes that she published in her popular and controversial travel books and that she would later continue in her own newspaper, *Paul Pry* (1831–36). Royall had developed her skills as a roving social and political critic during the production of a series of travel books, which will become the focus of this chapter, and had recently settled in Washington to turn that scrutiny on the workings of the government and on what she presciently saw as the increasing and dangerous influence of organized religion on national politics. Protestant church leaders were working toward the formation of a national Church Party, which would dramatically increase their already-significant influence on public policy. Royall vociferously protested the blurring of the boundaries

61

between church and state in print, on the streets of Washington, DC, and in the halls of the Senate and Congress. In fact, biographer Bessie Rowland James suggests that the "forum" and "publicity" the trial gave to Royall's warnings may have succeeded in ultimately defeating the Church Party.[2]

Royall clearly symbolized for her accusers the threats and problems of women stepping into new roles in public and print. Testifying in her own defense, Royall claims the real issue of the trial is censorship and describes in her own uniquely dramatic way the conspiracy she sees working against her:

> This prosecution was but one branch of the general conspiracy of the blue and black-hearted Presbyterians, the priests and missionaries, against the freedom of speech and of the press. If they were to succeed . . . nothing would be safe—bigotry and all the horrors of the inquisition would overwhelm the land; nothing would be left of all for which her husband and other worthies of the revolution had shed their blood.[3]

Royall imagines herself and her travel books standing between the success of the fledgling democracy, secured by the sacrifice and blood of veterans and patriots like her husband, William Royall, and a church police-state. Her sense of her own importance might invite us to agree with the phrenologist hired by the *New York Commercial Advertiser,* who concludes, "Gentlemen, she is beyond a doubt PARTIALLY insane."[4] Newspapers sold copies by playing up Royall's eccentricity; her opponents were even more interested in figuring her as a crazy old lady (she was sixty years old when the charges were brought) whose antics needed to be controlled for the sake of the public peace. Harkening back to a time when women were held in check through intimidation and violence, Royall's accusers called for the traditional punishment for the ancient charge of common scold, the ducking stool. The violence of the proposed ducking—a punishment used historically on accused witches who were dunked and held under water until they drowned or confessed—matched the violence of Royall's trespass against standards of appropriately feminine behavior, at least in the minds of her accusers. Jokes abounded about how Royall would find the cool water a relief from the summer heat of the capitol, but it was no laughing matter that the navy yard actually built the torture device in anticipation of her conviction.[5]

While censorship was a key element of the prosecution against Royall, the crime she was charged with was applicable only to women and specifically addressed her failure to live up to what were becoming increasingly rigid standards of behavior for white, middle-class women. She was an author before women's authorship entered the mainstream, primarily in the form of sentimental "women's" novels, which shortly became the literary territory and source of vast readership and success for authors such as Susan Warner and Maria Cummins. Royall's travel writing dealt instead with public institutions, local governments, and proposed legislation, not sentimental plots of orphan girls rescued by caring guardians, trained for proper womanhood, and finally appropriately married to suitable men. When women were supposed to be staying at home, she traveled widely around the country, funding her trips by selling subscriptions to her forthcoming travel books. When women were supposed to embrace middle-class consumerism and obsess about the latest fashions, she wore her poverty on her threadbare sleeve. Despite her "unfeminine" behavior, Royall's character witnesses shared the trial's focus on gender, asserting her femininity rather than acknowledging the censorship underlying the charges. Secretary of War John H. Eaton testified that "Mrs. Royall had always conducted herself like a lady when she came to his office seeking interviews," a paradoxical defense of her feminine deportment on her unladylike business of interviewing government officials for her self-published travel books. Mr. H. Tims, who served as doorkeeper for the Senate, offered an amusing reversal of the scold question with his testimony, quoted in the above epigraph, asserting that Royall's shrewish nagging, rather than an exception, was just like "all women." That neither defense witness questioned whether Royall's unladylike behavior was really the central issue illustrates how evaluating women on their conformity to or violation of an imaginary womanly ideal was fast becoming a cultural practice of the nineteenth century.[6]

Perhaps because of these feeble attempts at defending Royall's femininity, the court convicted her as a common scold, fined her ten dollars, and required that she raise a hundred dollars bond in guarantee of keeping the peace for one year. Fellow journalists paid the penniless Royall's fine, and the judge never actually imposed the punishment of the ducking stool. Undaunted, Royall embarked on more travels shortly after her trial—this time a trip south that would become *Mrs. Royall's Southern Tour, or Second Series of the Black Book, 3 volumes* (1830–31). She planned to capitalize on the notoriety the trial had generated, in order to sell her five existing travel books and subscriptions to the future volume as she traveled.

Royall did not intend for her travel to take her to new markets, as Prince and Bradley did, but she did intend for her travel to serve as a paying career. Sales were not brisk enough to pay for first-class travel (or even second- or third-class), and she had to combine book and subscription sales with begging for support from Masons' lodges and charities for Revolutionary War widows. Details of Royall's poverty during her journeys illuminate the material conditions of ragged-edge travel, and emphasize not only that poverty was a motivating factor in the decision of ragged-edge women to leave home, but that it was a very real risk to be calculated in the economies of travel. A savvy traveler and businesswoman despite her limited financial success, Royall cannily marketed herself and her texts. Examining the emerging literary market for women's travel writing and contemporary reviews outlining readers' expectations of the domestic focus of women's travelogues offers crucial context for evaluating how Royall negotiated these markets and expectations by occasionally couching her scolding and her transgressive travels in feminine sentimental language. However, her focus on public municipal institutions, portraits of women patriots and authors, and cogent critiques of national and local economic practices and policies highlight her unconventional use of travel writing both to critique and to promote nation-building. Her tours evaluate the practice of government on the local level, which she takes as ultimately reflecting the goals, practices, and administration of the larger nation.[7] Moving from her impoverished childhood on the Alabama frontier to her tours of Eastern cities and her eventual chosen home of Washington, DC, Royall reversed, in her travels, the course of manifest destiny, moving from the frontier back to the foundations of national government in order to call her readers and her nation to a return to the country's founding. She advocated a careful reassessment of the nation before it claimed new territory and moved still further from its democratic goals. Opinions like Royall's were most often unwelcome; her common-scold trial was a thinly veiled attempt to censor her, and the threatened punishment of the ducking stool was a blatant symbol of the violent consequences ragged-edge women often faced for their constructive criticism of the nation. Certainly a scold, but by no means common, Royall provoked extreme cultural anxiety, demonstrating just how threatening independent and mobile women travelers were to antebellum America's ideas about women's proper place.

Rags to Riches to Ragged Edge: Royall's Biography

Before focusing on Royall's first travel book, *Sketches of History, Life, and Manners in the United States* (1826), we need to consider a brief history of her eventful life, which showcases how unlikely her infamy and her literary success were.[8] Royall's tumultuous "rags to riches to ragged edge" story begins with the hardship and deprivation of life as a settler. In her *Letters from Alabama* (1830), Royall reveals the extreme poverty that marked her childhood on the Pennsylvania frontier:

> I suffered all that human nature could bear, both with cold and hunger. Oh, ye wealthy of those times, little idea had ye of what the poor frontier settlers suffered. Often running for our lives to the forts, the Indians pursuing and shooting at us. At other times lying concealed in brushwood, exposed to rain and snakes, for days and nights without food, and almost without clothes! We were one half of the time without salt or bread! pinned our scanty clothing with thorns; lived on nuts, bear's meat, and dried venison!

Royall is brutally honest (and perhaps a bit dramatic) about the reality of pioneer life; she sees it as a rite of passage that justifies her later criticism of the country she has helped to grow.[9]

Although her patriotic service on the frontier should have qualified her to share in the bounty of the new nation, her economic situation did not appreciably improve throughout her childhood and adolescence, until she finally married well above her own status. Royall's mother, Mary Butler, supported the family by working as a house servant following the deaths of Royall's father and stepfather. The account of Mrs. Eva Grant Maloney, a neighbor, describes the situation of Anne and her mother:

> The woman, Anne's mother, went to the Sweet Springs and was taken in by the wealthy and eccentric old Captain William Royall. She was

his wash-woman and menial—a subject of reproach to the slave-own-
ing aristocratic neighbors; for few white women on our frontier had
to be menials, and those only of the lowest class.

As the daughter of a servant, Royall occupied a low social position,
but surprisingly managed to continue her education by reading and
studying on her own, with the help of William Royall and his unusu-
ally extensive library. Although she arrived at Royall's household as a
servant's daughter, Anne eventually became mistress of his extensive
plantation in Sweet Water, Virginia, when she married him. A wealthy
landowner and Revolutionary War veteran, William provided Anne
with financial security. While biographer Sarah Porter's assessment that
"probably no other married couple ever found more happiness together
than Captain Royall and his pioneer-bred wife" may be an overstatement, the pair do seem to have overcome class and age differences
to achieve a marriage based on companionate interests and affection.
Porter finds evidence of Anne's devotion in her later travels, when "she
would go miles out of her way, often spending her last dollar for the
purpose, to look upon a spot of earth his feet had once pressed."[10]
    Despite William's efforts to protect Anne and assert her rightful
position as his wife, established families in the better social circles of
Sweet Water perceived her as an unsuitable match and ostracized her
from much of the area's social life. Greedy relatives went beyond ostracism and contested William's will in an effort to disinherit Anne. They
eventually succeeded, and left her penniless. A middle-aged widow at
the age of forty-three, Royall had to supply her own needs and pay back
considerable debts without the help of a husband or extended family.
In order to support herself and to evade her creditors, Anne decided to
travel and to write about her observations. She planned to sell subscriptions and to gather data for a proposed volume of travel writing, which
she eventually published as *Sketches*.
    Without any financial resources, Royall met the daily expenses of
her journey by begging. Her notes and observations on the places she
visited were made while she went from door to door petitioning for
financial support as the widow of a Revolutionary War hero and Mason.
Donations of money, clothes, and lodging sustained Royall at a level
just above abject poverty. Both her begging and her sightseeing were
often accomplished on foot, as she could not afford carriages or even
less-expensive public transportation. During her visit to Philadelphia

in 1824 during the composition of *Sketches,* she experienced the extreme physical consequences of her poverty-induced walking. She had four pennies in her pocket on her arrival and spent an entire day in search of subscriptions and donations, with little or no success, although she felt that since she was "determined to finish what [she] had begun, [she] might as well walk to death, as starve to death." After eight more miles the following day, she reports, "The skin of my toes bursted, my heels completely rubbed off, and both bled freely." When she falls into an exhausted sleep still in her clothes, she must spend most of the next day extracting her bloody feet from her shoes and stockings: "By bathing and soaking I separated the shoes from the stockings, but to get the stockings from the raw flesh was no easy matter and took several hours." This insight into the desperate state of Royall's finances and health during her travels compiling her *Sketches* does not emerge until her later *Black Book* series is published. Royall does not include the personal details of her suffering and poverty in *Sketches,* a choice that may have to do with her decision to publish her first volume of travels under the pseudonym "A Traveller." She may have found anonymity useful and protective with her first book, or she may have realized that her readers would distrust an author who was both poor and a woman. Regardless, this account of her suffering published in her later writing certainly suggests her very different perspective from the wealthy women tourists who will follow in her travel-writing footsteps (but not in her painful shoes) in the century's later decades. Most important, Royall's poverty and her struggle to support herself inform her criticisms of the nation and lead her to ask how each place that she visits succeeds or fails in protecting and supporting its most vulnerable citizens.[11]

The eventual publication and sale of her travel books at best temporarily improved her finances. Royall's standard of living never dramatically differed from poverty, according to biographer Bessie Rowland James: "Anne Royall had not lived like a princess during the months she prowled the halls of Congress. The evidence of how badly off she was crops up, from time to time, in bits of memoirs scattered through later works . . . She was wearing, as she had worn continuously since Alexandria days, the only dress she owned." While she did publish and sell her writing, she sold advance copies on her journeys and used that money as she traveled. Ultimately, Royall lived with constant economic uncertainty from her husband's death until her own passing.[12]

Despite her financial and social difficulties, Royall was an incredibly prolific author, publishing ten book-length travel texts and even a novel in the five-year period between 1826 and 1831. Her first travel book, *Sketches* (1826), was followed by her *Black Book* series, which emphasized portraits of people she met and snubs she endured as she traveled (*The Black Book; or, A Continuation of Travels in the United States*, 3 volumes [1828, 1829]; *Mrs. Royall's Pennsylvania, or, Travels Continued in the United States*, 2 volumes [1829]; and *Mrs. Royall's Southern Tour, or Second Series of the Black Book*, 3 volumes [1831]). She then founded two of her own newspapers, *Paul Pry* and *The Huntress*, which she published in Washington, DC, from 1831 to 1854, the incredibly long print run ending just three months before her death.

Sketches for Sale: Women's Travel Writing in the Literary Marketplace

As the public seem unwilling to lose an inch of ground I pass over or a single incident, I will be excused for a few brief remarks along the way.
—Anne Royall, *Mrs. Royall's Pennsylvania* (1829)[13]

[Emily] judged, rightly, that a girl of such keen intelligence as Gerty was naturally endowed with would suffer nothing by occasionally encountering what was beyond her comprehension; but that, on the contrary, the very effort she would be called upon to make would enlarge her capacity, and be an incentive to her genius. So history, biography, and books of travels, were perused by Gerty at an age when most children's literary pursuits are confined to stories and pictures. The child seemed, indeed, to give the preference to this comparatively solid reading; and, aided by Emily's kind explanations and encouragement, she stored up in her little brain many an important fact and much useful information.
—Maria Cummins, *The Lamplighter* (1854)[14]

We have named Miss Martineau's new work [Retrospect of Western Travel (1838)].—In her preface, she tells us, it is chiefly intended for her own countrymen, to enlighten them on the subject of American manners and character, especially those of our eminent men. She has made some clever hits, and, on the whole, these books are more amusing than her first publication. Still, there is much error, many partial, one-sided statements, and it is plain that she has gathered the hints for many of her sketches, from such prejudiced reports as coincided with, her own predilections.—If her English readers give credit to all she has written, their opinions respecting America and Americans, though different, will be scarcely more correct than those they gathered from Mrs. Trollope's speculations.
—*Domestic Manners of the Americans* (1832), "Editor's Table," *Godey's Lady's Book*, May 1838[15]

In Royall's own words, she offers a sense of her growing confidence as an author, and her own evaluation of the success of her unorthodox decision to travel and write. On the third page of her fifth travel book, Royall imagines her audience clamoring for every detail, fact, and impression that she can supply. By this point, she has sold her books, lived and traveled on the proceeds, and gained a level of notoriety and recognition (this is before she's branded a common scold). Four years before, after being disinherited and faced with poverty, Royall's decision to travel and fund her travels with her own writing anticipated with uncanny foresight the explosion of travel writing within the American literary marketplace. Between 1830 and the turn of the twentieth century, American authors published 1,765 books of foreign travel.[16] Of those published travel texts, women authored 195, although only 27 of those were published before the Civil War.[17] Royall's travel books, along with many other women's travel texts, are not included in these figures—Royall because she traveled within the United States rather than to a foreign country, other women's travel essays and sketches because they were published in magazines rather than in book form, making their numbers much more difficult to compile. The rise of travel writing as a popular genre did coincide with dramatically improved technologies of travel, such as steam-powered ships, new highways, and expanding railroads. Royall's success, however, has less to do with better means of travel than it does with her own insatiable curiosity about her country. Her readers shared that curiosity; the young nation was avidly interested in representations of itself. Even negative portraits sold books—Frances Trollope's *Domestic Manners of the Americans* (1832), her British view of the backwardness of American life, was published in four editions in its first year. Harriett Martineau, reviewed above in *Godey's Lady's Book,* was also successful, parlaying her travel books into a similarly thriving business. However, the fame and riches of Trollope and Martineau eluded Royall, and none of these female travel writers approached the success of later best-selling sentimental novels.

Royall's limited success does invite us to ask who was reading travel books and what audiences expected from the genre. Maria Cummins's *The Lamplighter* (1854) was a best-selling sentimental novel, so its recommendation of travel writing as appropriate for gifted young women readers suggests that women did read travel books and expected them to provide "important fact[s] and much useful information," since travel writing was closely associated with journalism. For instance, *Godey's Lady's Book,* the *Ladies' Home Journal* of its day, reveals its expectations that travel writing be objective and factual in its review of Martineau's *Retrospect of Western Travel* (1838). Mrs. Trollope, whose *Domestic Manners of the Americans* was such a success, also merits criticism for similar bias; however, the review demonstrates that women read and evaluated travel writing and discussed it in the pages of magazines directly targeting a mainstream female audience. In fact, *Godey's* published travel writing regularly, written by both men and women, some reprinted from other magazines and books and some commissioned specifically for the magazine. An 1841 editorial goes so far as to call for a new form of travel writing fast enough to keep pace with the new speed of travel itself:

> There must be some new way for tourists to communicate their adventures and impression.—Would that a Daguerreotype of the mind could be invented! This dull medium of pen, ink, and paper was only fitted for lumbering stage coaches and boats dependent on wind and tide. Now that the Fire King has lent his scepter to the locomotive, and his breath to the steam vessel, the traveller can only give a dash here and a jot there, and let readers fill up the picture from memory or fancy, as they choose.

The magazine's female editor, Sarah Hale, is speaking here to a female audience assumed to be familiar with travel writing; ten years before they may have been ready patrons for Royall's travel books.[18]

Royall did not take her audience, be they women or men, for granted. She actively and successfully marketed herself and her texts and even worked to create new and thriving avenues for literary sales. Biographer George Jackson describes her marketing methods in this fashion: "Adept early at publicity she visited the newspaper offices in the towns she passed through, so that an announcement of her presence would appear in the paper. Then, posing as a person of importance, she was able to sell more books." Sympathetic Masons also placed lengthy advertisements that described her long list of publications and included appeals to charity in local papers prior to her visits:

> The author is a female of respectability . . . the widow of . . . an officer of the revolution. This Lady, by one of those unforseen [*sic*] misfortunes common in the human family, has fallen into distress,

and appeals to the humane and benevolent citizens of this great and patriotic city [Albany, NY] for their patronage. These Works, we find, are patronized by the most distinguished men of the United States . . . Subscriptions will be received at the Bookstore of Messrs. Webster and Skinner, in this city.

The ad not only sparks curiosity about Royall and her books, but also plays on the community's sympathy and pride—do they want to be the city that abandons the down-on-her-luck veteran's widow, the city that is not sophisticated enough to join the country's "most distinguished men" in reading her books?[19]

In addition to her skillful advertising, Royall makes an argument for Americans to support and produce their own national literature, effectively creating a market for her own American text. In *Sketches* she calls on her readers to buy books written and printed in America, as opposed to reprinted British works (200–201). In her interviews with notable American authors, descriptions of Daniel Webster and Matthew Carey coincide with endorsements of Hannah Adams, "the glory of New-England females" (336); Miss Sedgwick, "an authoress of some reputation" (266); Mrs. Weare, "a poetess" (267); and Mrs. Sigourney, to whom "we are indebted for some of the finest specimens of poetry" (300). Including women in her canon of emerging American literary talent, Royall makes space for women's authorship generally and for her own books more specifically (and perhaps more self-servingly). Despite her construction of an emerging female literary tradition, Royall does not fit into the expectations for women writers in general, or women travel authors in particular, as we will see in the remainder of this discussion.

Beyond "Manners and Appearance": Travel Writing That Scolds the Nation

Who does not know the difference between their books—especially their books of travels—the gentleman's either dull and matter-of-fact, or off-hand and superficial, with a heavy disquisition where we look for a light touch, or a foolish pun where we expect a reverential sentiment, either requiring too much trouble of the reader, or showing too much carelessness in the writer—and the lady's—all ease, animation, vivacity, with the tact to dwell upon what you most want to know, and the sense to pass over what she does not know herself; neither suggesting authorly effort, nor requiring any conscious attention, yet leaving many a clear picture traced on the memory, and many a solid truth impressed on the mind! . . .

Every country has a home life as well as a public life, and the first quite necessary to interpret the last. Every country therefore, to be understood, requires reporters from both sexes. Not that it is precisely recommended that all travelers should hunt the world in couples, and give forth their impression in the double columns of holy wedlock; but that that kind of partnership should be tacitly formed between books of travel which, properly understood, we should have imagined to have to been the chief aim of matrimony—namely, to supply each other's deficiencies, and correct each other's errors, purely for the good of the public . . .

There is one set of female writers who having under the general name of tourists given the public an immense deal of extraneous information, who might be expected to occupy a prominent place in this article: the very nature of their services, however, compels us to pass them over in silence; for when one lady travels to Vaucluse to give us her views of mesmerism, another visits the German baths to describe the advantages of society in Russia; when one goes north to expatiate on the infant schools in England, another south to send home chapters of advice to the queen; and a fifth wanders generally at large, in order to bewail the waste lands within a few miles of London, and to reprobate the iniquity of a government who can suffer such resources to remain unapplied, "with a starving population under their very eyes, all ready to pay them five pounds an acre;" when, in short, ladies take all the trouble of travelling abroad merely to express those private opinions upon affairs in general which they could as well have given utterance to at home, we feel truly that it would be a grateful and very amusing task to bring their services before the public, but that it is not ours on this occasion to comprise them among so unpretending a class as that of the lady tourists. (Mrs. Johnstone, "Lady Travellers," *The Living Age*, 1845)[20]

For all her marketing savvy and efforts at publicity, Anne Royall stills falls short of Mrs. Johnstone's expectations of the "good" that "Lady Travellers" should do for "the public." Mrs. Johnstone's review, however, offers a contemporary touchstone of reader's expectations of women travel writers, and shows us the extent to which Royall either accommodates or revises those expectations. A reviewer and columnist for the *Living Age*, a weekly magazine published in New York from 1844 to 1900, Mrs. Johnstone confines the duties of lady tourists to describing the domestic affairs of the places they visit and amusing their readers with their clever observations of detail and their "ease, animation, [and] vivacity." Excluding women authors who waste her time with their "private opinions upon affairs in general," she argues for a sexual division of labor in travel writing, with men attending to politics and women to domestic matters. The pointedly political and economic focus of Royall's travel writing would certainly exclude her from Mrs. Johnstone's list of "Lady Travellers"; her *Sketches* would instead fit within the group of rejected texts that insist on writing about subjects Mrs. Johnstone wishes they would instead have "the sense to pass over." Despite condemning the texts she lists by content and not title (as if to protect her audience from mistakenly reading them), her review reveals the existence of five politically focused women's travel texts written around 1845 that use the genre to tackle issues ranging from school systems and agrarian reform to feudalism and faddish mesmerism. Although written two decades after *Sketches*, these texts constitute a cohort for Royall of other women travel writers voicing wide-ranging social and political criticism. Mrs. Johnstone's strategy, however, is to ignore texts that do not fit her formulation: "It is not ours on this occasion to comprise them among so unpretending a class as that of the lady tourists." She names twelve other texts that meet her standards, and her strategy of exclusion points to the similar manner in which troubling texts like Royall's have been erased from our consideration.[21] Mrs. Johnstone's assessment is not unique, but gains persuasive power because it resonates with midcentury understandings of women's travel writing; her repetition reinforces the accepted critical paradigm, and her use of that common currency bolsters the authority of her review.

Surprisingly, late-twentieth-century critics have continued to use the same model as Mrs. Johnstone. Critics such as Marion Tinling, Catherine Stevenson, and Jane Robinson argue that women travel authors focus on the details of domestic life and fashion while male authors include discussions of government and politics. Critic Mary Suzanne Schriber offers a more complex formulation in the introduction to her anthology of nineteenth-century American women's travel writing, *Telling Travels* (1995), arguing that women writers emphasized their gender to distinguish their texts in a crowded literary marketplace by providing "a woman's view of the world" that focused on aspects of domesticity in other cultures, a difference that they hoped would sell books.[22]

While Mrs. Johnstone clearly wished all lady tourists would confine themselves to domestic insights such as "Egyptian fine ladies . . . make their own sherbet, cook their own dishes, and wash their own floors" (she quotes at length from Mrs. Poole's account, which even includes the sherbet recipe), her counterexamples show that many women writers were not behaving like the apolitical, vivacious ladies she would have them be.[23] More-recent criticism has begun to pay attention to these political troublemakers, but the analysis has focused almost exclusively on women whose wealth and social position cushioned the consequences of their refusal to fulfill the expectations of new recipes and peeks at foreign household management. The politically focused texts studied are written only by women wealthier than Royall. These well-to-do tourists do not share Royall's worldview or specific approach to politics any more than they share her anxiety about attracting an audience with her unconventional political content or the extreme discomfort of her bargain-rate travel conveyances.[24]

While these more-recent approaches to the political content of women's travel writing begin to address the silences and limitations left over from the nineteenth-century logic of Mrs. Johnstone, Royall's travel writing offers crucial differences that call for still more complex theories of the relationship between women, travel, and nation-building. Writing decades before women such as Margaret Fuller, Royall provides an important precedent for the traveling women who follow in her footsteps and challenges our understandings of how and when images of politically minded mobile women entered the pages of newspapers and books and the cultural imagination. The specificity and detail of Royall's analysis of economic policy, social service facilities, and state and national legislation foreshadow her later muckraking journalism and far exceed, for sheer volume of information and breadth of subjects covered, the political travel writing that will follow. Her own experiences of poverty and hardship translate into a call for legislative solutions for economic and social injustices; her proposed political solutions are dramatically different from elite women's advocacy of reform through benevolence and charity, but she clearly imagines public roles for women as important to the new nation. Even as she is marginalized by her poverty and unconventional mobility, Royall figures herself as a patriot and her travel text as a document vital to the improvement of her beloved country. Travel and particularly a roving woman who serves as social and political critic are the antidotes she offers to corruption and injustice; the violent reaction to her traveling female presence suggests the alarming scope of the problem she fights.

If Mrs. Johnstone shudders at the thought of the woman author who has the audacity to "send home chapters of advice to the queen," imagine what she would think of Royall's unending stream of criticism leveled at everyone from small-business owners and local town managers to senators and the president. In her chapters on major Northeastern cities, Royall begins her assessment of the practice of American democracy by focusing on public institutions such as prisons, poorhouses, and hospitals. Framing her discussion of Washington, DC, Boston, New York, and Philadelphia in terms of their public facilities, Royall offers both criticism and approbation of each city's social services. "Manners and Appearance," the expected subject of women's travel narratives, is limited to only two pages in Royall's treatment of New York City, while her discussions of "Hospital," "Alms-House," "Penitentiary," "Asylum for the Deaf and Dumb," and "Bridewell and the Jail" constitute more than six pages all together (245–60). Royall makes a point to tour hospitals and prisons and to provide her assessment, which is directed not to an audience of would-be travelers, but to the residents and local governments of the cities she visits. Her travel writing is designed to embarrass the cities in question into improving their social services, and she intends for her work to change the locations she writes about, rather than passively record them for posterity. Frequently comparing cities and institutions ("The museum of Albany is a tolerable collection, much more so than I anticipated; but after seeing the museum of Philadelphia, it had not enough of interest in it to amuse" [278]), Royall assesses the progress of the nation in terms of its public management and cultural attainment. Her tour evaluates the spread and practice of the nation, and she assumes authority to judge failures and successes.

Tours of prisons, hospitals, and poorhouses are not unique to Royall's travel writing. Critic Mary Louise Pratt uses the term "social exploration" to describe the investigative trips that elite white European women make to public institutions and then record in their travel texts. Pratt describes these elite women's journeys away from safe, privileged domestic spaces as journeys "to explore the world in circular expeditions that take them out into the public and new, then back to the familiar and enclosed." While the elite women Pratt discusses do include an unexpected amount of political and social commentary in their travel texts, the position from which they make their criticism is very different from Royall's. These female social explorers have domestic space to return to, where "meals, baths, blankets, and lamps appear from nowhere." Royall, on the other hand, tramping through the streets of Philadelphia, New York, or Albany, has no safe domestic haven.[25]

Unlike her elite counterparts who have wealth to shield them from the scandal of traveling alone and becoming female authors, Royall carefully negotiates reader response to her trespass against femininity in her *Sketches*. For example, her critique of Washington's poorhouse is scathing: "This wretched establishment only exists to disgrace Washington" (143). Combining an emotional appeal with a fiscal reproach, Royall points to both human suffering and the mismanagement of public funds: "With an aching heart I turned my back upon those cheerless, friendless sufferers. Three thousand dollars are appropriated annually for the support of this establishment!" (143). Combining sentimental language and political criticism, Royall carefully manipulates gendered textual expectations. She justifies her political concern with an appeal to sentiment, an acceptable feminine interest and an increasingly popular women's literary strategy. This nod to women's concern with human suffering establishes her as appropriately feminine, despite the fact that she immediately expands the scope of her critique to include the masculine field of public management (the misspent three thousand dollars). In contrast, Pratt's elite social explorers do not "rel[y] heavily on the resources of sentiment," reinforcing their arguments instead with more-masculine language, such as "appropriating a few elements of economic rhetoric." Asserting mastery of masculine discourse, elite social explorers are anxious to move beyond feminine respectability to public and political participation. Since Royall, however, was already thrust into the public world by poverty, her self-presentation does not begin with the assumption of womanly privilege that might alleviate her trespass into politics for her readers. Rather, she deftly combines sentimental feminine language with her stinging political reproach.[26]

Even though Royall appropriates the language and sentimental appeal of women's domestic fiction, she is not advocating benevolence, the form of women's activism that became increasingly popular in the 1820s through midcentury. Built on notions of women's innate moral superiority, benevolence called for women to spread their moral influence outside the home to charities and social service work and simultaneously justified women's increasing participation in public life. Sentimental fiction could be tied to benevolence since some women authors used their texts to mobilize women who would lend their feminine moral might to a specific cause. The most famous example is Harriet Beecher Stowe's *Uncle Tom's Cabin* (1852), which sought to move its female audience to tears and then to action for the abolition of slavery. In contrast, Royall does not target middle-class women as the primary audience for her text, nor does she pose benevolence as a solution for the jails, maternity wards, and poorhouses she finds in need of improvement. Benevolence relies on a level of wealth and privilege that Royall herself does not have and which she knows many Americans lack. Rather than depend on charity, Royall instead targets governmental reforms to demand that the nation ensure a minimum level of protection for its most vulnerable members.

Royall's advocacy of a newly enacted law protecting women from debtors' prison brings the intersection of her concerns with gender, economics, and citizenship, as well as her literary strategies and themes, sharply into focus. In fact, Royall enthusiastically congratulates the nation's capital on its forward-thinking legislation:

> It is with the most heart-felt pleasure I advert to an act of Congress exempting females from prosecution for debt in the District of Columbia. This magnanimous and humane act in favor of the tender sex, has done them immortal honor, and ought to obliterate all their faults, were they as numerous as the sand on the shore. It is to be hoped that every state and city in the Union will imitate their noble example, and blot out for ever this foul stain upon the American character. The shameful practice of imprisoning men, is worthy [of] only the most despotic governments . . . but to subject females to cruel confinement is highly disgraceful to a free people;—it is high time this misguided imitation of European policy should be discarded from our shores. (154)

Once again employing sentimental language ("heart-felt," "tender sex," "immortal honor"), Royall tempers her hyperbolic criticism even while effectively labeling as "despotic" all local and state governments that continue to jail debtors. Following the itinerary and logic of her own travels, she returns to the nation's capital in search of a policy modeled on the true precepts of a "free people." She then appeals to legislators in "every state and city in the Union" to follow the capital's chivalrous and moral example. Effective government of established states and the frontier requires that new laws be constantly checked against the nation's founding documents to prevent "misguided imitation of European policy," a practice that will ensure the continued practice and expansion of democracy. Jailing women debtors is a "disgrace" to the nation, and Royall knows from personal experience—she was evading creditors and the possibility of debtors' prison in her former home state of Virginia at the time she wrote this. Despite her unfeminine competence as a traveler and her professional ambitions as a writer, Royall is all too willing to claim protection as a member of the "tender sex" on this occasion.

When Royall does focus on women, instead of recipes or household hints, she offers portraits of public accomplishments and patriotic service, a strategy that normalizes her own unconventional traveling behavior and fits with her sense of herself as a patriotic national watchdog. An important marketing ploy for Royall is to include interviews with prominent male politicians, writers, and public figures in her narrative in order to increase interest and sell more books, as well as to gain publicity for herself as an author. The most famous anecdote about her interviewing prowess involves her holding John Quincy Adams's clothes hostage, after he had been skinny-dipping, in exchange for an interview (biographer Bessie Rowland James debunks this colorful story as patently untrue, unfortunately).[27] And while Royall may have gone to great lengths to get her man, a pen portrait of Anne Bailey, female Revolutionary War veteran, argues for women's abilities and calls for new systems to support and protect them. Bailey served as a soldier, her skills surpassing many of her male counterparts: "Ann would shoulder her rifle, hang her shot-pouch over her shoulder, and lead a horse laden with ammunition to the army, two hundred miles distant, when not a man could be found to undertake the perilous task" (49). Royall's account emphasizes Bailey's fitness as a traveler, as well as her courage and military skill. The obstacles to successfully completing Bailey's military mission are similar to those encountered by other female travelers:

> But how, said [Royall], did you find the way,—"Steered by the trace
> of Lewis's army, and I had a pocket compass too." "Well, but how
> did you get over the water courses?"—Some she forded, and some
> she swam, on others she made a raft: she "halwys carried a hax and
> a hauger, and she could chop as well as hany man;" such was her
> dialect. (49)

Bailey masters the talents needed for travel—survival and tracking
skills—which she uses in service to the war effort. Her outstanding
service to the army highlights the value of those travel skills. Royall's
portrait of Anne Bailey as a female patriot and fellow traveler reminds
her readers of the sacrifices women make on behalf of their nation, and
places her own efforts to record the accomplishments and failings of
her country beside those of another patriot.

However, coupled with this laudatory portrait of Bailey as a female
patriot is a critique of the economic barriers that even extraordinary
women face. The former heroine, "now very old," lives in abject poverty,
as Royall notes: "When I saw the poor creature, she was almost naked"
(49). Royall admonishes the reader that although Bailey deserves to be
remembered for her service to her country, she more urgently needs
basic necessities and an income. As Royall argues, Bailey "deserves
more of her country, than a name in its history" (49). Royall calls for
the government to support Bailey, presumably in the form of a pen-
sion. Locating the solution to Bailey's financial problems in the political realm, she points to the failure of patriarchal systems, particularly
marriage, to offer women financial security. After losing her husband's
estate, Royall herself campaigned for many years to be granted a pen-
sion as a war widow.

"To Save the Odd Quarter": Royall's Fiscal Reproach of National and Individual Conspicuous Consumption

Descriptions of half-naked starving veterans are a far cry from the
accounts "recording wanderings of great length, undertaken solely for
pleasure and curiosity, consuming much time and money, and as such

indulged in especially by those who have both at their command," a group Mrs. Johnstone celebrates. She is atwitter with curiosity about how the other half lives and travels:

> We are naturally anxious to know how those who go clothed in purple and fine linen, and fare sumptuously every day, get on in the rude ups and downs of travelling life; for though yachts may be furnished with every luxury—though medical men and air-cushions, and ladies' maids and canteens, and portable tents and Douro chairs, and daguerreotypes, and every modern invention that money can procure, may be included in their outfit—yet the winds will blow, and the waves toss, and the sun beat down, and the dust rise up, and the rain soak through, and hunger, and thirst, and fatigue, and things their delicacy knew not of before, assail them as if they were mere flesh and blood like other people.[28]

While it would probably be more fun to join Mrs. Johnstone on her voyeuristic reading tour of the opulent yacht-owning set and their humbling encounters with "things their delicacy knew not of," Royall offers a very different glimpse into a very different mode of travel. Showing us how she negotiates the marketplace of budget public travel (transportation, accommodations, attractions), Royall criticizes the unequal distribution of wealth that she sees as threatening the economic and civic life of the nation. Demonstrating how she pinches pennies and castigating what she sees as wasteful individual spending and irresponsible public economic policy, she shows us that women are not incompetent or incapable in money matters, but well equipped to participate in the marketplace and in other areas of political and public endeavor.

Throughout her *Sketches* Royall inserts references to unscrupulous tavern owners and their efforts to overcharge travelers. She not only warns her readers about these "highway robbers," but she also portrays herself outsmarting numerous corrupt innkeepers (129). Moments of triumph over stagecoach drivers and innkeepers offer comic relief in Royall's text, even while making a serious point about her ability to protect and support herself. Congratulating herself on each penny saved, Royall invites readers to cheer her every victory. Bravado disguises her desperate financial straits in these passages, revealing Royall's pride and her unfailing determination. In her concerted efforts to "save the odd quarter," Royall refuses to pay inflated bills, citing a law requiring taverns to post their rates (186). She provides her readers with a practical guide to reasonable travel expenses: "He keeps a table spread with plenty and variety, and what was our bill? 50 cents per day, including extra charges" (22). By refusing to pay inflated rates, Royall demonstrates her travel savvy, which exceeds that of her male traveling companions. Paying twenty-five cents while her fellow male travelers pay seventy-five for the same stagecoach ride, Royall "prove[s] that men of genius and general science, are, for the most part, deficient in the common affairs of life" (127). Rather than being a victim of fraud, Royall "determine[s] not to be swindled" (127) and achieves a measure of economic independence and empowerment despite her vulnerable position as a lone traveling woman. As we have discussed before, she does not travel in style, but scrimps along, begging and walking her way through her tours. Wearing the same dress for years, Royall prizes her independence and mobility over the latest fashion or a more-comfortable mode of transport, and it is this philosophy of self-denial and self-reliance that she wants her country to share.

By condemning middle-class materialism, Royall frames conspicuous consumption as a danger to the economic health of the nation. She distances herself from middle-class women who are expected to know and buy the latest fashions, and claims in fact that the frenzy for fashion threatens the nation. Reproving the "pernicious effect of the growth of foreign luxuries," Royall points to the negative consequences of fashion on the health and pocketbooks of most Americans (57). She exaggerates in order to emphasize the high stakes involved in trade imbalances and impractical spending on both national and personal levels. By abandoning sturdy and warm homegrown fabrics for thin, expensive, imported silks, Royall argues, Americans risk not only their pocketbooks, but their health: "Twenty, perhaps forty, for one, die now to what was known when they lived on their own wholesome viands, and dressed in their own coarse but warm and substantial domestic cloths" (57). In her inflated account, the result is a death rate (presumably from colds and flu) increased two hundred to four hundred times. Despite her overstatement, she expresses in this passage an economic philosophy of national and individual self-reliance, advocating American products and rejecting dependence on foreign imports. While lace and silk may seem inconsequential in terms of national economic policy, Royall identifies the danger of trade imbalances and the subsequent erosion of American values (the abandoning of those instilled on the frontier).

According to her, middle-class young people imitating the fashions of the rich forsake the work ethic of their ancestors and weaken the future of the nation: "And what must our young fop do now? He is too fine to work, to be sure" (72). Employing an unexpected gender-role reversal here, she portrays the men as preoccupied with frivolous fashion, demonstrating their financial incompetence and poor work ethic,[29] whereas Royall's own economic savvy and tireless struggle to earn a living provide a stark contrast. With accounts of her bargaining "to save the odd quarter" and her warning against runaway material-ism, Royall provides an alternative model for middle-class women's economic participation beyond conspicuous consumption, whether it is of petticoats or extravagant chaperoned tours.

Clearly, Royall wouldn't share Mrs. Johnstone's interest in a yacht voyage, but she does offer a portrait of a sea journey that represents the best of the nation and the best of travel. She finds her utopia in the saloon of a steamship bound for New York City in which rigid gender roles and strict class consciousness relax:

> I found about fifty strange faces below . . . ladies and gentlemen all in one large room . . . The ladies, unembarrassed, modest, and discreet, conversing familiarly with the gentlemen, all mingled together, leaving it difficult to tell who were, or who were not their husbands . . . Here, society appeared in a new light, presenting a medium between those extremes under which I had been accustomed to view it, equally removed from impudent rusticity on the one hand, and repelling hauteur on the other. None seemed greater than his fellow, present-ing one of the most pleasing proofs of our salutary government I had hitherto seen. (236–37)

The snobbishness of Mrs. Johnstone and the ostracism Royall has expe-rienced while begging from house to house both give way to a glimpse of social equality achieved through the great social leveler of public transportation. Just as laws, in Royalls' view, should return to the wis-dom of the founding documents (as in the case of the legislation against sending women to debtors' prison Royall celebrates), so too should the social practices of the new nation be guided by the country's precepts of equality and fairness. Travel facilitated this process both literally and metaphorically, as passengers from all walks of life were thrown together in stagecoaches, in rapidly expanding cities, and eventually on the frontier. Before the country and its citizens followed the path of travel westward, however, they needed to evaluate carefully the practices and policies they took along for the journey. Anne Royall, traveling social and political critic, appoints herself to be their guide.

Leg Broken, Horsewhipped, Threatened with Dunking: The High Price a Scold Pays

At the beginning of this chapter, Royall faced the threat of the ducking stool as punishment for her outspoken opinions and her audacity in putting them in print. The threatened violence of the common-scold trial was actually nothing new for Royall. While she traveled collecting the material for *Sketches,* she was physically attacked on two separate occasions. In one instance, Royall was pushed down an icy set of stairs while visiting Vermont. Her leg broken, she relied on charity through long weeks of recovery, and the publication of her *Sketches* was subsequently delayed. In the 1820s, a broken leg was a near-catastrophic injury that could have easily resulted in death or permanent disability, and she did have a permanent limp as a result of the fall. The second attack occurred when a man Royall approached for subscriptions and charitable aid horsewhipped her, striking her on the head and shoulders as she retreated down a flight of stairs. The attack "left marks on her person, and drew blood from her face," according to a local newspaper. Royall credited her bonnet with saving her life, as the "heavy padding broke the force of the blows on her head."[30]

Why did an unpublished (both attacks predate the publication of *Sketches*), impoverished, itinerant woman writer generate such a hostile and extreme response? Newspaper coverage of Royall's arrivals in various towns created a buzz of notoriety, and her outspoken opinions were sometimes printed and were certainly freely given to those she met on her journeys, which may account for a certain level of negative reaction to her. She was pro-Mason (her husband was a member of the secret society, and many Masons gave her money as a result) and antichurch, two extremely unpopular views, but again, why were her opinions met with physical violence instead of counterarguments in the editorial pages? The reason lies in how her traveling and writing touched on the anxiety, already developing early in the century, surrounding women's appropriate role in the emerging American society. She challenged patriarchal authorities from church elders to town administrators, senators, and presidents well before Woman's Rights activists organized their membership and published their ideas. The violence of the physical and verbal attacks against her was most likely fueled by frustration that her outspoken opinions were so hard to censor. She sold quite a few of her books, and her newspapers were in print for an unheard-of length of time for the antebellum press—nearly thirty-three years of continuous publication despite constant financial struggle to keep them afloat and get them to the public. Ultimately, the vicious attacks on Royall reinforce arguments about the failure of the new nation to put its democratic philosophy fully into practice—the inclusion of diverse voices and opinions on political and social matters was not a reality, and many of her fellow citizens were not interested in the free speech of their neighbors. She may have found solace and possibility in the egalitarian steamship saloon, but to see principles of fairness and justice enacted throughout the country was to be her unfulfilled life's work.

Another traveler who would not have been included on the list of lady tourists, Mary Ann Shadd Cary took up her own political travel crusade at midcentury, when injustices even more pronounced than those Royall fought against threatened to rend the nation. Traveling to Canada to investigate that country's possibilities as a haven for disenfranchised free blacks and fugitive slaves, Shadd Cary uses travel writing for the political ends of uniting her black community and criticizing the racism of both the United States and Canada. She takes Royall's political travel writing in a new direction, building on Nancy Prince's discussion of black emigration to Jamaica and, as we will see, on Frances Wright's hopeful analysis of American democracy's potential to include white, middle-class women as full citizens, to call for economic, social, and political equality for African-Americans as well. All of these women authors, along with the unnamed political travel writers of Mrs. Johnstone's review, invite us to rethink our approach to women's travel writing and to look beyond the "lady tourist" to find her troublemaking predecessors and think about the ways they use travel and travel writing to scold nations.

· Three ·

Traveling Uplift

Mary Ann Shadd Cary Creates and Connects Black Communities

Feeling, as I do, that my destiny is that of my people, it is a duty to myself, setting aside the much-ridiculed maxim that "charity begins at home," to expose every weakness, to exclaim against every custom that helps prolong our day of depression. I shall, therefore, not by raillery or ridicule, seek to arouse; but as one who, by assent, if not by actual participation, has aided in this complexion of things, speak plainly and without fear. We thought, in connection with professional men, as the whites had such, we should, as they do, make a grand display of ourselves; we should have processions, expensive entertainments, excursions, public dinners and suppers, with beneficial institutions, a display of costly apparel, and churches on churches, to minister to our vanity; we forget that "circumstances alter cases;" we forget that we are, as a people, deficient in the "needful" to support such things.[1]

—Mary Ann Shadd, *Hints to the Colored People of the North* (1849)

It is well-known that the Fugitive Bill makes insecure every northern coloured man. Those *free* are alike at risk of being sent south. Consequently, many persons, always free, will leave the United States, and settle in Canada, and other countries, who would have remained had not that law been enacted.[2]

—Mary Ann Shadd, *A Plea for Emigration, or Notes from Canada West* (1852)

After a hurried and rapid journey by steamboat, railroad and wagon, without being able to stop at Hamilton, I find myself in the flourishing settlement called Dawn, on the Sydenham, enjoying the hospitality alternately of those staunch friends of our paper, Messrs. Hill, Cary and Johnson, and the active assistance of this respectable body of people generally. The appearance of the country is beautiful just now, and industry and progress mark every footprint made by our people, as well as those of their white neighbors. In the village of Dresden, carpenters are busy completing the fine buildings owned by Wm. Whipper, Esq.; smiths, wagon-makers, all are at work, and, to crown all, the farmers of the surrounding country have "demonstrated the problem" in connexion with the rest, whether the whites and colored people *can live together on terms of equality, and as independent freemen;* it has not to be proven here.[3]

—Mary Ann Shadd Cary, "Our Tour" (1854)

*A*lthough Mary Ann Shadd Cary was the first African-American woman to own and edit a newspaper in North America, a recruiting agent for the Union Army during the Civil War, one of the first women to enter law school at Howard University, and a noted lecturer and activist for abolition, racial uplift, and Woman's Rights, her extraordinary life has, until the late twentieth century, been forgotten.[4] A recovery of her story reveals how she both transgressed expectations for black women and literally transgressed borders between slave and free states and between the United States and Canada. Shadd Cary belongs among the ranks of women travelers presented in *Traveling Economies* because her travel writing describing her journey to Canada and her advocacy of Canadian emigration for American blacks, her trips to sell subscriptions for her newspaper, and her lecture tours all address issues of women's mobility and autonomy that the other authors here raise as well. At the same time, the form of her travel writing, newspaper editorials and an emigrant's guide, invites us to broaden our ideas about what antebellum travel writing was and how it reached its readers. Putting her travel writing to the purpose of racial uplift, intended to improve the economic and social condition of American blacks, Shadd Cary provides us with a unique example of politically motivated travel writing focused on improving the lives of an entire race.

The above excerpts from Mary Ann Shadd Cary's *Hints to the Colored People of the North* (1849), *Plea for Emigration; or, Notes of Canada West* (1852), and *Provincial Freeman* (1854) highlight her continuing advocacy of travel as a potential solution not only for herself, but for all American blacks, slave and free. Storming onto the black literary and political scene with the publication of *Hints*, the young, upstart, twenty-six-year-old Mary Ann Shadd proceeds to tell her black community exactly how their aspirations to middle-class privilege are undercut by their embrace of superficial displays of wealth (which they can ill afford). Urging free blacks to adopt instead the more-substantial values of hard work, thrift, and education, *Hints* acknowledges and analyzes the workings of racism in the North while also offering an immediate practical solution (cut down on showy, costly ostentation) and a long-term plan for community betterment (adopt the best values of the white middle class and eventually share in their economic and social privilege). Her audience may not have been ready for her criticism, even though her censure and remedy are fairly conservative; a letter to the *North Star* promoting *Hints* suggests that "its telling too much truth" may be the reason that the pamphlet "widely circulated in this city, but I believe very little money has been paid for it." While Shadd Cary may have begun to influence her community (at least by generating controversy through her criticism), the passage of the Fugitive Slave Law the following year added desperate urgency to her mission. Abolitionists who aided escaping slaves became criminals under the new legislation, and free blacks could be "claimed" by so-called "owners" with little or no proof. Shadd Cary recognized that the Fugitive Slave Law jeopardized community-building just as it jeopardized the freedom and safety of individual community members. Her proemigration tract, *Plea*, cites the Fugitive Bill as the impetus for her own emigration and for her advocacy of removal to Canada as an alternative to African colonization and other abolition plans. Travel became a survival strategy for the black community, and travel writing served as a means to inform and unite that community. Travel editorials published in the newspaper she subsequently founded and edited, the *Provincial Freeman*, continued to use travel and travel writing to support transplanted black settlements. Traveling between black communities "by steamboat, railroad and wagon," Shadd Cary evaluates local progress toward her original goal of black economic and social accomplishment and the erosion of racism and hostility she hopes will follow.

Shadd Cary self-consciously enters onto a world stage as she addresses the continuing effects of diaspora, the global dispersal of African-Americans as a result of the international slave trade. In their recent essay, "Unfinished Migrations: Reflections on the African Diaspora and the Making of the Modern World," Tiffany Ruby Patterson and Robin D. G. Kelley argue for an understanding of diaspora as a "process," the notion of process highlighting mobility and cultural construction: "As a process it is constantly being remade through movement, migration, and travel, as well as imagined through thought, cultural production, and political struggle" (20).[5] Shadd Cary's black travel writing can be read in terms of diaspora as process, since it both enacts mobility and imagines what that mobility means through the cultural production of texts. Traveling to Canada to evaluate the possibilities for black emigration in the wake of the Fugitive Slave Law, Shadd Cary uses her firsthand knowledge to claim authority in the high-stakes national and international debates on the necessity of establishing "a permanent nationality" for African-Americans (*Plea* 50). As she tours black Cana-

dian settlements and evaluates them in the pages of the newspaper she
has founded and edits, the *Provincial Freeman*, Shadd Cary both promotes emigration and discusses the specific threats and problems facing
existing Canadian black communities. Her travel writing illustrates the
complicated process of finding a national home for African-Americans
and insists on building communities despite the risks. The result is not
only a new practice of travel writing, but also a new version of black
nationalism focused on the creation and maintenance of local black
communities.

Black Travel Writing: Shadd Cary and Black Literary Traditions

While Shadd Cary's writing may seem by turns strident and didactic
and hopelessly optimistic, her two-pronged focus on simultaneously
chastising her community and inspiring it to improve fits well within
emerging black literary traditions. Slave narratives certainly constitute
an important African-American genre, especially with their emphasis
on representing black subjectivity and humanity, decrying the injustice of slavery and racism, and foregrounding themes of freedom and
self-determination for individuals, families, and communities. Poetry,
essays, autobiographies, and fiction written by and about free blacks
in the North constitute a second, equally important branch of black
literature of the mid-nineteenth century. Travel narratives fit within this
second branch, adding yet another genre in which black authors sought
to represent the complexity and richness of black experience.

From nineteenth-century explorations of alternative locations for
black communities to twentieth- and twenty-first-century investigations
of global black identity, black travel writing wrestles with fundamental
questions about race, mobility, and autonomy, then and now, locally and
globally. Shadd Cary's travel writing contemporaries include Nancy
Prince and Mary Seacole, whom we met in the introduction and first
chapter, as well as William Wells Brown, whose *An American Fugitive
in Europe* (1854) chronicled his own flight from the Fugitive Slave Law
and his subsequent residence in Europe. Paul Cuffe's *A Brief Account of
the Settlement and Present Situation of the Colony of Sierra Leone, in Africa*
(1812) predates the emigration debates Shadd Cary participates in at

midcentury and promotes the return of American blacks to Africa, a plan he followed by founding a small colony several years later in Sierra Leone. Martin Delaney's *Official Report of the Niger Valley Exploring Party* (1861), Robert Campbell's *A Pilgrimage to My Motherland* (1861), and Alexander Crummell's *The Relations and Duties of Free Colored Men in America to Africa* (1860) continue to evaluate the possibilities and benefits of a return to Africa. Crummell goes so far as to urge American blacks to usurp the place of white imperialists: "And now perhaps you ask—'How shall the children of Africa, sojourning in foreign lands, avail themselves of the treasures of this continent?' I answer briefly, 'In the same way white men do.' *They* have pointed out the way, let us follow in the same track, and in the use of the like (legitimate) agencies by which trade is facilitated and money is made by them." Emigration surfaces again in early-twentieth-century black travel writing. The popular resurgence of pan-Africanism and black nationalism inspired romanticized accounts of Africa such as W. E. B. DuBois's "Little Portraits of Africa" (1924), published in the *Crisis*, a major literary publication of the Harlem Renaissance. DuBois's idealized vision dreams of "when there will spring in Africa a civilization . . . where men will sleep and think and dance and lie prone before the rising sons, and women will be happy." But frustration and alienation replace romance as later travel writers such as Richard Wright (*Black Power: A Record of Reactions in a Land of Pathos*, 1954) and Gwendolyn Brooks (*Report from Part One*, 1972) describe the heartbreak of coming home to Africa to find that they are not welcome and that their status as Americans fundamentally separates them from their African ancestors. Present-day travel writers take up the problem of African-Americans in relation to the rest of world in texts such as June Jordan's "Report from the Bahamas" (1989), which describes her Caribbean vacation and theorizes about the potential and limits for alliances between first and third world black people. Colleen McElroy not only embraces her position as a black female traveler in *A Long Way from St. Louie* (1997), but also suggests that her experiences of racism equip her to be a better, more-considerate tourist. This abbreviated list only hints at the richness of black travel writing, and Shadd Cary occupies an important place as a foremother of the tradition.[6]

Early black travel texts like Shadd Cary's encourage us to ask how travel narratives fit within the textual and cultural production of black communities in the antebellum period. Abolition, while certainly the first and foremost priority of activists and subject matter of black writers, shared space in the pages of autobiographies, column inches of newspapers, and orations of black lecturers with the discussion of how to develop and protect the free black population. Black women participated avidly in theorizing the priorities and strategies free black communities should adopt; Shadd Cary extended these cultural conversations. Maria Stewart may be thought of as the beginning of this tradition, as her speeches (1833), subsequently published in pamphlet form and in the pages of William Lloyd Garrison's abolitionist newspaper, *Liberator,* exhort her community, men and women alike, to work for freedom and intellectual and moral improvement: "How long shall the fair daughters of Africa be compelled to bury their minds and talents beneath a load of iron pots and kettles? Until union, knowledge and love begin to flow among us." While Stewart is usually cited as the first black woman to lecture to promiscuous audiences of both men and women, Sojourner Truth, Jarena Lee, and Zilpha Elaw toured as preachers and combined traveling, lecturing, and life-writing with their advocacy of abolition and black community uplift. Frances Ellen Watkins Harper, Shadd Cary's better-known contemporary, actually shared lecture platforms with Shadd Cary and espoused through her speeches, poems, short stories, and novels a similar concern with racial uplift, whether that meant the education of black girls, promoting marriage and family, or supporting black industry. These women authors looked to a day when abolition would be accomplished and worked ahead to build communities ready for freedom. Not only Shadd Cary's lectures but also her travel writing fit within and expand this project to offer travel as a means to safety and security for her people. Her outspoken political and social analysis not only joins the debates of her day but also prefigures the analysis of sexism and racism that black feminists continue to produce. Shadd Cary's traveling journalism also predates Ida B. Wells Barnett's work throughout the South to expose the horrors of lynching at the turn of the twentieth century. Black literature and black activism often work together, and Shadd Cary adds to both traditions as she puts travel writing to the purposes of representing, educating, and promoting black communities.[7]

Even as Shadd Cary fits within traditions of race work and travel literature, however, she also expands those traditions. Her communal focus and her representation of a black female traveler change our ideas of who was traveling and for what purpose. Her texts call us to look for more unconventional travel writing and writers and call our attention to new political purposes for travel writing beyond the advocacy and support of U.S. imperialism. Shadd Cary prefigures later black travel literature's focus on returning to global black communities—largely the romanticized return to Africa—and goes it one better by helping to build the community she travels in search of. Her promotion and protection of black communities in Canada West and back home in the United States distinguish her travel writing and offer a unique contribution to the genre and to the project of racial uplift.

Shadd Cary Offers "Hints" to the Black Middle Class

Shadd Cary began her travels from a different place than the travel writers we have met so far—she was a member of a more-privileged segment of the black middle class, and enjoyed a level of comfort that eluded Nancy Prince, but less social security than white, middle-class Amy Morris Bradley. Her experiences of marginalization and economic insecurity, however, place her among the ranks of ragged-edge travelers studied in *Traveling Economies*. "Black middle class" is a category used by scholars and historians to describe free blacks who, through skilled labor or entrepreneurial efforts, secured a measure of economic stability for their families. Emphasis on education, activism, racial uplift, morality, and religion marked many black, middle-class communities. Unfortunately, upward social mobility for free blacks was often curtailed by racism, whether in the form of limited job opportunities, overt discrimination in hiring or purchasing from black merchants and laborers, or in legislated or de facto segregation. Even as free blacks "achiev[ed] high social positions as well-respected leaders of their communit[ies]," critic Carla Peterson points to the continuing (and often devastating) effect of race prejudice, which resulted in "their economic and occupational status [being] disproportionately lower" than their white counterparts. Free blacks responded to this economic and social pressure from the Northern white population by forming close-knit communities that tried to promote individual and communal self-sufficiency. While the black middle class created cultural and economic opportunities for elite free blacks, primarily in urban areas like Philadelphia and Boston, racial discrimination effectively limited the economic and social advances made in larger American society by its less-privileged members.[8]

Within the category black middle class existed a wide range of economic and social status, even within local communities. Peterson helpfully divides the black middle class into elite and subaltern subgroups, with the class divisions in free black communities based on education, free status, geography, occupation, and skin tone. Literate, skilled craftsmen, businessmen, and professionals such as doctors, ministers, and teachers formed the elite, while the subaltern group "was composed primarily of unskilled laborers, the men employed as sailors, waiters, or mechanics, the women as domestics and laundresses." Free black men and women worked across social and economic lines for the betterment of their communities, advocating reforms (temperance, racial uplift) and political enfranchisement (abolition). These common causes united diverse, black-middle-class communities in efforts to better the social and economic position of all African-Americans. Nonetheless, communities could also be divided by economic and social issues, and by vastly different experiences of wealth and poverty. [9]

Shadd Cary was fortunate to benefit to a certain extent from black-middle-class economic stability and educational opportunities. Not sharing in the wealth of the black elite, Shadd Cary's family nevertheless had a high standing in their community, as biographer Jane Rhodes notes:

> Like her parents and grandparents, Mary Ann would reap the benefits of a mixed ancestry that offered certain privileges—they were mulatto, they were free born, they worked in the skilled trades, and they owned property. The Shadds escaped the worst of slavery while living in a slave state [Delaware], and benefited from a color-conscious social system in which light-skinned blacks had more status, wealth, and power than their dark-skinned relatives.

Shadd Cary's mix of privilege (within the free black community) and oppression (limits placed on her career and financial stability by race and gender) shaped the priorities of her later activism, which focused on economic, social, and educational opportunities for black Americans.[10]

Wealthier free black men and women enjoyed a high level of influence and donated time and money to racial-uplift programs and other social-reform movements; in fact, Shadd Cary may have become acquainted with many such race leaders when her family lived outside Philadelphia.[11] Unfortunately, the majority of free blacks struggled financially, as Nancy Prince's efforts to support herself and her family demonstrate. Black literature of the period depicts the wide economic continuum of the black middle class. Frank Webb's novel *The Garies and Their Friends* (1857) represents a diverse, black-middle-class community with characters who range from manual laborers, domestic servants, clerks, and professionals to a black millionaire real estate investor. Shadd Cary falls between the deprivation experienced by Prince and the affluence achieved by the elite vanguard represented by successful black entrepreneurs.

However, a letter from Shadd Cary's father illustrates a level of emotional support not available to most ragged-edge women, white or black:

> I therefore advise you to come home as soon as you can prudently leave the place. Thank God you yet have a home where you are welcome[;] therefore do not sacrifice your remaining health if you can posibly [sic] help it, be cautious how you inform your school patron that you are about to leave lest you put in thier [sic] power to wrong you either in your money matters or your character ... I remain your affectionate Father.[12]

Offered financial and professional advice, as well as love and refuge, Shadd Cary was fortunate to have the emotional, if not necessarily financial, support of her family. She remained close to her family, in fact, for her entire life, living and working with them in Canada after they emigrated and joined her. At the time she received this letter, she was working as a teacher, and according to Rhodes, "Her race and gender meant that her income was among the lowest for teachers in [New York], requiring her to exist on a meager salary with little job stability."[13]

Despite her ragged-edge experiences of continuing financial struggle, Shadd Cary promotes a philosophy of racial uplift based on assimilation to white, middle-class values in her earliest publication, *Hints to the Colored People of the North* (1849). A self-published twelve-page pamphlet, *Hints* presents Shadd Cary's "direct analysis of the condition of northern blacks," and begins Shadd Cary's career as an outspoken critic of both the nation and the black community. Unfortunately, no complete extant copy of *Hints* exists, but it is excerpted in the *North Star*, Frederick Douglass's newspaper. Disparaging ostentatious and economically imprudent displays of fashion, Shadd Cary encourages blacks to adopt the white, middle-class virtues of modesty, decorum, and education. She asks, "What profits a display of ourselves? . . . How does that better our condition as a people?," chastising her fellow black community members for squandering resources on fashion that they can ill afford. According to Shadd Cary, "expensive entertainments, excursions . . . [and] a display of costly apparel" drain free blacks' bank accounts and incite the scorn, rather than the desired admiration, of white society, whose response Shadd Cary provides for her readers when she insists that the white middle class "say[s] 'the colored people are spending their money for velvet and gold now, and in winter they will be dependent on public charity.'" Shadd Cary claims that her community's actions reinforce the racist assumptions of the surrounding white society, which she again recreates for her audience: "Negroes and Indians set more value on the outside of their heads than what the inside needs: 'They are glad when one of their number dies that they walk in procession, and show their regalia.'" Shadd Cary was only twenty-six years old when she penned this outspoken criticism of her own community; her scathing remarks set the stage for a career of unabashed challenges to the United States, Canada, and her own black communities. The underlying premise of her argument, however, was that the Northeast could be a viable home for African-Americans and that racism could be overcome by evidence of black morality and industry. Shadd Cary believed that blacks would eventually secure a place as both citizens and members of the comfortable middle class. That idealistic view changed with the passage in 1850 of the Fugitive Slave Law, which marked the beginning of her travels and her promotion of emigration as a solution for her community.[14]

After attending the November 1851 "Great North American Anti-Slavery Convention" held in Toronto, Shadd Cary was convinced by proponents of Canadian emigration and made plans to stay. She took up residence in Windsor, Canada West (across Lake Erie from Toronto), and founded a school to support herself, although the poverty of the students she sought to serve necessitated finding funding from the American Missionary Association in order to keep the school open. After nine months of residence in Canada, Shadd Cary published her *Plea for Emigration* and entered into Canadian and U.S. debates about emigration formally. She continued to live and work in Canada West for nine years, eventually founding and editing her newspaper and continually touring Western Canada and the U.S. Great Lakes region to sell subscriptions to her paper and to lecture for supplemental income.[15]

A Plea for Emigration:
Defining Community, Beginning the Work

Shadd Cary's *Plea for Emigration* begins with a unifying vision of community based on shared interests, but quickly complicates that formulation to include the diversity she experiences while traveling among various black settlements. Adding urgency to her call for removal to Canada, Shadd Cary figures both free black and slave populations as under attack, threatened specifically by the Fugitive Slave Law and more generally by the U.S. government's failure to abolish or even to curtail the spread of slavery. The risk has become more serious "since the passage of the odious Fugitive Slave Law has made a residence in the United States to many [blacks] dangerous in the extreme" (43). The legal support of the re-capture and re-enslavement of fugitive slaves characterizes a central government she terms "a pro-slavery administration" whose policies will have a "fatal effect" on free and fugitive populations alike (43). Working hand in hand with the hostile administration is the "Colonization Society," an "immoral influence" that in supporting emigration to Africa, "teeming as she is with the breath of pestilence, a burning sun and fearful maladies," constitutes one of the black population's "most bitter enemies" (43). In opposition to both slavery and the convenient removal of blacks to what she views as distant, unsuitable, and potentially deadly Africa, Shadd Cary offers her own assessment of Canada as a solution for her global black community.

Shadd Cary's global solution, however, is fundamentally rooted in local knowledge. She authorizes her text by virtue of her firsthand experience in the location she advocates: "I have endeavoured to furnish information . . . believing that more reliance would be placed upon a statement of facts obtained in the country, from reliable sources and from observation . . . [therefore] I determined to visit Canada, and there to collect such information as most persons desire" (44). Shadd Cary's authority thus rests in her declaration of specific working knowledge of the new potential home for her broadly defined African-American community. She can speak to the viability of Canadian emigration because she has been there and seen it herself. Travel authorizes her writing and her political commentary on major issues facing blacks in both the United States and Canada. By defining black communities as in peril, Shadd Cary can then figure herself as their guide out of danger and into the utopian possibilities of Canadian settlement.

In evaluating Canada as a viable new home for her displaced African-American community, Shadd Cary focuses on the pragmatic matters of climate, agriculture, and land prices. Recognizing "our ideas of comfort and pecuniary independence" as community priorities, she unites her audience with the collective pronoun *our* and with detailed answers to emigrants' practical questions (49). Shadd Cary begins by addressing what she identifies as the foremost objection to Canada as a viable location, the climate. She corrects misinformation with the specifics of temperature charts and the perhaps overly sanguine assurance of her own evaluation: "I believe that climate poses no obstacle to emigration, but that it is the most desirable known in so high a latitude, for emigrants generally, and coloured people particularly" (48). With headings such as "Soil, Timber and Clearing Lands" (49), "Grains, Potatoes and Turnips" (53), "Garden Vegetables" (54), "Prices of Land in the Country and City Property" (57), and "Labour and Trades" (59), *Plea* offers assurance to a very specific audience that their basic needs can be met in the proposed new homeland.

Although the practical concerns of agriculture and climate figure prominently in the decision to emigrate, Shadd Cary identifies the protection of black civil rights as the most crucial benefit Canada provides would-be emigrants. Any land might do "if the questions of personal freedom and political rights were left out of the subject, but as they are paramount, too much may not be said on this point" (49). To achieve the goal of "a permanent nationality," both soil and civil rights must be amenable to newly arriving black emigrants (50). Shadd Cary highlights extensive discussions of laws guaranteeing access to education and voting rights. She quotes legislation directly in an effort to prove that emigrants are not relying solely on Canadian sympathy for fugitive slaves, but that law, rather than sentiment, is the solid bedrock upon which the community can build its future. If the Fugitive Slave Law constitutes the impetus for black exodus from the United States, then Canadian laws guaranteeing black civil rights are the best motivation for choosing the site of the new black nation.

Shadd Cary is aware that her audience is skeptical after the disparity they have already encountered in the United States between legislated freedoms and the continuing social practices of racism. She attempts to overcome this reservation by including portraits of black accomplishment in Canada, balancing her practical discussion with inspiration for would-be immigrants. She reassures her community that Canadian social practice matches the guarantee of civil rights she celebrates. Scholar Richard Almonte argues that her emigrant's guide provides her audience with "reassurance that the journey was worth it." The specificity of Shadd Cary's definition of community informs her selection of examples of what makes emigration "worth it," and modifies the generic form of an emigrant's guide to include racially specific assessments of the proposed destination. Thus, her vision of a global black audience becoming local black communities in settlements throughout Canada West shapes her advocacy and her guide's advice.[16]

Shadd Cary speaks directly to her audience's experiences of racism in an effort to calm their fears and to assure them that she understands their concerns and that Canada will meet their individual and communal needs. Writing for an audience of fugitive slaves and free blacks whose labor has been stolen, unpaid, undervalued, and segregated, she presents a utopian vision in which black workers do not suffer discriminatory labor practices, advance due to their merit and hard work, and even become the managers of white labor. Shadd Cary compares the racism of the United States to the promise of Canada in this way:

> All trades that are practiced in the United States are there [in Canada] patronized by whomsoever carries on: no man's complexion affecting his business. If a coloured man understands his business, he receives the public patronage the same as a white man. He is not obliged to work a little better, and at a lower rate. There is no degraded class to identify him with, therefore every man's work stands or falls according to merit, not as is his colour. Builders and other tradesmen of different complexions work together on the same building and in the same shop, with perfect harmony, and often the proprietor of an establishment is coloured, and the majority or all of the men employed are white. (59)

In the space of several sentences, Shadd Cary has claimed for her dis-placed black community the freedom and equality the United States fails so miserably to provide.

Hoping ultimately to unite her community literally on Canadian soil, Shadd Cary begins by ideologically uniting them through common goals of social, economic, and political freedom. Although she addresses her text to "emigrants in general—men of small means, or with no capi-tal" (52), she paints a grand picture of future economic security. Foretell-ing the future of black Canadians, Shadd Cary optimistically asserts: "The conviction, though, is irresistible that indigence and moderate competence must at no distant day give place to wealth, intelligence, and their concomitants" (53). Dedication and hard work, she insists, will ultimately be their own reward: "From the many instances of suc-cess under my observation (particularly of formerly totally destitute coloured persons) I firmly believe that with an axe and a little energy, an independent position would result in a short period" (52). From the lowest to the most ambitious, emigrants, including Shadd Cary herself, find in Canada opportunities for building a new individual and com-munal future.

Uniting her community with her vision of success for all, despite the hurdles of discrimination, poverty, and lack of education, Shadd Cary's proemigration tract nonetheless reveals potential and existing divisions among would-be community members. Shadd Cary extends the authority she has gained by traveling and authoring her guide-book, offering her views on how the community should behave once it arrives. Her stances in *Plea* on segregation, "begging" (the practice of soliciting charitable donations from the United States for fugitive-slave settlements), and the management of black settlements offer valuable insight into the development of her political and social philosophies. However, her pointed arguments for her own uplift agenda simultane-ously showcase the presence of opposition to her opinions, and thus the diversity of viewpoints within the black community. Critic Carla Peterson has drawn attention to this feature of Shadd Cary's editorials in the *Provincial Freeman*, and *Plea* foreshadows this development in her later newspaper publications. For example, Shadd Cary critiques "the course of the coloured persons, in pertinaciously refusing overtures of religious fellowship from the whites," which she identifies as "tend[ing] to perpetuate ignorance" (61–62). Demonstrating her prointegrationist stance, she questions any institutionalized segregation, but also reveals the strong support among segments of the black community for separate black institutions.

Deeper rifts among the black community are suggested in Shadd Cary's discussion of the Refugee's Home, a settlement for fugitive slaves founded and administrated by fellow emigration advocate and abolitionist Henry Bibb. Like many settlements, the Refugee's Home distributed a large block of communal land in small parcels to newly arriving emigrants, who benefited from an initial gift of land and help with buying adjacent land. The distinctive feature of the Refugee's Home, however, was that it served "fugitives from slavery *only*" (70, emphasis in original). Shadd Cary's status as a free black may underlie her objection to the exclusive nature of the Refugee's Home, as she declares that there is little advantage free blacks have "from the accident of nominal freedom" (71). More important, however, than economic benefits free blacks lost by being excluded from the Refugee's Home was the growing schism in the black community. According to Shadd Cary, distrust and disdain between fugitives and free blacks constitute a harmful continuing legacy of slavery: "The policy of slaveholders has been to create a contempt for *free* people in the bosom of their slaves, and pretty effectually have they succeeded" (71). Shadd Cary's definition of community starts with the premise that fugitives and free blacks share common interests and will work together to achieve a safe communal home place.

Her text, however, reveals the lingering impact of proslavery rhetoric that demonizes free blacks to discourage slave escape. The community she targets may be tenuous at best, a construction that she hopes to strengthen and make real through her emigrant's guide, and later through her newspaper. Shadd Cary figures the situation in terms of family conflict: "Thus, discord among members of the same family is engendered; a breach made that the exclusive use by fugitives of the society lands is not likely to mend" (71). Rather than emphasizing the familial ties of all blacks as a basis for black nationhood, Shadd Cary reveals the fragility of her transplanted black community. The project of uniting so many local constituencies (not just free black and fugitive, but probegging vs. self-sufficiency, segregationist vs. integrationist) is formidable. Shadd Cary addresses this continuing challenge by moving from her emigrant's guide to travel writing published in the black press in a newspaper that she has founded and edits to reach a global black and white audience.

Creating and Connecting Community:
The Provincial Freeman

An even more complex portrait of the multiplicity of political and social viewpoints within the local black communities of Canada West emerges through the pages of Shadd Cary's newspaper, the *Provincial Freeman*. The genesis of the paper itself reinforced the complexity of the community that constituted its audience. Founded in 1853, Shadd Cary's newspaper directly competed with Henry Bibb's existing *Voice of the Fugitive* (1851–54). Bibb's paper was already struggling to survive, given competition from other Canadian papers and U.S. black and abolitionist newspapers such as Frederick Douglass's *North Star* and Garrison's *Liberator*. Nonetheless, Shadd Cary insisted on entering the crowded newspaper marketplace because she felt that she and other black Canadians were not fully represented by existing publications. Her ongoing feud with Bibb and his wife, Mary, over their opposing views on the funding and maintenance of black settlements, particularly the Refugee's Home, meant that she, and those who shared her opinions, would not be represented in the pages of the *Voice of the Fugitive*. While Shadd Cary was most interested in having a forum in which to present her own viewpoint, the *Provincial Freeman* also succeeded in representing a wide range of black opinions and in portraying the diversity and complexity of local black communities.

Of particular interest are Shadd Cary's travel editorials, letters written to the *Provincial Freeman* during her frequent and sustained subscription tours throughout Canada West and the Midwestern United States (1854–56). Travel and community intersect in Shadd Cary's editorials to reinforce her claims of specific local knowledge and to represent fully local black communities. The impetus for these travel editorials was, as Peterson notes, "most often a debate entertained with an opponent who did not share a similar program of uplift." By recording these debates, Peterson argues, Shadd Cary represents opposing viewpoints, as her travel editorials "explode into a polyphonous discourse that underscores the heterogeneity of black communit[ies] and [their] racial uplift agendas." The political and social agendas of black settlements in Canada (or of black communities in the United States) cannot be simplified to one issue or to one proposed program of reform. Rather, black communities were dynamic, and issues and potential solutions were hotly debated and constantly being reevaluated. Critic Elizabeth McHenry argues that the black press provided a forum for black communities "as they struggled to maintain their focus on communal change while remaining true to differences in perspectives on race and nation, political vision and public stance." Shadd Cary's travel and travel writing highlight the tension between common cause and community divisions; her journeys to individual towns and settlements spotlight local survival strategies that can be shared with the wider community through the pages of the *Provincial Freeman*.[17]

Community survival, according to Shadd Cary, means that black women as well as men need to assume their rightful place as citizens and community members. Her travel editorials link her political views on emigration and legal rights for American and Canadian blacks with her critique of sexism. Shadd Cary celebrates the black women's political activity she observes on her journeys and admonishes reluctant women to take part in public racial uplift efforts as well. For example, she makes special note of women present at a political rally: "Attended the meeting held by the voters, last night, at Chatham, at which I saw quite a large numbers [*sic*] of females. I like that new feature in political gatherings" (5 Aug. 1854). By the time Shadd Cary writes her travel letters for the *Provincial Freeman,* she has become a spokesperson for emigration and the first African-American woman to publish and edit her own newspaper. With so public a career, not to mention one dealing with such controversial political topics, she steps outside the bounds of conventional feminine behavior, going beyond critiques of black women's exclusion from middle-class domesticity to redraw the boundaries of appropriate female behavior to include traveling, writing, citizenship, and even nation-building.

Encouraging other women to join her, Shadd Cary represents female activism in her travel writing as logical and necessary to the cause of racial uplift, the female support of which, according to her, is a growing trend: "The women—God bless them—see the work of reform to be theirs too, and good sisters in the places I have mentioned, will go to work for an Annual Bazaar" (22 July 1854). By showing black women in Canada West actively participating both in political rallies and in the more-traditional role of orchestrating fund-raising bazaars, she illustrates that Canada offers black women like herself unprecedented opportunities for public activity and leadership.

At the same time that she presents these new opportunities for women, Shadd Cary disparages those who offer traditional middle-class gender roles as an excuse for political inactivity. She castigates black women who invoke gender and class privilege at the expense of the cause of racial uplift:

> Nothing can exceed the interest shown by the women in [the *Provincial Freeman's*] success—a hopeful sign, when one calls to remembrance the apathy of our females generally and especially in the great City of Toronto, until very recently. If there is any one thing that tends to intensify one's contempt for the *muslin* multitude, it is the nothingness the delicate creatures display when invited to aid in a work for the general good. (21 Oct. 1854)

Shadd Cary sarcastically refers to the performance of femininity demonstrated by these women; working to "impress you with their 'feebleness,'" these reluctant race workers shrink from public gatherings and require the approval of men (21 Oct. 1854). Instead, Shadd Cary argues that these women should use their comparative wealth and influence (as discussed earlier, their status was still low compared with their white, middle-class counterparts) for the political cause of racial uplift and should further expand the possibilities open to women by their example.

Shadd Cary makes few personal references in her travel editorials, but those she includes show that she practiced what she preached. Shadd Cary's representations of her own unfeminine behavior challenge the limits of domesticity for women as well as doctrines of racial inferiority that dismiss black women's accomplishments as thinkers and activists. One incident in particular, a debate between John Scoble, trustee for the Dawn Settlement, and Shadd Cary, illustrates her strategies of self-presentation.[18] Attending a public meeting of the Dawn Settlement, one of the black settlement communities founded for fugitive slaves and free blacks, Shadd Cary hoped to secure subscriptions and pledges for future fund-raising from the residents. Instead, Scoble, a white man of considerable influence both in the region itself and in emigration debates, disparaged the "spirit of the paper" and recommended that "it should be stopped" (22 July 1854). He then turned his attention to Shadd Cary, whom he termed "of no position, and comparatively unknown" and therefore unfit to edit the paper.

Shadd Cary's reply to Scoble's attack debunks gender and race stereotypes at the same time that it reveals her own defiant disregard of social conventions. Her ironic description of the confrontation emphasizes her low social status compared to Scoble's:

> Your humble agent was suddenly the insignificant body. Imposing scene! Mr. John Scoble, the would-be member for Peel, or *anywhere*, if you please, trying to do battle against a negro *woman, in a log schoolhouse at Dawn!* Conflict of Russian and Turk, how comparable with it! (22 July 1854)

Shadd Cary uses Scoble's attack on an insignificant "negro *woman*" to make him appear ridiculous and ungallant. Her caustic critique also indicts Scoble as a political opportunist ("would-be member" refers to his ambitions to hold public legislative office). As a white trustee of a troubled and mismanaged black settlement, Scoble seeks to gain power by exploiting Canadian blacks, according to Shadd Cary's argument. Scoble's tactics of intimidation, used here on Shadd Cary, whose race and gender make her a vulnerable target, demonstrate reprisals she faced for her activism and for her autonomy.

Even though Shadd Cary portrays herself as undeserving of Scoble's attack, she and her newspaper are threatening. She undercuts the seriousness of their confrontation with irony, comparing it to the ongoing war in Crimea. Regardless, Shadd Cary and her newspaper clearly troubled established leaders in the region, such as Scoble. Invoking the modesty and powerlessness associated with her gender, Shadd Cary deflects attention from her transgressive behavior and simultaneously belittles her enemy. However, her growing power and influence are evident, as illustrated by her presence at the meeting, her position as editor and publisher of her own newspaper, and her publication of her version of the conflict. Shadd Cary succeeds in voicing her political opinions, and in controlling the medium through which they reach her audience. Thus, she had more power than many black men and white, middle-class women of her time, and her defiance of feminine restrictions on her actions and writing is a model for her female readers. By describing her travels and her public debates with men in the columns of the *Provincial Freeman*, Shadd Cary connects politics, race, and gender in a way that promotes black female autonomy.

Shadd Cary's battle of words with Scoble is one of many scathing critiques of other race leaders and uplift programs that demonstrate the complexity of the issues facing African-Americans and the multiplicity of proposed solutions, which the *Provincial Freeman* effectively documents. For example, Shadd Cary disparages Frederick Douglass's position on black emigration, which, perhaps because of the influence of Shadd Cary and others, changed from outspoken opposition to belated endorsement: "Frederick Douglass, Esq., and some great guns are to come from the States, I am told, whose policy, so recently 'changed,' will be told by themselves" (22 July 1854). Criticizing John Scoble's management of the Dawn settlement and his probegging philosophy, Shadd Cary argues for her own cause of black economic self-sufficiency (22 July 1854, 22 Sept. 1855).[19] Another African-American leader, Rev. C. C. Foote, advocates separate black schools and churches, contrary to Shadd Cary's integrationist stance (8 Dec. 1855).[20] Shadd Cary also alerts her readers to corruption, exposing Rev. Hiram Wilson's fraudulent missionary efforts: "Mr. Wilson's prosperity only confirms one in the irresistible conclusion, that no missionary field is more *profitable* than that in which the fugitives of Canada are the *victims*" (3 Nov. 1855). She also uses her travel editorials to condemn ill-conceived abolitionist efforts, such as those of Henry Garrett, who attempted to raise funds in support of his plan to buy the freedom of American slaves (8 Dec. 1855). Shadd Cary's strongly worded denouncement of opposition (and even friendly) race leaders and their alternative views on emigration, self-sufficiency, and abolition nonetheless show the range of political positions present in the relatively sparsely populated western provinces of Canada.

In addition to illustrating the variety of opinions held by African-Americans and their leaders, Shadd Cary reveals that these differences threaten to erupt into violent confrontation: in one city, she claims, "Begging is openly advocated, and threats against the life and security of those who do not agree with them, are quite common" (6 Oct. 1885). Although Shadd Cary never represents herself as being in physical danger, her mention of the threatened violence echoes the threats that Nancy Prince confronted, as well as the violence that Anne Royall experienced. The very mobility that enables Shadd Cary's participation in her community's volatile debates on crucial issues also makes her particularly vulnerable, as does, of course, her outspokenness.

As the list of opponents and issues covered in Shadd Cary's editorials suggests, the format and genre of her travel editorials lend themselves to changing, quick, and evolving responses to the needs of local black communities. Shadd Cary literally takes her show on the road, addressing the most pressing issues facing the particular locality in which she finds herself. In an editorial refuting criticisms of the *Provincial Freeman* by a rival, white-owned newspaper, the *Kent Advertiser,* Shadd Cary condemns the *Advertiser*'s failure to represent and support the black residents of Chatham and displays her own superior knowledge of specific community needs. This personal familiarity with the local political scene trumps the feigned concern of the *Advertiser:*

> When have you [the editor of the *Kent Advertiser*] asked for equal school privileges, in your public schools, for the children of the respectable colored voters of Chatham, the people whom you seem to love so dearly, and how frequently have you urged that point? When did you allude to the black injustice done colored passengers on your Chatham boats, by the contrivance of the "Colored Cabin?" What measures have you opposed to the unequal division of the town into wards, by which the influence of colored voters would be weakened—eh? What have you had to say about the insults offered to the entire colored population of your town, by "Negro Serenaders," with their caricatures of the colored people, and which are so well known to your citizens, and so distasteful to the colored people? When has your influence been extended in favor of the section of Chatham, so much occupied by them, so as to increase their convenience on wet weather? Your readers have read plenty about side walks in other directions! Has your interest in them made you ask for a bridge or a plank for their accommodation? (8 Sept. 1855)

This lengthy passage demonstrates Shadd Cary's extensive knowledge of both the large and small issues facing the particular black community in Chatham. From the serious threat of unequal and inadequate access to education and the gerrymandering of voting districts compromising black political representation, to the social practice of racism exhibited in segregated transportation and minstrel performances, Shadd Cary offers Chatham's black community more-accurate textual representation that will hopefully lead to political and social change. The discussion of sidewalks, which may at first seem trivial, further testifies to her intimate knowledge of the local communities in which she lives and works, and demonstrates her commitment to improving the everyday lives of her fellow community members through her newspaper and her travel writing.

While Shadd Cary's travel gained her unprecedented insight into the workings of local black communities, the format of her editorials, published quickly in her newspaper, allowed her to address urgent issues immediately. Critic Todd Vogel argues that the ephemeral nature of the black press was a decided advantage: "It made the writers nimble. They could plunge into the public conversation and get their views out nearly immediately." Shadd Cary frequently takes advantage of her ability to address immediate controversies and threats facing black neighborhoods. In her account of her trip to the Dawn Settlement, for instance, she limits her description of the actual location in favor of alerting her readers to what she sees as an ill-conceived and dishonest begging scheme that is shortly to be adopted by the settlement. Arriving in Dawn a few weeks before the announcement of the plan, Shadd Cary can warn her community about the "grand scheme by which poor gentlemen, as well as rich ones, may line their pockets" (22 July 1854). She therefore effectively steals the thunder of the Dawn administrators' upcoming announcement and galvanizes her community, who "will yet arise in their might and seep these pretenders from amongst them" (22 July 1854). Quick response to such threats is possible because, as Shadd Cary declares in the next sentence, "The *Freeman* is read here, and the people pay for it." The financial support she receives from the community allows her to fully represent its up-to-the-minute concerns and to organize an effective response to continuing and emerging threats. Her extensive travel authorizes and informs her analysis and directs efforts to ensure communal survival.[21]

Despite the firsthand evidence of social and political discrimination Shadd Cary uncovers on her travels, ultimately she focuses on strengths—specifically on practical strategies to combat racism—rather than on community vulnerability. Attributing discrimination to a few isolated "enterprising American[s], with more brass than brains," she dismisses the threat, saying, "I assure you [they do] not have an influence" (21 Oct. 1854). Moreover, she insists that growing black political power will quickly overcome prejudice if blacks combine their influence to resist racism, encouraging the black community to "meet the minion[']s prejudice at the polls" (3 Nov. 1855). As evidence of the power of black community solidarity, she cites the example of victory by "faithful colored compeers in the colored school election" (3 Nov.

1855). Historians Robin Winks, William Pease, and Jason Silverman have effectively documented the virulence of race prejudice in Canada in the mid-1800s, findings which suggest that Shadd Cary deliberately emphasized the promise rather than the practice of racial tolerance in Canada. Peterson claims that Shadd Cary's underestimation of racism's power is an evidence of the "practical limitations" of her theories of uplift and black nationalism. Rather than underestimating racism, however, Shadd Cary's travel writing presents various local strategies for combating prejudice, ranging from organizing voting blocks to buying black newspapers. Her strategy is to build black communities strong enough to withstand and ultimately defeat the serious threat of racism in Canada and, by extension, the United States and the globe.[22]

Shadd Cary effectively represents black communal achievement in her travel editorials, a different emphasis from the celebration of individual achievement that traditionally characterizes travel writing. While she does certainly represent her own successful battles with opposition race and political leaders, her text foregrounds her dispersed community's tenacious will to survive and prosper despite the hostile political, social, and physical climate. Hence, rather than offering herself as a model belying notions of racial inferiority, Shadd Cary offers instead the endurance and success of black settlements as proof of her communities' competence. The focus of the travel narrative shifts, then, from the heroic feats of the white male traveler conquering new lands and people, or even the celebration of female accomplishment found in Lillian Leland's *Traveling Alone*, to a representation of community that highlights diversity and persistence in specific localities.

Shadd Cary's focus on community-building and survival constitutes a unique revision of the travel genre. Shadd Cary believes the growing strength of black communities, united through the pages of her newspaper, will eventually supply the safe haven that free blacks and fugitives so desperately need. Her warnings are intended to ensure that black communities thrive on the local level, that they might provide national and global solutions for African-Americans. Shadd Cary's advocacy of Canadian emigration negotiates the tension between local and global black needs. The global goal of a black nation requires an influx of black emigrants whose numbers will provide protection against the practices of discrimination. Until the population of emigrants reaches that critical mass, however, fledgling local communities need to combat threats to their survival so that they can eventually accommodate those new arrivals.

The apparent paradox of Shadd Cary's description of the St. Catherine's community perhaps best reveals this double purpose of her travel writing: to promote emigration and to protect emigrants who have already arrived. Her first mention of St. Catherine's offers a dire warning at its conclusion: "There is certainly neither British justice nor laws to be had in and about this section, and the colored people look 'down-hearted.' More about this place in my next" (6 Oct. 1855). Her warning here proclaims that legislation guaranteeing black civil rights is not being enforced, and that black community members are dispirited and failing to effectively protest the problem. Such a description would seem to condemn St. Catherine's as an inhospitable community for potential emigrants. However, in her following travel editorial Shadd Cary presents a seemingly contradictory description: "It may not be too late yet to urge upon emigrants and others, the claims of that thriving town [St. Catherine's]" (3 Nov. 1855). Her seeming reversal is paired with more evidence of curtailed rights, specifically a lack of access to schools. But rather than depicting black residents as "down-hearted" and discouraged, in this editorial she describes the successful resistance employed by black community members during the colored-school election. Presenting warnings and strategies for reform, Shadd Cary invites blacks to claim their share of the potential bounty of St. Catherine's. Thus, her message is not contradictory but two-pronged: she is urging emigrating blacks to take advantage of desirable and economically viable locations in Canada West at the same time that she works to strengthen the communities already existing in those locations. Consequently, travel becomes a political tool that serves Shadd Cary and her community in their struggle to articulate the local, national, and global issues facing black communities and to propose and implement solutions.

Travel and travel writing, however, are not only political tools for at-risk black communities. Critic Katherine Bassard's formulation of "performing community" illuminates the ways in which Shadd Cary's literary production constitutes an aesthetic and cultural production that does not merely reflect community, but actively re-creates it. Bassard articulates the relationship of cultural production and community this way:

The forms and practices we designate African American culture are active and constitutive of African American community rather than passive indicators of race/group identity . . . [pre-Emancipation African Americans] are *performing community*, engaging in and (re)producing cultural forms and practices whose central function is community building and the production of the terms by which African Americans come to identify themselves as "a people."

Bassard's discussion highlights the dynamic relationship between cultural production and community formation, an ongoing process we can certainly trace in Shadd Cary's travel writing. In her analysis of the black press, Historian Elizabeth McHenry suggests the power of reading as early black newspapers understood it: "[Reading] was an invitation to participate, a means of orienting the individual toward social and communal models of exchange, be they written or oral, that would enhance civic life and facilitate involvement in the public sphere." Reading the travel writing of Shadd Cary literally connected her readers across the miles of difficult Canadian terrain and galvanized them for political action. As the example of her description of St. Catherine's demonstrates, Shadd Cary's literal displacement as a black female traveler made possible a creative response to the threats facing her community and ultimately created and connected that community through her aesthetic and textual production. Shadd Cary is able to textually displace the threat of increasing racism in St. Catherine's in order to foreground communal possibility, and by considering Shadd Cary's travel writing in this light, we gain new insights into the practice of the genre and the powerful role black travel writing can play in black communities and in the process of representing and remedying diaspora.[23]

Conclusions:
Implications for Theorizing Travel Writing

Shadd Cary's full representation, protection, promotion, and, ultimately, creation of black communities in Canada West applies the uplift mission of black newspapers to the genre of travel writing. In the process, Shadd Cary revises uplift projects, the scope of the black press, and the narrative form of travel writing. Stressing the diversity of black political and social agendas, she represents black communities as dynamic and constantly changing, a powerful antidote to static portrayals of black unity and solidarity that shied away from any presentation of discord or conflict. Shadd Cary's focus on local black communities models her

larger national and global uplift goal: to create a black nation of independent black thinkers and activists. Rather than construct her community on a foundation of inflexible and unchanging political mottoes,
Shadd Cary equips her community to adjust to new ideas, new threats,
and new strategies for survival. Eschewing uplift models of "lifting
as we rise," Shadd Cary locates her activism on the ground in local
places instead of as a hierarchy of upward mobility. Thus, her travel to
settlements and black neighborhoods becomes a crucial element of her
textual and political production. It is her knowledge of local places, in
fact, that lends authority and insight to her radical revision of uplift. By
focusing on protecting and promoting those communities, Shadd Cary
changes the parameters of travel writing to highlight communal rather
than individual achievement.

In the pages of the *Provincial Freeman*, Shadd Cary promoted her
community and described her own traveling exploits. Travel writing
and the black press may at first seem unlikely partners. However, writing for an audience of fugitive slaves and free blacks struggling with
the forced mobility of escape or relocation, Shadd Cary does more than
promote another possible place to run. Her travel and mobility instead
create a home place, promoting the survival of viable and sustainable
black communities. Elaborating on her earlier *Plea for Emigration*, the
Provincial Freeman works toward her goal of creating community by
connecting the often geographically isolated black settlements through
her emigrant's guide, her subscription tours, and the pages of the newspaper. Study of the *Provincial Freeman* demonstrates the potential of
the black press to operate in sophisticated ways to express the diverse
voices within the black community and to connect that community
while still respecting the divisions and fractures among its members.
Although we often think of newspapers as ephemeral, new attention to
the black press underscores how recovering black periodicals can provide local community histories that capture the diversity of viewpoints,
concerns, and possibilities. Shadd Cary's emigrant's guide, travel editorials, and newspaper provide fascinating examples of how the black
press and black travel writing can work to represent and even create
dynamic black communities, both yesterday and today.

Shadd Cary shares with Amy Morris Bradley and Nancy Prince the
freedom and potential danger of being a ragged-edge woman traveler
as well as the quest for a safe, secure home. She shares with Anne Royall
an overt focus on nation-building that belies the expectations of separate spheres—with women confined to domesticity and the home—and

provides female readers with models of mobility and activism. Shadd Cary expanded the role of travel writing, using it to become a spokesperson for her community and to work for liberation and social justice both inside and outside that community. Early feminist Frances Wright also sought to expand women's roles and their place, and imagined that the new nation would provide unprecedented opportunities for white, middle-class women like herself. While her education, wealth, and social connections initially facilitated her travels throughout the Northeast, her public advocacy of Woman's Rights, abolition, and free love made her a figure of public ridicule and scorn, and perhaps the most infamous woman of the early nineteenth century. An examination of Wright's early travel writing, her subsequent activism and abolitionist work, and the extremely negative public response she generated documents the extent of antebellum culture's distrust of mobile, autonomous women. The following chapter will examine the unwelcome and unexpected figure of the ragged-edge female traveler as both a challenge to middle-class definitions of appropriate femininity and a convenient counterexample that effectively reinforces middle-class notions of proper womanhood.

·Four·

A "Singular Spectacle of a Female"

Frances Wright's Traveling Figure[1]

As to Fanny Wright, you said you believed her to be honest in her opinions, amiable in her disposition, philanthropic in her efforts, and endowed with rare intellect. Allowing that you are as near right as partisans usually are, in estimating leaders, still I must compliment you by saying, that I believe you have secret *feelings* that would present a very different picture of this strange excrescence of female character.

Every man of sense and refinement, admires a woman *as a woman;* and when she steps out of this character, a thousand things that in their appropriate sphere would be admired, become disgusting and offensive.

The apropriate [*sic*] character of a woman demands delicacy of appearance and manners, refinement of sentiment, gentleness of speech, modesty in feeling and action, a shrinking from notoriety and public gaze, a love of dependence, and protection, aversion to all that is coarse and rude, and instinctive abhorrence of all that tends to indelicacy and impurity, either in principles or actions. These are what are admired and sought for in a woman, and your sex demand and appreciate these qualities as much as my own. With this standard of feeling and of taste, who can look without disgust and abhorrence on such a one as Fanny Wright, with her great masculine person, her loud voice, her untasteful attire, going about unprotected, and feeling no need of protection, mingling with men in stormy debate, and standing up with barefaced impudence, to lecture to a public assembly. And what are the topics of her discourse, that in some cases may be a palliation for such indecorum? Nothing better than broad attacks on all those principles that protect the purity, the dignity, and the safety of her sex. There she stands, with brazen front and brawny arms, attacking the safeguards of all that is venerable and sacred in religion, all that is safe and wise in law, all that is pure and lovely in domestic virtue. Her talents only make her the more conspicuous and offensive, her amiable disposition and sincerity, make her folly and want of common sense the more pitiable, her freedom from private vices, if she is free, only indicates, that without delicacy, and without principles, she has so thrown off all feminine attractions, that freedom from temptation is her only, and shameful palladium. I cannot conceive any thing in the shape of a woman, more intolerably offensive and disgusting.

—Catherine Esther Beecher, *Letters on the Difficulties of Religion* (1836)[2]

112

*J*ust who was Frances "Fanny" Wright, and what did she do to be described as a wart ("strange excrescence"), an amazon, and a monster in the space of a single page? Wright's complicated life includes travel writing; owning and editing her own newspaper; gaining a national reputation for her lectures and writings on freethinking, Woman's Rights, labor reform, abolition, and, most shockingly, free love; not to mention rumors of affairs with famous men, an illicit pregnancy, and a subsequent, disastrously unhappy marriage. While Anne Royall grabbed headlines for several months with her common-scold trial, Wright spent two decades as a lightning rod for cultural anxiety about women's roles and women's place. Catherine Beecher was not Wright's only critic; rather, she joined a chorus of clergy and mainstream media who found in Wright a convenient target for their strict policing of gender roles. By the late 1820s, biographer Celia Morris Eckhardt argues, Wright was "the symbol of most things women should not be," and her name became an epithet used to "discredit liberal causes" ranging from abolition to labor reform.[3]

Other women lectured publicly to "promiscuous" audiences (comprising both men and women) during the same period, for example, the abolitionist Grimke sisters and the African-American spokeswoman Maria Stewart. The extreme reaction to Wright centered on the radical content of her speeches and writing and the radical fact of her travel and mobility. An analysis of Wright's travel writing, her later Woman's Rights theorizing and activism, and the contemporary media's reaction to her traveling female presence illuminates how travel informed and shaped her feminism and how she responded to and attempted to revise the cultural response to her traveling female body. While her detractors were more comfortable seeing Wright as an isolated and extreme example, her experience and writing, on the contrary, connect with the work of other writers featured in *Traveling Economies*—specifically Anne Royall and Mary Seacole—to show how women travel authors represent their own mobile bodies in the pages of their texts. Although Wright was economically and socially more privileged than these other travelers, her outspoken political commentary and activism compromised her social position and therefore placed her on the ragged edge of middle-class respectability.

Wright's public career began eighteen years before Beecher castigated her in the pages of *Letters on the Difficulties of Religion* (1836), with her decision to travel. Leaving Scotland accompanied only by her younger sister, Camilla, Wright toured the northeastern United States for two years and published her praise of the new nation in an epistolary travel narrative, *Views of Society and Manners in America*.[4] She shared the political focus of Royall's slightly later travel writing, as evidenced by Wright's chapter descriptions: "Remarks on the conduct of the first American Congress," "Internal government of the states," "National Government," "Federal Constitution," and "Effect of political writings." She devotes more than two-thirds of her narrative to a celebration of the country's democratic social and political principles; the last third of the book shifts to consider the place of women in the new republic. With improvements in education, Wright argues, American women (white, middle-class women, at least) stand poised to reap all the benefits democracy has to offer, a promise Wright hopes to claim for herself in the not-too-distant future. Thus, at the end of her travelogue, women's bodies claim center stage as Wright recasts white, middle-class women as citizens and works to populate the body politic with female thinkers, leaders, and voters. This is just the beginning of Wright's radical feminism, but even here her travel and travel writing constitute a crucial first step in her thinking. The public will continue to link her radical ideas with her physical mobility, and the negative reaction to her reveals the virulence of cultural hostility to traveling women.

Asking "Who can look without disgust and abhorrence on such a one as Fanny Wright?," Beecher reconfirms the conspicuousness of the female traveler and the viciousness of the rhetoric policing proper femininity. Beecher's rant is pure hyperbole, its very excess betraying the anxiety that the image of an independent, outspoken, unconventional traveling woman generated in the 1820s and 1830s. Wright is Beecher's Frankenstein, an ill-advised experiment with women's autonomy that has gone monstrously wrong. Her body marked with unfeminine strength, independence, and opinions (not to mention bad fashion sense), Wright in Beecher's estimation shares "the shape of a woman," but none of the morality, decorum, domesticity, or subservience that is the substance of femininity. Alternatively, Wright represents her own traveling female body, in the process revising the limited notions of what women can do and where they should go, a project and practice shared by Royall and Seacole. All three women present their strong, capable female bodies for the purpose of challenging prevailing assumptions about women's unfitness for travel or public life.

Claiming expertise on "all that is pure and lovely in domestic virtue," Beecher argues that properly feminine, white, middle-class women belong in the home. Ironically, Beecher herself was fast becoming a public figure: "At the height of her career in the mid-nineteenth century, Catharine Esther Beecher was one of the most famous women in America," according to historians Jeanne Boydston, Mary Kelley, and Anne Margolis.[5] An advocate for women's education, Beecher founded three schools for women and actively published her opinions on women, education, religion, and home management. Her *Treatise on Domestic Economy, for the Use of Young Ladies at Home, and at School* (1841) was so popular it was published fifteen times in fifteen years, and was later expanded into *The American Woman's Home: or, Principles of Domestic Science; Being a Guide to the Formation and Maintenance of Economical, Healthful, and Christian Homes* (1869). The Martha Stewart of her day, Beecher built her career on telling other women how to manage their homes, while she managed her public career. Her attack on Wright conveniently deflects attention from her own public life and work through the skillful depiction of Wright's inappropriate, unfeminine public work and travel. Using Wright as the counterexample to "what [is] admired and sought for in a woman," Beecher defines appropriate middle-class femininity by explaining what it is not. Problematically, Wright, Royall, and Seacole use similar strategies in their travel writing, drawing attention to the bodies of "other" racially different or poor women to assert their own femininity by means of the contrast. An analysis of this strategy as it works across their diverse texts further illustrates the complex ways that women travelers negotiate their audiences' response to their traveling bodies.

The violence of that cultural response to women travelers often took the women themselves by surprise. A cartoon featuring Wright with a woman's body and the quacking, nagging head of a goose reinforces Wright's monstrosity; she is an experiment in new roles for women gone wrong. Editorials proclaiming her "the Red Harlot of Infidelity" and "a bold blasphemer, and a voluptuous priestess of licentiousness" share Beecher's strategy of linking Wright's sexualized body with her transgressive behavior and ideas.[6] The *New York Evening Post* refers to Wright as a "singular spectacle of a female, publicly and ostentatiously proclaiming doctrines of atheistical fanaticism, and even the most abandoned lewdness."[7] Infidelity in the early-nineteenth-century sense referred primarily to heresy (Wright openly questioned religious hypocrisy and argued that religion should be replaced by rational free-thinking), but as historian Lori Ginzberg points out, "Labels linking irreligion with sexual and domestic instability seemed to 'work'" during the period. In other words, linking harlotry with heresy made sense; expressed sexuality and a lack of pious devotion were both crimes against the emerging standards of middle-class femininity that women like Beecher were enshrining and empowering. While Ginzberg argues that the most important use of Wright's public image was to convince women of "the utter evil—the absolute unthinkableness—of irreligion," I argue that embedded in Beecher's rant and the media diatribes is an equal measure of anxiety about mobility and travel for women.[8] Cumulatively, the media attacks reduce Wright's problematic body and her ideas to an insult to be hurled at other women who overstep their bounds. Ginzberg observes the peculiar potency of the "epithet" of "Fanny Wright" or "Wrightism" that was applied at least until 1848 to people and causes as varied as Woman's Rights advocate Antoinette Brown and the New York Working Men's Party, and concludes that "Frances Wright, both the woman and her philosophy, exemplified the fears and anxieties of her age."[9] The media treatment of the unconventional, outspoken female traveler was designed to deter other women from following in her traveling footsteps.

Although Wright's traveling body was ultimately co-opted by a cultural vision of women devoted exclusively to domesticity, an examination of her travel writing offers insight into the development of her own vision of women's autonomy and citizenship. Comparing her strategies for negotiating audience response to her own traveling independent female body with the strategies of Royall and Seacole shows how ragged-edge travel authors challenged definitions of femininity by including their own performances of unfemininity. Finally, a discussion of women travelers' troubling reliance on denigrating "other" women's bodies demonstrates the limits of their traveling revisions of gender roles. The notoriety of all three ragged-edge travelers ensured that new ideas about white women and black women traveled almost as widely as the women themselves. However, their traveling accomplishments were overshadowed by their experiences of public censure and ultimately taught other women more about the risks than the rewards of public travel and public life.

"In the Shape of a Woman":
Imagining the Female Citizen

Beecher's list of femininity's greatest hits—"delicacy of appearance and manners, refinement of sentiment, gentleness of speech, modesty in feeling and action"—does more than set out a nearly impossible standard for women's behavior. The terms she uses also evoke the travel genre and implicitly criticize Wright's travel writing as well as her unfeminine demeanor. "Appearance and Manners" are not only the superficial concerns to which women should devote themselves, but are also the acceptable content of women's travel writing, as we saw in chapter 2 with the discussion of the decidedly different political travel writing of Anne Royall. Wright shares with Royall an overwhelming focus on politics and the workings of government, eschewing expectations that women's writing focus on "sentiment." Outspoken in her critique of European social, economic, and political practice and in her celebration of American democracy, Wright is neither gentle nor modest as she proclaims herself a twenty-three-year-old sage fit to judge and evaluate nations. But while Beecher sees Wright as a traitor to femininity disguised in "the shape of a woman," Wright and her travel writing in fact unveil a citizen with a female body.

Breaking with the prevailing school of European "grumbletonians" (16) who find only fault with the young upstart nation, Wright instead depicts America as "the very palladium of liberty" (81), including lengthy and detailed explanations of the plan and workings of the United States government—everything from the "history of the Federal Party" (172) to the Declaration of Independence (53). Her extensive discussions of the plan of American government present an idealized picture of the liberating potential of democracy. In Wright's view, liberation will inevitably extend to women who "are assuming their place as thinking beings" in the new republic (218). The political participation of women is the likely, if not inevitable, outcome of Wright's utopian vision.

Wright constructs not only a new world, but also a new female traveler. Traveling is no longer the exclusive province of "a *preux chevalier*, in olden time, setting forth in a new suit of armor, buckled on by the hand of a princess, [seeking] adventure through the wide world"

(91). Wright rejects chivalry, with its underlying assumptions of female weakness, claiming instead the masculine prerogative of "adventure through the wide world" for herself. The image of the roving knight is replaced by that of the "peaceful traveller of these generations, who goes to seek waterfalls instead of giants and to look at men instead of killing them" (91). Usurping the perspective of the masculine explorer, Wright asserts her competence as a female traveler and claims a wider sphere of "adventure" and public activity for women.[10]

A female explorer setting out to discover a country that already exists, to project onto it her own constructions of freedom and equality, Wright romanticizes American politics, economics, citizens, and attitudes toward women, all in service to her utopian vision. Critic Paul Baker suggests the limits of Wright's representation, "distorted as it was by her prejudices and enthusiasms." In Wright's text, according to Baker, "The spotless cities and smiling countryside of the East . . . [are] viewed through the distorting lens of classical imagery." While Baker notes that modern readers may find Wright's hyperbole "sometimes difficult or impossible to accept," I argue that for Wright accuracy takes second place to finding (and creating if she has to) a place where women can be citizens.[11]

For Wright, America is "a country where the dreams of sages, smiled at as utopian, seem distinctly realized" (188). Describing America as "animated" by the "spirit of liberty" (169), Wright compares the new nation to a "young Rome" that she envisions taking its place among the great republics of history (261). American government represents a "triumph of virtue and good sense over the vices and follies of human nature" (171). America's economic and political systems are egalitarian and extend to every citizen, regardless of birth or social position. The result, according to Wright, is a country of equals rather than a nation of masters and servants, "where all men are placed by the laws on an exact level" (237). Class distinctions are not erased under the American system, but are based on "education and condition" rather than on aristocratic lineage (237). Meritocracy replaces aristocracy in the new nation, Wright asserts, and her construction of America as a land of economic and social opportunity sets the stage for her argument that women should be the next group to benefit from the political advances of the American system of government.

Wright imagines a future full of possibility for women, rather than increasing limitations on what they can do and where they can go. She declares, "It would be impossible for women to stand in higher estimation than they do" in America (218–19). Emphasizing the "public attention" focused on "the improvement of female education," Wright lauds America's "liberal philosophy" and the consequent place the nation "award[s] to women" (218). Of course, by "women" Wright means white, middle-class women like herself. Her description of New York City having "neither poor nor uneducated" residents, for instance, indicates that her focus is mainly on the middle class. And her observations on "Appearance and Manners of the Young Women" are chiefly drawn from studying "large evening assemblies," social events attended by girls wearing "showy and costly" dresses (21–24). The reforms Wright advocates, particularly women's education, would primarily benefit white, middle-class women, fitting them to participate in public life. It is not until later in Wright's life that she will work for abolition and working-class labor reform, issues directly affecting black and poor women.

For the new nation to achieve its utopian potential, in Wright's view, it must continue to foster the development of women both educationally and politically. Wright notes that the country owes its independence to women who contributed to the Revolutionary War: "The women shared the patriotism of the men . . . actually buckling on the swords and cartridges and arming the hands of their sons and husbands" (183). Her argument here echoes Royall's celebratory portrait of female Revolutionary War heroine Ann Bailey, whom Royall includes in her text to support her underlying theme of women's fitness for citizenship. It is important that Wright's discussion of women does not appear until page 218 of her 270-page text, because she spends the first three-quarters of her narrative constructing a nation where women can eventually participate in governing and in citizenship. She has built her utopia with the object of populating it with white, middle-class women.

The final barrier to women's participation in the public life of the new nation is education, an issue Wright addresses by advancing in her travel text her own "utopian plan of national education" for women (222). While she leaves the particulars to "the republic herself," she outlines the basic components of education that will be needed by the future female citizens of the nation (222). Arguing that women should be taught "the principles of government, and the obligations of patriotism," Wright advocates a system of education that will fit women to participate in civic life (23). She initially camouflages her radical call for political education for women by framing it in terms of republican motherhood. According to Wright, "In a country where a mother is charged with the formation of an infant mind that is to be called in future to judge of the laws and support the liberties of a republic, the mother herself should well understand those laws and estimate those liberties" (218). But even when cast in terms of supplementing women's traditional role as mothers, Wright's demand for women's education radically critiques the existing educational systems in the United States and Europe. Pointing to the "European manner" of educating women that focuses on "personal accomplishments and the more ornamental branches of knowledge," Wright calls for a reformed system that emphasizes "solid information" (218). Her plan for female education would replace studies of "French, Italian, dancing, [and] drawing" with "philosophy, history, political economy, and the exact sciences" in order to produce women of "powerful intellect" who could engage the political and social issues of the day (218). While Wright does not advocate female suffrage in her text, she is clearly advocating reform that would produce educated women suited to assume the responsibilities of both citizenship and public administration. Ironically, Beecher shares Wright's focus on women's education, having founded three schools for the instruction of women. Needless to say, Beecher's curriculum is quite different.

Women's bodies, as well as their minds, need cultivation to fit them for citizenship. Wright's plan for female education is not limited to introducing "solid information," but also includes a physical education component (218). Linking mental and physical development, Wright declares that "to invigorate the body is to invigorate the mind" and that women need to pursue both mental and physical exercise (220). Linking mental and physical independence, Wright identifies sexism in the cultural tenet that women remain physically weak and mentally passive: "The vanity [of men is] soothed by the dependence of women: it pleases them better to find in their companion a fragile vine, clinging to their firm trunk for support, than a vigorous tree with whose branches they may mingle theirs" (221). Rather than clinging vines, women need to be physically powerful and self-reliant if they want to assume their place as citizens of the new republic. Wright's program of physical education, advocating that women "be taught in early youth to excel in the race, to hit a mark, to swim, and in short to use every exercise," is designed to "impart vigor to their frames and independence to their minds," and signals a radical departure from traditional gender roles (222). The notion of mobility is important here, as women running and jumping represent movement across social and physical boundaries. Their bodies and minds are vehicles for the advancement of womankind and the new nation. Wright's own travels throughout the Northeast and Midwest illustrate the mental and physical vigor she describes. She models her new woman-citizen on herself; she is the thinking, active woman who will assume her rightful place in the halls of American democracy.

"Brazen Front and Brawny Arms": Risking Danger and Performing Unfemininity

Describing Wright's "great masculine person," Beecher embellishes her portrait with "brazen front and brawny arms," as if Wright has followed her own program of physical fitness to an extreme. Beecher's word portrait, however, certainly does not match contemporary likenesses of the attractive and unmuscled Wright. Rather than accurately representing Wright's body, Beecher follows the logic of "embodied deviance," Jennifer Terry and Jacqueline Urla's term for the nineteenth-century ideology that figured social transgressions as a mark or disfigurement on the transgressor's body.[12] According to Beecher, Wright's unfeminine behavior—"mingling with men in stormy debate, and standing up with barefaced impudence, to lecture to a public assembly"—blurs the line between masculinity and femininity. Beecher finds this gender-blurring particularly unsettling because she locates power for white, middle-class women in their essential difference from men. Notions of women's moral superiority and innate capacity for nurturing granted women like Beecher a certain amount of leeway to enter the public sphere in the name of expanding the moral influence of the home outward into the community and the nation. Beecher therefore jealously guards the power she gains by promoting her version of femininity and policing the behavior of other women. She labels Wright's behavior masculine to guarantee that it will be off-limits to other middle-class white women. Wright, in contrast, argues that male and female are equal rather than different, a philosophy she believes will gain women greater power as citizens than they can exercise from the confines of a moral domestic sphere.

Femininity is a performance, as feminist theorist Judith Butler argues and as Beecher's list of appropriate feminine behavior demonstrates, and Wright will not limit herself to the scripts of domesticity and subservience.[13] Wright seeks to redraw the social boundaries that limit women's behavior and autonomy, making space in restrictive definitions of femininity for the kind of public life she lives and that she claims for future women citizens. Demonstrating what educated, outspoken, mobile women can accomplish, she performs unfemininity, providing audiences with a model of expanded roles for women that complement the utopian vision of her travel writing. Travel is a crucial part of Wright's unfeminine behavior, as travel often requires women to demonstrate the physical strength, quick thinking, and independence that violate the expected performance of femininity. Performing unfemininity instead, Wright and other ragged-edge travelers work to expand possibilities for women and to rewrite the meaning attached to their traveling female bodies.

Wright recognizes the ways in which perceptions of women's physical weakness limit their mobility and autonomy. Cultural ideas that emphasize women's physical and sexual vulnerability work to confine women to the safe space of the home, effectively cowing them by what critic Kristi Siegel terms the "rhetoric of peril."[14] It is that rhetoric, the constant repetition of stories of rape and physical harm suffered by women outside the home, rather than the women's actual physical weakness, that limits where they can go, as Wright argues:

> I apprehend that thousands of our countrywomen in the middle ranks, whose mothers, or certainly whose grandmothers, could ride unattended from the Land's End to the border and walk abroad alone or with an unmarried friend of the other sex armed with all the unsuspecting virtue of Eve before her fall—I apprehend that the children and grandchildren of these matrons are now condemned to walk in leading strings from the cradle to the altar, if not to the grave, taught to see in the other sex a race of seducers rather than protectors and of masters rather than companions. (219)

Women's abilities have not changed; they could still ride the length of the countryside. The difference, according to Wright, is a shift in cultural ideas about women—they are no longer able to take care of themselves when they "ride unattended" or "walk alone," but instead are limited by both fear of seduction (or more frightening still, rape) and the increased control of men who install themselves as "masters." Since women are "condemned to walk in leading strings" from birth until marriage and beyond, the goal of the scare tactics is to preserve their virginity, marriageability, and, ultimately, docility. Indoctrinating women to believe in and practice their subordination to men, the "rhetoric of peril" centers on limiting women's physical movement. Let them wander, the logic goes, and there's going to be trouble. Wright and her fellow ragged-edge travelers suggest just how much trouble uncontrolled, mobile women can get into—Seacole endures racist taunts from ship stewards, and a toast ostensibly in her honor declares that bleaching would be her best route to social acceptance; Royall sparks so much controversy and outrage that she's thrown down icy steps, breaking her leg, and on another occasion is horsewhipped by another angry opponent of her outspoken opinions.[15]

Scenes of physical danger in Wright's text highlight female travelers' simultaneous competence and vulnerability, a representational strategy also found in later texts and throughout those included in *Traveling Economies*. By representing her own body facing and overcoming physical danger, Wright contests the "rhetoric of peril," even as scenes of risk also draw attention to her vulnerable and out-of-place female form. These episodes focus attention on the writers' female bodies by describing their unexpected and unfeminine stamina and skill (as in the case of Bradley riding her mule on treacherous cliff sides in the first chapter). The rugged nature of most early-nineteenth-century transportation frequently made travel dangerous for both men and women. Recounting successful negotiations of life-threatening situations, women writers argue for their fitness as travelers and present important counterevidence to the prevalent stereotype that white, middle-class women were weak, timid, and unintelligent and were therefore justifiably confined to the relative safety of hearth and home.

Describing a near plunge down the Genesee Falls in upstate New York, Wright displays not only her physical strength and quick thinking, but also her vulnerability and impulsiveness. Wright and her female companions descend down the side of the falls to perch on a narrow ledge "formed by the roots of a blasted pine" (116–17). The adventure produces in Wright "a sensation of terror that I do not remember to have felt in an equal degree more than once in my life" (117). The women then make a narrow escape from the precipice:

> Our sight sw[am], our ears filled with the stunning roar of the river, the smoke of whose waters rose even to this dizzy height, while the thin coating of soil which covered the rock and had once afforded a scanty nourishment to the blasted tree which sustained us seemed to shake beneath our feet . . . To restore our confused senses and save ourselves from losing balance, which had been the loss of life, we grasped the old pine with considerable energy, and it was at last, with trembling knees and eyes steadily fixed upon our footsteps, neither daring to look up nor down, that we regained the height from which we had descended. Having regained it, I thought we never looked more like fools in our lives. (117–18)

The episode focuses the reader's attention on the vulnerable female bodies clinging to the cliff, hanging on despite their trembling limbs and unsure footing. Nonetheless, the women do survive, rescuing themselves without the help of male guardians and displaying their strength, courage, and competence, if not their prudence, in going down the precipice in the first place. Risking their lives "to see what [they] could," Wright claims the daring and adventure that was usually reserved for male travelers (117).

Even though Wright survives the danger and lives to write about it, the description of the near slip down the falls draws the reader's attention to her female body, for although she and her party demonstrate their "considerable energy" and strength, which succeeds in restoring them to safety, the incident nonetheless emphasizes their out-of-placeness as much as it does their traveling competence. The moment, then, offers readers an opportunity to question whether women traveling alone (or in a group of other women without men) is a good idea, a question that a male traveler who sees the women almost fall to their death in fact asks directly, as Wright records in her text: "A young man, who the next day become our fellow traveller, told me that he had seen us take this position [on the precipice] with such alarm that his blood ran cold" (118). Couched as chivalrous fear for the women's safety, the male traveler's words reinforce the rhetoric of peril (see what trouble women get into on their own?). Women travel writers had to walk a fine line between sharing a thrill with their audience and alienating them with accounts of their unfeminine, risky behavior. Travel readers expected at least a few brushes with danger, and female authors may have felt market pressure to meet those expectations, regardless of their gender. Women travelers in peril could titillate a leering audience and thereby sell more books. Yet women authors were taking a writerly risk by portraying their own daring; they could either engage readers or shock them. Examining other representations of physical danger on the road or ship or mule begins to answer whether the writerly risk was worth the publishing danger. Comparing similar scenes in ragged-edge travel texts exposes the variety of hazards women travelers confronted and the complex ways that female authors used moments of danger to craft their self-representations. Ultimately, women authors could not control their readers' or fellow travelers' responses to their traveling bodies, and such scenes serve to reinforce the constant scrutiny women travelers underwent on the road and on the page.

As a female traveler, Wright was conspicuous; her female body attracted as much attention as, if not more than, her words. As discussed in chapter 1 of *Traveling Economies,* Amy Morris Bradley and Nancy Prince both include accounts of the scrutiny they endured while traveling alone. Bradley's interrogation by fellow passengers who helped her over a bout of seasickness demonstrates how chivalry thinly disguised the true purpose of monitoring women's movement and behavior. The social scrutiny that Nancy Prince experienced was much more sinister and threatening. A black woman traveling alone, Prince was threatened with enslavement and beating when her ship docked at a Southern port. While black women travelers could be particularly conspicuous, white women's mobility could also bring them to the attention of a culture that preferred women to stay at home. Hoopskirts and black faces drew attention when in places they were not expected to be, such as on steamships or in railcars. While chapter 1 investigated why women travelers (particularly ragged-edge women travelers) elicited a strong reaction from their fellow passengers and even from their readers, Wright invites us to ask how and why women travelers represent their own bodies in their travel accounts. Wright is not really surprised by her own strength when she scrambles off her dangerous scenic overlook of the falls; instead, she shows her audience her strong female body in order to rewrite the meaning that the culture reads there.

We have seen how women travelers sometimes cushion their transgressive adventurous behavior by deploying femininity—insisting on their respectable manners and dress, for example, as Mary Seacole does in *Wonderful Adventures of Mrs. Seacole in Many Lands* (discussed in chapter 1).[16] Despite female travelers' gender-bending behavior, an exaggerated performance of femininity can support status quo women's subordination by reinforcing cultural ideas about proper behavior for women. While women travelers do sometimes deploy "proper" femininity strategically in their texts, at other moments they challenge gender norms by performing unfemininity. They demonstrate their strength, competence, and will, qualities that serve them well not only when rescuing themselves from a slip over the falls, but also in the public life Wright envisions as women's future. Rewriting the meaning supposedly written on women's bodies, women travelers challenge the rhetoric of peril, with its emphasis on bodily vulnerability and traveling incompetence. Later tourism will erase their subversion and redouble the power of the rhetoric of peril to sell more chaperoned tours and contain the problematic social and physical mobility of women like Wright.

Seacole would at first glance seem to be almost nothing like Frances Wright. A self-described Jamaican mulatto, Seacole traveled through Central America and to the Crimean battlefront thirty years after Wright's journey to the United States. What Seacole and Wright share are similar strategies for representing their own fitness for citizenship and public life. A comparison of Wright and Seacole illuminates aspects of *Wonderful Adventures* that would otherwise be obscured and traces textual strategies across the emerging field of antebellum women's travel writing. Wright's plan for women's physical education and her own successful negotiation of the jeopardies of travel support her plan for women to become active members of America's democracy. Seacole's project is complicated by race, as she works to deconstruct negative racial stereotypes and restrictive gender norms. Showing her black, mobile female body surviving the deadly hazards of the Crimean battlefront, Seacole claims space for women travelers in the most masculine of public spaces—a war zone.

In chapter 1 we observed Seacole's performance of femininity in Central America as she described her fashionable dress and decorum. Once she arrives at the Crimean battlefront in the second half of *Wonderful Adventures*, her portrayal of her body and her unfeminine behavior highlight her determination and success as a traveler. Seacole climbs aboard a ship stocked with munitions—docked in the Black Sea to convey supplies to the battlefront—and encounters a mode of transportation designed with the male body, rather than an ample female form, in mind: "Time and trouble combined have left me with a well-filled-out, portly form—the envy of many an angular Yankee female—and, more than once, it was in no slight danger of becoming too intimately acquainted with the temperature of the Bosphorus" (86). The picture of Seacole almost falling into the water provides a moment of comic relief before the narrative proceeds to the description of more life-threatening situations "under fire" at the front lines (157). Even in this comic moment, however, the discussion of physical danger shifts the focus onto her body, which—black, female, portly, overdressed—should not be climbing up the side of a ship near a battlefront, or anywhere else for that matter. She is trespassing into the masculine war zone, and her presence threatens her own safety, as well as the stability of socially prescribed gender roles. With every trip up the ship's ladder, Seacole successfully negotiates another barrier to black women's mobility and freedom. The negotiation is often difficult and perilous, as both the Bosphorus and society wait for her to misstep. Perhaps the next time they meet her in person in a remote corner of the globe or on the streets of London, she will not be an oddity, and she will not be the only woman traveling.

An unplanned bath in the Bosphorus is only the beginning of the dangers Seacole faces in the Crimean battlefront. Her independence and determination continue to serve her well, but the stakes are clearly higher the longer she remains "unprotected" in a war zone (112). Increasing the danger to herself and defying gender constructions, Seacole risks her life by journeying to the front lines of the war. She leads her mules laden with refreshments and medical supplies, gaining entry into the nexus of masculine power and violence—the battle sites. Mother Seacole's portly form would seem to be totally unsuited for dodging bullets, "but each time [her] bag of bandages and comforts for the wounded proved [her] passport" (157).[17] While her womanly mission of mercy gains her access to this dangerous masculine arena, her survival of the gunfire challenges the widely held notion that women are weak, timid, and unsuited to the rigors of battle (or public life, for that matter). Bandaging wounds and selling sandwiches, Seacole fearlessly serves on the front lines, painting a vivid picture of her black female body diving for cover: "I was 'under fire.' More frequently than was agreeable, a shot would come ploughing up the ground and raising clouds of dust, or a shell whizz above us . . . and with very undignified and unladylike haste I had to embrace the earth and remain there" (157). The dictates of the battlefront require the performance of unfemininity, or in Seacole's terms, an "unladylike," but successful, duck and cover.

Surrounded by death and danger, Seacole not only enters the war zone, but also copes with it more successfully than many of the male combatants. Her only wound during the entire Crimean campaign is a dislocated thumb, which "did not inconvenience" Seacole, although it "never returned to its proper shape" (158). A slightly scarred battle veteran, Seacole moves through the forbidden territory of the front lines, collecting shell casings for souvenirs (171). Describing herself as "a lioness in the streets of Simpheropol," she trades feminine docility, domesticity, and fear for unfeminine strength, self-determination, and mobility (190).[18]

"I Cannot Conceive of Anything in the Shape of a Woman, More Intolerably Offensive and Disgusting": Representing "Other" Bodies

While Seacole dodges the bullets of race and gender, Wright puts her own body and those of other white, middle-class women front and center in her imagined democratic utopia. Despite her plan for female education (including physical education for stronger female bodies to complement stronger female minds), an education gap was not the only problem preventing the full public participation of women in the fledgling democracy. Political and social injustices, particularly the enslavement of African-Americans, threatened to destroy Wright's utopian vision and the nation itself. Wright does decry slavery in her travel text—an early call for abolition, given the 1821 publication date. Furthermore, she follows up with her own abolition activism, founding Nashoba, an experimental abolition colony that intended to educate, manumit, and resettle freed slaves outside the United States. Critic Carolyn Karcher celebrates Wright's "intrepidity that led her to act publicly against slavery at great personal and financial risk, nearly a decade before either the formation of a radical abolitionist movement . . . or the rise of women antislavery writers and speakers."[19] While Wright may have been daring and high-minded in her proabolition writing and activism, a fundamental flaw limits the efficacy as well as the humanity of her theory and later practice. In *Views* Wright dismisses and ignores the problematic bodies of African-Americans, limiting her physical travel through the United States by canceling a Southern leg of her tour and blaming blacks for their own victimization. In fact her travel writing celebrates the mobility and independence of traveling white, middle-class women at the expense of African-Americans, an agenda that had disastrous consequences for the slaves who were victimized by Nashoba when Wright actually put her travel text's theories into action.

View's rhetorical construction of the United States as the land of the free fails Wright, finally, when she confronts the real-world injustice of slavery, as her constructed utopia threatens to disintegrate in the face of the "impure breath of [slavery's] pestilence" (267). The "free winds of America" that Wright imagines allowing white, middle-class women to soar to new heights of personal and political freedom are tainted by the "odious" presence of slavery, which represents the complete denial of liberty (267). If African-Americans could be denied citizenship and human rights based on their skin color, then women could be denied political participation on the basis of gender. The meritocracy that Wright envisions allowing women to enter public life on the basis of their education and refinement crumbles in the face of a society that accords the full benefits of democracy to only a few wealthy white men. Wright recognizes the threat that slavery poses to her potential utopia and ultimately avoids directly confronting the injustice that her vision cannot brook. Refusing to travel to the South and downplaying Northern racism, she can preserve her utopian vision only by ignoring the institutionalized racism of the land of "freedom for all." She admits, in fact, that she has "ever felt a secret reluctance to visit" the Southern states, and curtails her physical journey through the new nation (267). Avoiding a direct confrontation with the "breath of evil" that threatens the nation and her utopian view thereof, Wright upholds America as a land of opportunity and freedom, rather than representing the undeniable oppression and exploitation that also mark the new republic (267).

Wright goes so far as to argue that race prejudice no longer exists, turning away from the realities of race politics in America. She finds "much satisfaction [in] the condition of the negro" in the Northeast and chooses to "rejoice in this visible decay of prejudice" rather "than to dwell on what remains" in the rest of the Union (42). Wright further de-emphasizes the effects of race prejudice by suggesting that free blacks in the Northeast enjoy conditions that make social elevation possible and likely. According to Wright, free blacks "are equally under the protection of mild and impartial laws," and opportunities abound for economic success: "Nothing indeed is here necessary but his own exertions to raise him in the scale of being" (44). Nancy Prince and Mary Ann Shadd Cary provide compelling counterevidence about the pernicious results of racism on free black communities through their travel narratives, as discussed in the first and third chapters.

Justifying the fact that very few "Africans" have, in fact, taken advantage of the opportunities that she imagines are so abundant, Wright enumerates stereotyped character flaws that inhibit black progress: "greater laxity of morals," "[un]frugal," "singularly cheerful and good humoured," and "immoderately fond of dancing" (43–44). In a later description of black domestic servants, Wright adds "indolence," "intemperance," and "petty dishonesty" to her list of racial character defects (238), thus absolving the fledgling republic of responsibility for its African-American citizens and placing the blame on those citizens themselves rather than on institutionalized racism and slavery.

However, describing America's democratic political system, in which "every individual has an equal sovereignty," Wright must acknowledge that slavery is "a grievous exception to this rule" (188). Although her acknowledgment of slavery is made here only in a footnote to the main body of her text, it does signal the profound challenge that slavery presents to her view of America. The institutionalized denial of human dignity and human rights sanctioned in slavery jeopardizes the claims of women to status as full and equal human beings and citizens, dimming the brightness of America's utopian potential:

> Had you studied with me the history and character of the American republic, did you see in her so many seeds of excellence, so bright a dawning of national glory, so fair a promise of a brilliant meridian day, as your friend imagines that she can discern, you would share all that regret, impatience, and anxiety, with which she regards every stain that rests upon her morals, every danger that threatens her peace. (270)

Found in the final paragraph of *Views of Society and Manners*, this admission of a fundamental flaw in the republic is minimized by Wright, who trumpets the optimistic view that "'the day is not very far distant when a slave will not be found in America!'" (270). Once slavery's "stain" is washed from the new nation, in the literal form of the removal of problematic black bodies, its utopian potential can be realized.

While Wright works to erase problematic bodies and to put her own in the spotlight, other women travel writers use the bodies of racial and class "others" to mitigate their readers' response to their unfeminine behavior. Objectifying other women even as they contest cultural notions that they should be only domestic ornaments themselves, the authors undermine their argument that travel is liberating and empowering. Instead, these authors rely on the same hierarchies of race, class, and gender that marginalize them to claim power over those below them on the social ladder. Travel may be a source of freedom for these women, who, as we have seen, have the courage, stamina, and determination to travel in spite of the social and physical dangers; however, they are willing to sacrifice other women for the sake of their own hard-won liberation.

Anne Royall and Mary Seacole, for instance, both use the bodies of other women to buttress their own claims to feminine respectability, despite their transgressive behavior. Even though she figures the ship's saloon as a model of egalitarian democracy, Royall also relies on racist and classist depictions of women and immigrants to reinforce her own authority as a writer. Very likely due to her marginal class position, Royall makes an effort in her text to distinguish herself from women she deems inferior. For instance, although Royall wore the same threadbare dress during the entire period she researched her *Sketches,* she presents poor women as fundamentally different from herself. On seeing a destitute woman, Royall declares, "O poverty, to what shifts art thou reduced! I looked at her and shuddered!" (95).[20] Royall's own experiences of extreme poverty do not temper her response. While her sentimental language is charged with emotion, the poor woman's plight evokes revulsion rather than sympathy. Royall works to disassociate herself from poor women because poverty was frequently linked to immorality by nineteenth-century social ideology, and she would risk losing her slippery grasp on middle-class femininity and respectability by revealing her own brushes with poverty. In her study of "the economically comfortable American woman" traveling abroad, Mary Suzanne Schriber finds similar representations of foreign women peasants: "[The wealthy female tourist] is able to see in 'them' her worst nightmare [of lower-class status]. She counters her fear by underscoring 'their' difference simultaneously magnifying and securing her superior place." The difference is that Royall's vehemence instead stems from her own closenss to the poor woman she describes; she is separated from her by neither nationality nor economic security.[21]

While we might expect white women like Royall to use racially different women as foils to bolster their questionable femininity, Seacole's use of negative portraits of traveling white women is a surprising strategy designed to combat racial stereotypes. Seacole jealously guards her claim to femininity by comparing her own decorum with the license white women take with gender expectations: for instance, the white women on the Central American overland route to the Gold Rush "appeared in no hurry to resume the dress or obligations of their sex. Many were clothed as their men were, in flannel shirt and boots; rode their mules in unfeminine fashion . . . and in their conversation successfully rivalled the coarseness of their lords" (20). Seacole equates feminine "dress" and "obligations"; her own adherence to conventional dress standards signals to her audience her adherence to conventional morality, despite her unconventional mobility. She presents herself as a moral agent of femininity who is not tainted by her experience of independence and travel. Seacole attempts to reduce the threat of women's increasing participation in public life by presenting herself as morally unscathed by her journey.

Seacole contests the "deviance" culturally assigned to her by emphasizing her own high moral standards. While she does not completely reject "the idea that moral character is rooted in the body," she challenges the social structures that construct black women as always already deviant.[22] Thus, as critics Farah Griffin and Cheryl Fish assert, it is important that "Seacole must distinguish herself from the 'camp followers' and prostitutes" in Panama and Crimea.[23] By locating deviance in the bodies of white traveling women, Seacole disrupts the systems of power that construct "whole categories of people [as] fundamentally deviant, not by virtue of particular symptoms they manifest, but simply because of their subordinate location in systems for distinguishing gender, ethnicity, class, and race."[24] Her emphasis on traveling white women's lack of femininity deconstructs the idea that femininity is tied to biology or, more specifically, to a particular race. In her text Seacole can then construct herself as feminine, even more feminine than women whose skin color should grant them the privilege and status of middle-class womanhood. She deflects attention from her black female body, and the deviance her audience would read there, by focusing on the inappropriate bodies of traveling white women.

Is She "Free from Private Vices"?
Troubling Sexuality and the Female Traveler

Since Wright was "going about unprotected, and feeling no need of protection," her trespass against proper femininity is cast by Beecher in terms explicitly associated with women's travel and linked to traveling women's sexuality. Women traveling unaccompanied by men were referred to as "unprotected," a term that was code for, among other potential weaknesses, sexual vulnerability.[25] Unmoored from the safety and confinement of the snug harbor of home, women travelers would encounter men, a circumstance that could compromise their sexual purity, through rape or seduction. Emerging ideologies of white, middle-class women's "passionlessness"—a term used by historian Nancy Cott to describe the denial of sexuality that was necessary to reinforce ideas of women's moral superiority—were at odds with the mobility and independence of women travelers.[26] Women who would put their reputations and their bodies in jeopardy might as well be guilty of "private vices," as Beecher snidely suggests.

Royall's efforts to establish her respectability stem from her first-hand knowledge of popular conceptions of women travelers. In her *Letters* Royall includes a reference to prevailing views of traveling females: "What are you travelling alone for? It is a bad sign—you must be a bad woman" (217).[27] In response, Royall continues to emphasize her high moral standards throughout her *Sketches*. Encountering a group of women in New York City's prison, she makes an effort to distance herself from their corrupt influence, as well as their low status: "They were the most abandoned, vicious, lewd, impudent . . . alas! for frail woman. They laughed, they romped, they gigled [*sic*], and saluted me with the familiarity of an old acquaintance! asked 'if I came to keep them company?' I would have suffered the guillotine first" (252). Royall assigns deviant sexuality to the women prisoners using terms of vulnerability ("frail") and of vulgarity ("romp," "giggle," "familiarity"). She reserves for herself, the "proper" woman traveler, not only propriety, but the stance of social judge. Royall charges the women not only with being "lewd," but also with failing all standards of middle-class womanhood—decorum, modesty, and reserve. She, by contrast, is a proper middle-class woman who would rather lose her head than be lumped in with "bad" women. Royall's later sensational trial as a "common scold" (discussed in chapter 2) did actually land her briefly in jail and almost resulted in torture on a ducking stool built specifically for her. And even as she wrote about the women prisoners, she was herself evading debtors' prison in her home state of Virginia, a fact she conveniently overlooks in her discussion of lawbreaking women.

Black women, even before they traveled, were perceived as sexual objects and ascribed overblown and predatory sexuality. Seacole was familiar with racist assumptions about black female sexuality, and thus made a concerted effort to assert her own purity and respectability in order to challenge and debunk the stereotypes. While Seacole worked to dismantle the hypersexual image assigned to black women by the popular imagination, Wright in her controversial and outspoken discussions of free love extends her program for women's sexual emancipation at the expense of black women by reinforcing the debilitating Jezebel stereotype.[28]

For Beecher, Wright's most objectionable travels take her out of polite society and into the realm of expressed female sexuality. "Feeling no need of protection," as Beecher would have it, Wright rejects the image of middle-class women as passionless or helpless and argues instead for women to express their sexuality without the restriction and servitude of marriage. In so doing, she commits, in Beecher's estimation, "broad attacks on all those principles that protect the purity, the dignity, and the safety of her sex." To choose mobility and sexual autonomy over safety and domesticity is evidence of Wright's pathology ("offensive and disgusting"), and her popularity threatens to spread her "private vices" to other women. More women might suffer contagion if women travelers continue to circulate unchecked through antebellum America. Joining Beecher in denouncing Wright, the *Advocate of Moral Reform*, another media source, dramatizes the contagious effect of her immorality during her previous lecture tour:

> Wives, once happy in their husbands' arms, seduced by her diabolical doctrines, parted from the peaceful and lovely paths of virtue and

affection at home, strayed in to the mazy meanderings of sinful pleasure, abandoned themselves to indiscriminate indulgence in libidinous practices, and are now among the mass of moral putrefaction
that tenant the temples of infamy.[29]

Wright's critics again link an image of travel, "mazy meanderings," with
her "libidinous practices," connecting traveling women with immorality that promises to spread wherever they go.

Wright's most controversial ideas about female sexuality were not
spread through her lecture tours, where she expressed the ideas much
more subtly, but in the pages of the *New Harmony Gazette* (which she
would soon buy and rename the *Free Enquirer*), in response to a series
of scandals at her abolitionist colony, Nashoba. Wright's colony was
intended to provide a model for the education, vocational training,
and eventual colonization of slaves that would solve the problem of
the "stain" of slavery on the nation. Instead, the marshy, mosquito-rid-
den location; inadequate slave labor-force (made up primarily of slave
women and young children); mismanagement and limited farming
knowledge of the white trustees and residents; and Wright's frequent
and extended absences to raise much-needed funding turned the utopian project into a dystopian nightmare in which slaves were beaten and
exploited.[30] Answering charges that slaves were being beaten, that the
white overseer had taken a slave woman as a concubine, that Wright's
sister was practicing free love with another white male resident, and
that Isabella, a female slave, had suffered an attempted rape by a male
slave, Wright took the occasion to explain her theory of female sexuality
rather than to address the exploitation occurring at Nashoba.[31]

Wright's "Explanatory Notes on Nashoba" showcases her groundbreaking early feminist theory as well as the disastrous and damag-
ing limitations of her exclusive focus on white, middle-class women.[32]
Wright's notion of white, middle-class women's independence included
her formulation of women's sexual independence. Wright endorsed the
doctrine of free love, as Elizabeth Bartlett notes: "Wright advocated
that rather than shrouding their bodies, desires, and faculties, women
address them openly," a philosophy that shocked her Victorian audience, whose "dictums of propriety . . . rendered the mere mention of
an arm or leg indecent." At a time when white, middle-class women
were "viewed as having no bodies at all" and considered to be without
sexual feeling or passion, Wright's emphasis on women's expressed

sexuality was radical. Believing that this expression was natural and necessary, Wright argues for rethinking accepted notions of morality and for sanctioning sexual passion in her "Explanatory Notes": "Let us not teach, that virtue consists in the crucifying of the affections and appetites, but in their judicious government! Let us not attach ideas of purity to monastic chastity, impossible to man or woman without consequences fraught with evil, nor ideas of vice to connexions formed under the auspices of kind feeling!" This statement is included in a section justifying Nashoba's repudiation of marriage and advocacy of free love, or sexual union founded on "mutual inclination" rather than on matrimonial or legal compulsion.[33]

Wright's insistence that "the marriage law . . . is of no force within [the] pale" of Nashoba is meant to secure white, middle-class women's freedom within the bounds of the colony. Wright argues for this independence by saying, "No woman can forfeit her individual rights or independent existence, and no man assert over her any rights or power whatsoever, beyond what he may exercise over her free and voluntary affections." Free to express their sexuality, according to Wright, women should no longer be "condemned to the unnatural repression of feelings and desires." She links the end of sexual repression with the end of the sexual double standard that "condemn[s] one portion of the female sex to vicious excess, another to as vicious restraint . . . and generally the male sex to debasing licentiousness." Wright seeks to undermine the power of institutionalized sexual mores and, with them, institutionalized gender inequity.[34]

The colony's response (and Wright's lack of response) to the attempted rape of Isabel, a slave woman at Nashoba, demonstrates how the policies that Wright supported at Nashoba secured the sexual freedom and bodily self-control of white women at the expense of the slave women she was ostensibly trying to assist. Reporting the near rape to the white trustees of Nashoba, Isabel requests a lock for her door to prevent future attacks. The trustees refuse her request. Declaring the "proper basis of the sexual intercourse to be the unconstrained and unrestrained choice of *both* parties," Camilla Wright denies Isabel the lock in order to promote an ideal of mutual respect and community, "which will give to every woman a much greater security, than any lock can possibly do." But the freedom of sexual choice that Camilla and Wright claim as their prerogative is based on an assumption of bodily and sexual integrity that is not the experience of all women. The Wright sisters enjoy privilege as white, middle-class women, which offers them a level of protection from sexual abuse and violence. For slave women like Isabel, however, control of their bodies and their sexuality is not assured.[35] The refusal of the lock for Isabel's door after repeated threats and an actual attack clearly favors Camilla's expression of female desire (taking a lover) over Isabel's desire for bodily integrity and safety. Moreover, the response to Isabel's request for a lock on some level sees Isabel, a black woman, a slave whose body and sexuality are property, as unrapeable. Nashoba provides the occasion for Wright's expression of female desire, and that message is privileged over the sexual integrity of a slave woman.

As Deborah Gray White notes in her discussion of the stereotype of the slave woman as "Jezebel," black women are always present in constructions of white female sexuality, lurking as the dark, sexualized foil to white women's virtue.[36] Wright, despite her abolitionist project, does not succeed in revising sexual stereotypes of black women, relying on them instead to secure her own sexual freedom. She borrows this strategy from her earlier portrayal of African-Americans in her travel writing—and her later feminism continues to depend on race privilege that reinforces status quo social power structures. Wright's travel writing and her radical philosophy and reform work are linked by both their vision of liberation for middle-class white women and their failure to include diverse women in their formulation of Woman's Rights. Despite her pioneering journeys across social boundaries, then, Wright's flawed attempts to change cultural scripts of femininity and sexuality ultimately fail.

While Wright co-opts female slave bodies in service to her radical feminist agenda, her own traveling female body is used by Beecher and her other conservative critics to limit the mobility and autonomy of white, middle-class women. Beecher's venom reveals her investment in a construction of femininity based on conservative, middle-class values. In order to promote and sustain this gender ideology, Beecher appropriates Wright's person and words as she seeks to consolidate the power of middle-class white womanhood. Wright's disregard for social boundaries and expectations of "proper" feminine behavior that was first evident in her travel writing makes her a target for Beecher, and for a society threatened by women's autonomy and mobility.

Wright spent her later life in Europe, writing *England, the Civilizer* (1848), a history that traces the abuse of male power and that offers in its last chapter a return to her earlier utopian writing, with an imagined world run with the participation of women: "Come! in this last extremity let woman's voice obtain a hearing. Woman! who never asked, nor asks for self . . . Who never felt, nor feels, saving for others and for collective human kind." While Wright herself may have "obtain[ed] a hearing" among the American and British publics, she could not control the reception of her troubling message or her disconcertingly unfeminine presence.[37] Simultaneously ostracized and scrutinized, Wright was held up as a "singular spectacle" of indecency, a warning that other women considering rebellion should heed. The controversial figure of Fanny Wright continued to haunt the nineteenth century even after her death in 1852.

Woman's Rights leaders recognized the legacy of her feminism and used her picture as the frontispiece of *History of Woman Suffrage* (1881), but not before her own daughter joined in the chorus defaming Wright's character and activism. Eckhardt describes daughter Sylva's condemnation: "In 1874 [Sylva] testified before a Congressional committee against female suffrage. 'As the daughter of Frances Wright, whom the Female Suffragists are pleased to consider as having *opened* the door to their pretensions,' Sylva begged the Speaker and the members of the House committee 'to *shut* it forever, from the strongest convictions that they can only bring misery and degradation upon the whole sex, and thereby wreck human happiness in America!'" The struggles of Frances Wright may have paved the way for later feminists, but her life and work, and even her body, were also co-opted by her adversaries, including her own daughter, and used to reassert ideologies that limited the freedom and power of all women.[38]

Royall and Seacole each achieved notoriety as well, although on a smaller scale than Wright. Royall's trial as a "common scold" (discussed in chapter 2) was front-page news in national newspapers, and she ensured that her name would continue to be in the news and in the shaping of news by founding and editing her own newspapers, *Paul Pry* and the *Huntress*. Largely forgotten, Royall is now being recovered as an important female pioneer in the field of journalism. Seacole gained a certain level of fame because she was featured in war correspondents' reports on the Crimean War (the Crimean was the first war to be extensively covered by reporters stationed on the front lines of battle). *Wonderful Adventures* was intended to trade on her notoriety; the abrupt end of the war bankrupted Seacole when she could not sell the expensive cheese and champagne she had stocked for the British officers, and she wrote in an attempt to recoup her financial losses. Supportive cartoons and advertisements in *Punch*, a popular British magazine, called for patronage of Seacole's book and there was even a benefit held in her honor (although unfortunately it did not raise much money for her).[39] Additionally, a favorable review of her book appeared in the *Illustrated London News* on 25 July 1857. However, the review did not acknowledge Seacole's challenge to ideologies of race and gender in *Wonderful Adventures*, instead referring dismissively to her text as a "little book," and concluding that it could be "safely recommended." She remained in England during her last years, where she was received in prominent homes and by the Princess of Wales.[40] She died in 1881, leaving a substantial inheritance.[41] She remained in obscurity until the centenary of the Crimean War, in 1954, when the Jamaican Nurses' Association named their headquarters Mary Seacole House. More recently, the 1980 exhibition *Roots in Britain* included Seacole in its chronicle of black British history.[42] However, her white, middle-class counterpart Florence Nightingale (who started her now-famous corps of nurses during the Crimean War and refused Seacole's offer to serve) clearly eclipses Seacole's limited fame.[43]

All three of these notorious ragged-edge travelers demonstrate that new versions of femininity—or perhaps more accurately, unfemininity—circulated widely through antebellum culture via the pages of travel narratives and the bodies of the women travelers themselves. While these authors challenged the rhetoric of peril, their reception—ranging from benign neglect to ostracism and even violence—reinforces for other women the risks involved in traveling and public life. Ultimately, all three remain flamboyant exceptions to the rule of "proper" femininity and domesticity, rather than trailblazers paving the way for more women to follow. Their unsettling mobility and autonomy may have had precisely the opposite effect, generating enough anxiety to inspire the control and commodification that characterized later women's tourism of the nineteenth century, which was designed to combine travel and femininity rather than to test the limits of unfemininity.

The first woman to climb Pikes Peak certainly tested limits, whether they were of physical endurance, gender roles, or Woman's Rights politics. The next chapter features Julia Archibald Holmes's ascent of Pikes Peak in 1858 and the early feminist newspaper, the *Sibyl*, in which she published her travelogue. Wearing bloomers for her trip across the Midwest and to the summit, Holmes declares herself a radical feminist and shares her accomplishment with the reform-minded readers of the *Sibyl*. In a more-explicit way than any of the other writers in *Traveling Economies*, Holmes directly links travel and early feminism. Similarly, the *Sibyl* uses the travel genre to support its feminist platform. Reform newspapers, and certainly radical feminist periodicals, are an unexpected and underanalyzed place to look for women's travel writing. The final chapter of *Traveling Economies* takes us across the prairie and across the pages of the *Sibyl* to investigate how feminism works with the travel genre.

· Five ·

To the Summit of Equality

A Feminist Traveler, Bloomers, and the Antebellum Feminist Press

Sister Sayer—I think an account of my recent trip will be received with some interest by my sisters in reform, the readers of The Sibyl—if not by the rest of mankind—since I am, perhaps, the first woman who has worn the "American Costume" [bloomers] across that prairie sea which divides the great frontier of the states from the Rocky Mountains . . . I traveled in an ox wagon and on foot upwards of eleven hundred miles during the last three summer months . . . I wore a calico dress, reaching a little below the knee, pants of the same. Indian moccasins on my feet, and on my head a hat. However much of it lacked in taste, I found it to be beyond value in comfort and convenience, as it gave me freedom to roam at pleasure in search of flowers and other curiosities, while the cattle continued their slow and measured pace.[1]

—Julia Archibald Holmes, "A Journey to Pikes Peak and New Mexico" (1859)

*A*ll of the women travel writers in this study tested the limits of what women should do and where they should go. Frances Wright's early evaluation of the practices and theories of American democracy certainly laid the foundation for her later Woman's Rights and suffrage activism; Mary Ann Shadd Cary began to include reprints of Woman's Rights articles alongside her own arguments for black emigration and black civil rights as the *Provincial Freeman*'s publication run drew to a close; and Amy Morris Bradley defined herself in terms of mobility and independence rather than marriage and domesticity, and offered her life as a model for her young nieces and female cousins. While none of these authors directly linked their travels to an explicitly feminist agenda, antebellum Woman's Rights rhetoric with its call for women's increased physical and social mobility invites a connection between early feminism and women travelers. Julia Archibald Holmes with her account of her ascent of Pikes Peak in 1858 frames her journey in feminist terms and represents herself as a traveling standard-bearer

141

for the spread of Woman's Rights across the frontier. She revises the travel genre to represent herself as a feminist traveler and to convey her political agenda. Her version of traveling nation-building recasts national expansion in service to feminism.

Julia Archibald Holmes begins her travel narrative with what she considers the most salient information, her identity as a dress reformer and feminist and her target audience of "sisters in reform." Publishing her travel account in the *Sibyl* (1856–64), an antebellum newspaper dedicated to promoting dress reform (bloomers to replace corsets and hoopskirts) and Woman's Rights, Holmes addresses herself to an audience of like-minded feminists. Her travel narrative directly connects reform dress, feminism, physical fitness, and the participation of women in public civic life. Crafted to encourage her "sisters in reform" to follow in her mountain-climbing and activist footsteps, Holmes's account features a feminist traveler who revises expectations of the domestic focus of women's travel writing, and serves as a role model for her audience. Holmes advocates for women's equal abilities on the wagon train or in the voting booth, pairing action with theory and articulating an equality-focused feminism, in contrast to competing formulations of benevolence or abolitionist feminism, that offers the figure of the strong Western woman as inspiration for Woman's Rights activists and for the nation itself.

The *Sibyl* published Holmes's narrative because it fit so closely with the periodical's own complex formulation of Woman's Rights and because it shared Holmes's vision of the frontier and eventually the nation promoting women's equality. However, the newspaper strictly policed membership in its reform community; therefore, the choice of Holmes as a model of their theories put into practice offers just one example of the impossibly high standards for membership, which I term "exclusive sisterhood." As a feminist traveler who linked women's independence and mobility and reinforced the philosophy of the *Sibyl*, Holmes—and the bloomer-wearing figure she cut—inspired readers at the same time she demanded that would-be reformers prove willing to climb mountains in service to the cause and have the resources to conquer peaks. Holmes and the *Sibyl* used feminist travel and travel writing to bridge the gap between the theories and practice of women's equal participation in public civic life, beginning with an audience of sympathetic reformers, but also circulating images of women travelers and feminists more widely through antebellum culture.

New Traveler, New Politics: A Feminist Traveler Theorizes Women's Equality

Just as the *Sibyl* proposes bloomers as a practical first step to Woman's Rights, Holmes represents feminist travel as a practical demonstration of women's fitness for the rigors of public life. Fashion in Holmes's text functions as a code for middle-class white femininity; by rejecting hoopskirts in favor of pants, she opts out of it and into independence and expanded social and political participation beyond the scope of what was considered "proper for a woman among so many men" in society and on the largely male wagon train to Pikes Peak (522). Holmes directly connects physical mobility, dress reform, and women's autonomy, claiming that her bloomer offers her "comfort," "convenience," and, most important, "freedom" (522). Her feminist travel demonstrates that bloomers and Woman's Rights work together. Refusing to limit herself to the expected domestic focus of women's travel writing and claiming instead the accomplishment and perspective usually attributed only to male travelers and explorers, Holmes portrays her own strength, thereby justifying her claims to gender equality. Her articulation of feminism differs from simultaneous formulations of benevolence or abolitionist feminism, stressing equality and presenting herself as a model of emancipated womanhood.

Holmes's ascent of Pikes Peak is the culmination of a journey that has tested her physical limits and proved her fitness as a feminist traveler. She begins her trip west on 2 June 1858, as a member of the Lawrence Party, "the first Kansas party of gold-seekers to visit what is now Colorado," traveling in the group's wagon train with her husband, James H. Holmes, and her younger brother, Albert W. Archibald.[2] Once at the Peak, she uses the physical strength she has acquired by walking to climb to the summit, a trek that involves a scramble through sandy soil, a near-vertical climb up the mountain's fourteen-thousand-foot altitude, and even the peril of clinging by her toes to the rocky mountain face.

Her bloomers' comfort and convenience allow Holmes to follow a program of physical fitness that has prepared her for all of these challenges, eventually enabling her to achieve the summit. She emphasizes her formidable will and her impressive physical accomplishment in her description of the trek from Kansas to Colorado and eventually to

New Mexico: "I commenced the journey with a firm determination to learn to walk. At first I could not walk over three or four miles without feeling quite weary, but by persevering and walking as far as I could every day, my capacity increased gradually, and over the course of a few weeks I could walk ten miles in the most sultry weather without being exhausted" (522). Even as she highlights her impressive daily mileage across the sunbaked prairie, what Holmes offers her readers is not so much an exceptional example, but a model for them to follow. Extensive walking is a learned skill, one that other women, with dedication and perseverance, can develop themselves. The reward for Holmes, and potentially for her readers, is "the liberty to rove at pleasure," not only a vision of autonomy but also one of joy worth the work of building the necessary stamina (522). The dismal alternative is to be "confined . . . the long days to feminine impotence in the hot covered wagon," the chosen fate of the only other woman on the wagon train, whom Holmes describes as "unable to appreciate freedom or reform" (522). What is at stake is not whether to walk or ride across the scorched prairie, but whether one makes the journey as an independent traveler or essentially as a piece of baggage. Both options are choices; Holmes effectively shows that the other woman performs appropriate femininity (frail, dependent, conservative), while she casts herself as a feminist traveler who contests and revises stereotypical gender roles.

"Vigorously attacking the mountain," Holmes applies the same commitment and resolve to summiting as she did to her trek across the plains (530). In a climbing party with three men, she presents herself as an equally able member of the group: "The first mile or so was sandy and extremely steep, over which we toiled slowly, as we frequently lost all we gained. But by persevering and every rod laying, or rather falling on our backs to rest, we at last reached the timber where we could obtain better footing" (530).[3] Holmes shares the difficulties of the climb with the men; she is the recipient of neither chivalrous attention nor assistance. Her use of *we* emphasizes that the men, too, struggle with the incline and the sandy soil, and she as a feminist traveler has undertaken the same difficult journey and kept apace with them. Describing their first campsite "on the east side of the Peak, whose summit looming above our heads at an angle of forty-five degrees, is yet two miles away towards the sky," (530) she provides still more detail about the arduous nature of the climb, with the steep, vertical two-mile stretch awaiting the climbers. But even with the summit hike "looming," Holmes does not focus single-mindedly on the peak; she takes the opportunity to explore the side of the mountain and further prove her mettle as an adventurer. This side trip takes her around the mountain and into considerable danger: "We went in search of a supposed cave about three fourths of a mile along the side of the mountain. We penetrated the canyon with much difficulty, being once obliged to take off our moccasins that we might use the toes and balls of our feet in clinging to the asperities of the sidling [sic] rock" (530). Again, both her drive and her dedication are on display here. She risks her life, clinging by her toes to the cliff face—not for the achievement of the summit, but for the thrill of discovery. Here Holmes casts herself in the mode of explorer, moving beyond travel or even equality.

Holmes's travel narrative defies generic expectations for women's travel writing, replacing a focus on domesticity and exceptionalism with her emphasis on feminist politics and an empowerment of her female audience. When women's travel and exploring was acknowledged, it was often in service of an expansionist agenda that celebrated the spread of domesticity to as-yet-uncivilized territory. Scholar Susan Kollin identifies this "'first white woman' trope" as operating in many late-nineteenth- and early-twentieth-century women's travel texts. Kollin describes the function of the trope in white, middle-class women's travel writing as "announcing the appearance of a pioneering figure who ventured where no other white female had gone before." She maintains that "the 'first white woman' trope effectively broadened the horizons of the new white womanhood, doing so in service of western expansion." Representing themselves as carrying the banner of middle-class femininity to the far corners of the globe, the women travel writers Kollin discusses often frame their travels in terms of civilizing missions meant to spread the doctrine of domesticity. The unorthodox nature of their dangerous trips to remote locations is effectively tempered by their performance and celebration of proper domesticity, often in inhospitable and challenging locations. Women travelers' performance of this domesticity supports and extends the spread of U.S. territorial expansion, couching conquest as the spread of enlightenment and improvement by demonstrating the "proper place" of civilized women and the correct way to run a comfortable home. However, promoting feminism rather than domesticity, Holmes's account offers a very different spin on the promotion of manifest destiny, as a tool to spread gender equality to the frontier and beyond.[4]

While her contemporaries and even late-twentieth-century scholars frame Holmes in terms of the "first white woman trope," her insistent promotion of a feminist agenda changes the terms on which women travelers participate in expansion and imperialism.[5] It is important to note that neither Holmes nor the *Sibyl* uses the "first white woman" formulation; both instead emphasize Holmes's identity as a dress reformer and feminist. Holmes and the editors and publishers of the *Sibyl* do, however, reveal "their yearning to assert agency and authority in nation-building projects," according to Kollin's formulation.[6] The crucial difference is that Holmes and the *Sibyl* want to participate in claiming and shaping the West as a land of opportunity for women. They do not want to see status quo gender relations recreated in the United States' new Western territories; rather, expansion must be predicated on gender equality.

As a feminist traveler, Holmes goes beyond revising stereotypes of women travelers to claim and revise the exclusively male role of explorer. Explorers are often key agents of imperialism and expansion, laying the groundwork by surveying land and resources and in their travel narratives laying claim to land through their assertions of discovery and cultural superiority. Holmes casts herself as an active explorer, a position she sees as asserting power normally reserved for white men: "[I] felt that I possessed an ownership in all that was good or beautiful in nature, and an interest in any curiosities we might find on the journey as much as if I had been one of the favored lords of creation" (522). She usurps the place of the "lords of creation," effectively adopting what critic Mary Louise Pratt identifies as the masculine "monarch-of-all-I-survey" perspective. Narrating the "peak moments at which geographical 'discoveries' were 'won,'" the white male traveler, according to Pratt, conquers territory merely by viewing it. Holmes similarly declares "ownership" by virtue of her active physical presence in the territory between Kansas and Pikes Peak. Emphasizing the physical fitness she has developed thanks to her bloomer outfit, Holmes replaces Pratt's "seeing-man . . . whose imperial eyes passively look out and possess" with a representation of herself as an active agent. The result is a justification of both her "ownership" of the land she crosses and of her trespass into the masculine territory of travel and adventure. Pratt's formulation, tied as it is to the explorer's role in the expansion of patriarchy, does not imagine a woman in the role of seeing-man. However, I argue that Holmes offers a feminist revision of this model as her travels focus on the expansion of Woman's Rights.[7]

Holmes also displays her physical travel competence, which is equal to that of the men who accompany her, as well as her savvy understanding of the way that travel and exploration can be tied to the exercise of individual and national power. Her death-defying risk of clinging by her toes is repaid with a "discovery":

> We found no cave but a tremendous amphitheater shaped space, whose perpendicular walls rose seven or eight hundred feet high. Piled around this vast circle at the foot of the walls, were granite boulders of all sizes and shapes rising against the walls like the terraced seats of a circus or theater. Deep in the center is a circular spot of green grass, with flowers, and a silvery stream winding through it. We called the place Amphitheater Canyon. (530)

Her reward is an exclusive view of this hidden sight, a place she lays claim to through her description. She creates the metaphor that connects her new discovery to her own and her readers' frame of reference, an amphitheater suggesting importance, culture, and even the theatricality of her own daredevil performance. Her ownership of her accomplishment and of the place she has seen is further cemented by the process of naming, an act that erases any previous knowledge of the canyon and any other name it might have had. Traveling, seeing, and naming reinforce Holmes's "ownership" of the canyon and her authority to write about it, in much the same way that the westward spread of the Lawrence Party and other settlers effectively claimed Western frontier territory for the expanding nation.

Holmes conquers the West through her accomplishment of the summit of Pikes Peak—not only for herself but also for the readers and activists who make up her audience. After the dangerous detour into Amphitheater Canyon, her description of the climb to the summit on 5 August 1858 is anticlimactic:

> Arriving within a few hundred yards of the top the surface changed into a huge pile of loose angular stones, so steep we found much difficulty in clambering up them. Passing to the right of a drift of snow some three or four hundred yards long, which the sun and wind had

turned into coarse ice, we stood upon a platform of near one hundred acres of feldspathic granite rock and boulders . . . It was cold and rather cloudy, with squalls of snow, consequently our view was not so extensive as we had anticipated. A portion only of the whitened back-bone ridge of the Rocky Mountains which forms the boundary line of so many territories could be seen, fifty miles to the west. We were now nearly fourteen thousand feet above the sea level. But we could not spend long in contemplating the granduer [sic] of the scene for it was exceedingly cold, and leaving our names on a large rock, we commenced letters to some of our friends, using a broad flat rock for a writing desk. (530–31)

The final rocky stretch to the summit, while difficult, constitutes only several hundred yards, a small portion of the climb. As the final push to the summit lacks drama, Holmes redirects her audience's attention instead to the total height of the peak, and thus to the enormity of her achievement. Weather limits her feminist-of-all-I-survey view, but she does manage to see as far west as the Rockies, which are significant not because of their beauty but because of their function as boundary markers for frontier territories that her gaze claims for herself and for the readers of the *Sibyl*. She immediately turns from the view to the crucial job of documenting her accomplishment by inscribing her name on the boulder and writing letters that will reach family, friends, and the pages of the feminist magazine. The emphasis on writing, even as she is literally on the snow-squall-whipped mountaintop, recognizes that the written record she is producing is as important as the climb itself, for herself and, in turn, for the readers she would have follow her.

Holmes's travel writing is carefully crafted to encourage those readers to climb mountains of their own. In comparison to a more-candid version of the climb recorded in a letter to her mother, Holmes downplays the physical challenge in her piece for the *Sibyl* in order to present her climb as arduous but certainly replicable by other dedicated bloomer wearers. Her letter to her mother, on the other hand, emphasizes the transformation in her physical strength during her walking and the difficulty of the climb: "Two days of very hard climbing has [sic] brought me here [to the last campsite before the summit climb]—if you could only know how hard, you would be surprised that I have been able to accomplish it. My strength and capacity for enduring fatigue have been very much increased by constant exercise in the open air since leaving home, or I never could have succeeded in climbing the rugged sides of this mountain."[8] Holmes's own mother might not recognize her physically fit daughter, thanks to her bloomer-aided exercise program, but that increased ability has been put to the test by the mountain, a fact Holmes deemphasizes for the readers of the *Sibyl*. The description of the first mile-long climb up the sandy soil at the base of the Peak offers the most vivid account of the physical challenge Holmes faced in the version she presents in the *Sibyl*, but for that audience she focuses on her ability to keep up with the men. To inspire the *Sibyl*'s readers, Holmes wants to portray her accomplishment as extraordinary, but also within the reach of all (bloomer-wearing, reform-minded) women. Her ascent was actually repeated two years later, in 1860, by two other white women reportedly wearing bloomer dress, but they apparently had no knowledge of Holmes, believing themselves to be the first women to summit.[9] Although the women were not, in fact, following the trail she had blazed up the peak, Holmes and the *Sibyl* imagine their "sisters in reform" proving themselves by doing no less.

Those high expectations applied to words as well as deeds. Holmes serves as a role model not only of mountain climbing, but also of theorizing and articulating a feminist message through her travel writing. She refuses formulations of gender difference that figure women as weak, vulnerable, and in need of male protection. With her emphasis on mobility and autonomy, Holmes's feminism differs from simultaneous formulations of benevolence, which justified women's increasing participation in charity and social service work based on a view of women's innate moral superiority. Rather than relying on a notion of essential difference to expand women's sphere from the home outward, Holmes insists on a view of women's equality that highlights women's equal competence and skill and their rightful place in public life. Her argument for equal rights and equal responsibilities is what underlies her request to be assigned a watch with the rest of the male guards of the camp: "Believing, as I do," she writes, "in the right of woman to equal privileges with man, I think that when it is in our power we should, in order to promote our own independence, at least, be willing to share the hardships which commonly fall to the lot of man" (523). The captain of the guard refuses Holmes, saying that "it would be a disgrace to the gentlemen of the company for them to permit a woman to stand on guard" (523). Recording the vehement reaction of the men on the wagon train to her would-be trespass into the masculine realm of guard duty, Holmes recognizes that masculinity is defined in terms of male roles as protectors and defenders of both property and women. She criticizes the sexism that persists despite her demonstrated physical competence and identifies the workings of social power evident in the guard master's argument: "He believes that woman is an angel, (without any sense,) needing the legislation of her brothers to keep her in her place; that restraint removed, she would immediately usurp his position, and then not only be no longer an angel but unwomanly" (523). Holmes is well aware that white, middle-class women are supposed to remain "angels of the hearth" confined within the domestic sphere. By both traveling and writing about her journey, however, she demonstrates that she is capable of participating in public life and is intelligent enough (with "sense") to author her travelogue.

Holmes's articulation of feminist politics through her travel narrative foreshadows later Woman's Rights discourses that link mobility and independence with liberation, as well as subsequent travel writing that incorporates arguments for suffrage and women's public participation. Theorizing "women's writing of travel-as-politics," critic Mary Suzanne Schriber identifies several approaches taken by women authors toward "deliberately" political subjects in their travel texts. But even though Holmes fits within Schriber's framework as a woman travel writer for whom "gender politics occup[ies] center stage," Holmes is ultimately more radical in her re-visioning of gender than the women that Schriber identifies as "aim[ing] to shape the culture's attitudes toward the sexes and, in this way, to expand the boundaries of domesticity." Her rhetoric of feminism does not rely on an expansion of domesticity; rather, as we will see, she argues that she has proven her mettle as an abolitionist activist and is therefore fit for citizenship.[10]

Demanding opportunities to participate in public civic life, Holmes figures herself not only as equally competent, but also as already experienced in public service and reform work. Her own history of dedication to abolition activism has prepared her as a reformer. In her discussion of being refused for guard duty, for instance, Holmes cites her experience and the participation of other women in the Kansas abolitionist movement as proof of fitness for public service and, more important, the vote: "He [the captain of the guard] would vote against the question of universal franchise, were it to be submitted to the people, although he was a hero in the struggles of Kansas, and must have witnessed the heroic exertions of many of the women of that Territory to secure for their brothers the boon of freedom" (523). Holmes herself moved to Kansas with her family as activists working to end slavery in the territory and see it enter the Union as a "free" state. As her work and that of other abolition activists attests, women were not unfit because they were untested; rather, they had already demonstrated the courage and dedication to the principles of freedom and justice required of American citizens. Her direct reference to suffrage links her theory of women's equality with her own practical experience as an activist and proposes the specific remedy of votes for women.

While the connection between women's empowerment through physical fitness, travel, and feminist activism seems logical today, Holmes's travel writing prefigures the later turn-of-the-century shift in feminist rhetoric identified by Jean Fagan Yellin as foregrounding the liberator figure of the strong white woman.[11] With the rise of eugenic feminism at the turn of the century, white, middle-class feminists stressed their difference from other races rather than comparing the oppression of slavery and patriarchy, as the rhetoric of abolitionist feminism had. According to critic Victoria Lamont, "feminized versions of the western male hero" found in women's Western fiction in the early twentieth century fit with the feminist movement's changing rhetoric and racial politics: "The West displaced abolitionism as the origin of American feminism, supporting the desire of Anglo-American feminists to distance themselves from their African American counterparts."[12] Holmes, however, predates by nearly fifty years the figures and the discourse of Western women as feminist models in popular literature and culture that Lamont proposes. She and the *Sibyl* were prescient in their vision of the West as a land promising expanded roles for women—Colorado, the state Holmes viewed from the top of Pikes Peak, enfranchised women in 1893, and the territories of Wyoming (1869) and Utah (1891) ratified woman suffrage even earlier. Holmes's early experiment replacing the rhetoric of abolitionist feminism with the liberator figure of the strong white woman fit with the *Sibyl*'s view of its readership as a uniquely dedicated and limited group.

Holmes anticipates the later representations of strong, white, Western women, which, Lamont argues, found their fictional expression in portraits highlighting the "female individualism of [Western cowgirl] figures such as Annie Oakley."[13] Holmes becomes a larger-than-life Western heroine not only because of walking across the prairie or even summiting Pikes Peak, but also because of facing a series of dangers on her journey. For example, at one point she bravely stares down a buffalo: "There within forty yards of me stood a venerable buffalo bull, his eyes in seeming wonder fixed upon me . . . His gaze was returned with equal astonishment and earnestness. Much as I had heard and read of the buffalo, I had never formed an adequate idea of their huge appearance" (522). "The grand emperor of the plain" is no match for the unruffled Holmes, who coolly returns his gaze and then records the successful hunt of her large visitor (522). Trying to feed a buffalo calf orphaned by a subsequent hunt, Holmes does suffer an attack, but is only momentarily rattled: "The savage little animal advanced toward me and gave me such a blow with its head as to destroy the center of gravity" (522). The narrative doesn't even pause for Holmes to pick herself up before celebrating the strength and valor of another strong Western female, the mother buffalo who sacrificed her life for the ornery calf "and presented a beautiful illustration of the triumph of maternal feeling over fear" (522). Throughout her journey Holmes emulates the fearlessness of the mother buffalo, whether by swimming in the Arkansas River, where "a number of large rattlesnakes were killed"(530), or by dismissing the threat of kidnap by Native Americans: "It was of no use to hide now, for every Indian within a mile knew of my whereabouts" (529). A model of female strength, dedication, and courage equal to, if not surpassing, the men in the Lawrence Party, Holmes replaces formulations of benevolence that figure women as morally superior and fundamentally domestic, as well as formulations of abolitionist feminism that highlight the patriarchal oppression of slaves and women, insisting instead on a vision of gender equality that will be not only liberating but also practical and necessary to settle the untamed frontier. Even though her accomplishment and strength are extraordinary, she is not meant to be a singular example; her "sisters in reform" are meant to follow her daunting example, out West and at home.

Circulating Women, Circulating Texts:
The *Sibyl* as a Context of Publication

The women who would follow Holmes on her literary and literal travels were the readers of the *Sibyl*. Travel writing by reform-minded women fit well within the *Sibyl*'s call for women's physical and mental autonomy as necessary antidotes to sexism. In the same issue in which the second and final installment of Holmes's travel account appears, for instance, the *Sibyl*'s outspoken editor, Lydia Sayer Hasbrouck, articulates the direct connection between mainstream fashion and women's subordination. According to Hasbrouck, "the latest fashion," by diverting women's minds from reform and exhausting their bodies, stunts women's moral and intellectual development: "We ask what can woman do towards fitting herself for a higher development, so long as her mind is narrowed to the study of the latest fashion, and her intellectual powers have no higher aim than to construct garments to prostrate the little physical power she has remaining, after lugging and lifting and drabbling her load of dry goods through the streets?" Holmes's account featured on the issue's front page suggests exactly what women freed from both corsets and stifling definitions of femininity can accomplish. By traveling, Holmes is able to escape the domineering social conventions that Hasbrouck finds as pervasive as the air women breathe: "Not only her skirts, her whalebones, her stays, but the very atmosphere she breathes, destroys her energies and leaves her only a shadow of what she should be." According to critic Patricia Smith Butcher, by identifying the operations of sexism and offering new models for women, the *Sibyl* and other women's reform periodicals served as "relentless catalysts [that] assisted in the evolution, dramatization, and celebration of new roles for women." Thus, Holmes's travel account reinforces the goals of the *Sibyl,* and the newspaper's stories of warning confirm Holmes's own experience of gender oppression.[14]

A symbol for its supporters of white, middle-class women's autonomy, mobility, and competence, the bloomer provided opponents of Woman's Rights with a potent image of female silliness that they used to undercut and ridicule calls for feminist reform. The bloomer's emergence in the late 1840s was lampooned for more than a decade, as historian Gary Bunker catalogs in his discussion of the themes of anti-bloomer cartoons:

> Enormous, domineering wives led frail, hen-pecked husbands around by the nose; comely partisans of liberal inclination showed signs of moral decline; "real" men spurned the advances of "strong-minded ladies"; . . . a "model bloomer . . . was in such a darned hurry to get on her rig, that she forgot her pants"; and the inherent inferiority of women was claimed by the failure to produce great paintings, sculpture, poetry, drama, opera, and mechanical inventions.

To combat popular press images of the bloomer in particular and women's inferiority in general, women themselves founded, edited, and published a number of newspapers dedicated to Woman's Rights, including *Una* (1853–55), the *Pioneer and Women's Advocate* (1852–53), the *Genius of Liberty* (1851–53), and the *Woman's Advocate* (Jan. 1855–58 or 1860). Amelia Bloomer's *Lily* (1849–56) is perhaps the most well-known early feminist reform periodical; however, a consideration of less well-known women's reform newspapers such as the *Sibyl* suggests the breadth of participation by women in the public rhetoric surrounding women's issues in the mid-nineteenth century.[15]

The *Sibyl* (1856–64) deserves particular attention among antebellum feminist periodicals for its longevity, its promotion of uncompromising stances on dress and gender reform, and its strict policing of membership among its cadre of dedicated reformers. A growing scholarly conversation about the cultural work performed by nineteenth-century periodicals has begun to assess the central role such publications played in the construction, perpetuation, and dissemination of social and political ideologies. An examination of the *Sibyl*'s radical message and editorial strategies complements Patricia Okker's study of *Godey's Lady's Book,* with its focus on that mainstream publication's formulations of appropriate white, middle-class femininity. Placing the *Sibyl*'s long editorial life and thriving and geographically diverse distribution in this context suggests both the surprising reach of the early feminist newspaper and the limits of its vision of social and political reform. The paper's mission statements, editorials, letters, features, and travel writing articulate a sophisticated feminist agenda, create a widely dispersed audience for its message, and ultimately demand an almost impossibly high level of dedication from its readers.

An analysis of the *Sibyl* and Holmes demonstrates that bloomers were part of a complicated and multifaceted feminist agenda that had dress reform at its center, but that also offered critiques of the economic, educational, sexual, and political barriers that white, middle-class women faced. Despite many women's shared experience of gender oppression, the sisterhood envisioned by the feminist reform press was complex and problematic, demanding uncompromising dedication from its members, and ultimately it may have excluded many more women than it welcomed.

Linking mainstream women's fashion to impaired physical movement, poor health, and a preoccupation with conspicuous consumption, the *Sibyl* argues for the increased health and physical fitness to be gained from dress reform, a prerequisite for public service and participation for women. The newspaper presents its critique in the form of satiric verse, publishing a poem entitled "Miss Alice" in the column next to Holmes's travelogue. The poem traces the sad story of Alice, who insists on wearing her finery despite a cold, wet storm and suffers the ensuing negative health effects:

> Next day, poor Alice was sick and sore,
> Pain in spots and pain all o'er;
> Pain in the head, and pain in the teeth;
> Pain in the lungs, and stomach beneath;
> Pain in the limbs, above and below;
> Pain in the shoulder, and pain in the hip,
> Pains to pay for the dip, dip, dip.
> Yet Alice and all, both young and old,
> Wondered how Alice had caught such a cold!

The humorous account of Alice's suffering nonetheless conveys the message that women's dress reform and women's full and equal social participation are necessary, concomitant changes dictated by common sense.

Unlike the mainstream media's cartoons, it is not the reformers who are silly in the *Sibyl*; rather, fashionable women are ridiculous. A much more dire account of the health effects of women's fashion appears in "Madge Moody's Lectures, No. 7": "But what provoked me most, was, to hear Mrs. Showoph talk about the 'mysterious ways of providence' in taking her little girl from her, who died with scarlet fever not long since. I wanted to ask her if she thought Providence would advise her to let her child go all winter with cotton stockings and pantalets that just come to the top of them, and thin shoes." As dramatizations of the fashion-conscious attitudes of most women, "Madge Moody's Lectures" exaggerate but also illluminate the very real consequences of white, middle-class women's and society's lack of common sense.[16]

According to critic Lori Duin Kelly's analysis of bloomers in the popular press, "For Dress Reformers, clothing, far from innocent and frivolous, was a 'symbol' of woman's inferior position in society." Although adoption of reform dress was often a symbolic rejection of restrictive gender roles for white, middle-class women such as the readers of the *Sibyl*, dress reform was also more complicated than a straightforward critique of woman's sphere. Not merely symbolic, bloomers constituted a practical and tangible first step toward wide-ranging social change. Reform would not be limited to Woman's Rights; this workable start for women's activism was intended to lead to other areas of reform advocated by the *Sibyl*, including temperance, abolition, and labor reform.[17]

Perhaps because of their direct connection to reform work and potentially revolutionary social change, bloomers generated an immediate and general hostility that was directed toward both reform dress and women's activism more generally. Bunker's analysis of antebellum caricature identifies dress reform as the catalyst for an unprecedented reaction: "What whetted the cartoonist's appetite for misrepresenting women's themes more than anything else was the introduction of 'the bloomer.' Its adoption by the leaders of the movement . . . fixed an image of contempt for [reform-minded] women . . . that endured for generations." The extensive lampooning of bloomers reveals the threat that dress reform and Woman's Rights discourses posed to mid-nineteenth-century American society. Ultimately, bloomers and dress reformers were jeopardizing the status quo of women's subordination, and potentially undermining systems of power based on white male dominance. Reconsidering bloomers in this light suggests their power, rather than their laughability.[18]

For Holmes on her trip, bloomers facilitated access to the masculine territory of travel and adventure. For the *Sibyl* and its readers, such masculine territory included education and suffrage. The newspaper's extensive coverage illustrates the various ways in which American society was institutionalizing women's subordinate status. A column titled "Educational Development" locates the solution for women's subordination in educational reforms that would produce true companionate marriages and true equality for women: "Let man and woman be educated *alike* in *everything* . . . [and the result will be] a nobler life in all respects." Lack of access to education is a frequent subject of letters printed in the *Sibyl;* correspondents complain of scarce educational opportunities and of the way women's limited education is used to justify their exclusion from politics and public life. A correspondent identified as "Luna" traces the specious logic of such arguments against woman suffrage: "Such reasoning reminds me of the anxious mother who wished her son to learn to swim, but he must learn before going into the water or he might get drowned. So, if woman is allowed to vote before she is 'well educated' and had 'proper political training,' she might make a mistake." It is clear that the *Sibyl* and its readers were well aware of the circular logic that was often used to exclude women from full citizenship.[19]

In addition to lack of suffrage and education, the *Sibyl* identified the sexual double standard and limited economic opportunities as other obstacles to women's autonomy. Publishing a caution to its readers against Lord Napier, who was renowned for his "libertine career," the *Sibyl* recognizes that women are often placed in an "equivocal position" when seducers exercise their "peculiar and fascinating power" over vulnerable women. The argument echoes the earlier analysis of the New York Female Moral Reform Society, whose newspaper, the *Advocate,* published the names of seducers in an effort to ameliorate the sexual double standard. Addressing gendered economic injustice as well, the *Sibyl* includes an article entitled "Pecuniary Dependence," suggesting the limited occupations open to women and the hiring discrimination they face by wearing reform dress. The *Sibyl* offered both theoretical and practical solutions to women's experiences of economic injustice; for instance, it eventually hired an all-female staff, as this ad for a female printer under the heading "A Chance for a Dress Reformer" emphasizes: "We now have an opening for another apprentice should any thorough reformer be desirous of learning the printer's trade . . . None but an active, working, dress reformer need apply." The masthead illustration of the *Sibyl* also reinforces this view of the necessity of expanding women's work opportunities by picturing women operating a printing press. With its wide-ranging discussions of the various factors operating against women's full and equal social participation and its presentation of practical solutions, the *Sibyl* presents a complex analysis of gender oppression.[20]

Exclusive Sisterhood in the Feminist Reform Press

So whom did Holmes's narrative and the feminist analysis of the *Sibyl* reach? The newspaper's first issue boldly proclaims, "We circulate Two Thousand copies of our first issue, scattered everywhere throughout the Union." Although the *Sibyl* clearly sought to compete with other reform periodicals—intending "to make it the leading reform journal in the country"—Kathleen Endres and Therese Lueck conclude that it "never had a large, national circulation." For comparison, Frank Luther Mott's *A History of American Magazines* puts the circulation of Bloomer's successful women's reform magazine, the *Lily* (1849–56), at four thousand at the height of its popularity in 1854. Despite the *Sibyl*'s lower circulation, Amy Beth Aronson still places the newspaper among an elite group of "national players" that constituted "the first generation of American feminist magazines." While not as successful as the *Lily*, the *Sibyl* did reach a surprisingly wide audience, especially considering its radical feminist content.[21]

The *Sibyl* succeeded in connecting women in various and often isolated rural locations. Mary Craig writes from Iowa, declaring her intention to found "The Oskaloosa Dress Reform Society," and documenting her early success. Similar letters from Faribault, Minnesota; Meadville, Pennsylvania; South Bend, Indiana; Willoughby, Ohio; Waterloo, Wisconsin; and Polo, Illinois, offer further evidence of the various communities linked by the newspaper. Guila, writing from Huntley Grove, Illinois, suggests that her town has "many about here who would be reformers if they had a little help; there are some bold ones as it is." The mission statement of the *Sibyl* declares an intention to unite a reform community: "Believing there are many scattered up and down the earth, who think with and like us, we call upon them to aid our undertaking, and thereby advance the good cause." Holmes imagines herself as part of this geographically dispersed reform community and writes with that audience in mind.[22]

In contrast to the geographically diverse (but unswervingly dedicated) community of activists and liberal thinkers the *Sibyl* considers its audience stand what Holmes calls "the croakers against reform," those opposed to gender and social reforms (522). Following the lead of the *Sibyl*, Holmes includes references to the opposition she encounters from conservative men and women. These conservative characters serve, both in Holmes's travel narrative and in the *Sibyl*, to personify the obstacles to social and political change and to emphasize the need for dedicated reformers to join forces in order to accomplish their common goals. Conservative women in particular caused Holmes and the *Sibyl* the most disappointment and frustration. Particularly because so much of the movement's rhetoric centered on building a coalition of women supporting their own enfranchisement and autonomy, women dissenters presented a potent threat to images of white, middle-class women allied behind a shared cause.

Strategic representations of antireform women pepper the columns of the *Sibyl*. Frequently, unsympathetic women are rendered as merely backward and powerless. A letter from Miss Fidelia R. Harris, MD, describes the contrast between her own independence and fitness for public life and that of a group of fashionable women gathered at the scene of a fire:

> Among the women who were standing with me on the corner, were hooped ones and hoopless ones, some with skirts held in their hands to an altitude not comporting with popular ideas of decorum, (it was a muddy, sloppy, sleety, night,) and some with robes trailing in the mud, in accordance with the most approved and sensitive ideas of gracefulness, (?) and I stood among them, in the proudly dignified consciousness of being clothed in accordance with the dictates of reason and propriety.
>
> "Oh, dear, dear!" said my good neighbor Mrs. B. as she stood with both hands full of cumbersome skirts, "Oh dear, dear! Can't we do something!" "No," I replied, "you see there is nothing can be done for the burning building, and there are plenty of men at work for the others." "Oh, dear, well I wish WE could help!" I involuntarily laughed at the idea. Poor, fettered creature! How could you help, be the necessity ever so great. And yet, that is but the echo of the heart-cry that is going up all over our land from thousands of just such fettered women.

Reason, grace, dignity, decorum, and usefulness are all counted on the side of the author and the readers of the *Sibyl*; Mrs. B., on the other hand, provides a humorous (if not ridiculous) example of women who have not yet awakened to the cause of dress reform and Woman's Rights. While congratulating the *Sibyl*'s audience on its good sense and independent spirit, the author's use of fire also suggests the urgency of the reformer's mission and the need for increasing dedication. By presenting a foolish woman character who does not support reform, the author and the *Sibyl* galvanize their existing audience and create an image of prestige and a sense of like-minded community for insiders who support their cause.[23]

Representations of conservative women complicate the *Sibyl*'s version of sisterhood, for not all white, middle-class women are automatically considered allies; rather, the readership of the *Sibyl* constitutes an elite group of awakened women who understand the need for gender and dress reforms and who dedicate themselves to action. The *Sibyl*'s standards for membership are, on occasion, impossibly high. A diatribe against Lucy Stone, for instance, one of the most prominent leaders of the Woman's Rights crusade, penned by editor Hasbrouck, suggests the expectations the newspaper has of its readers. In response to Stone's abandonment of reform dress in the interest of protecting herself from what she called "the pressing curiosity of the public," Hasbrouck proclaims: "We have a high regard for Lucy Stone; we respect her talents, we honor the many good things she has done for reform, but we know she has made a grand mistake as regards the reform dress. She has not only injured the cause, but she has caused the mass to look upon her as lacking in the true, strong elements that should constitute a reformer." According to Hasbrouck, Stone's return to long skirts overshadows the accomplishments she has made while publicizing the cause of Woman's Rights. As such a public figure, Stone could have been held to an extreme standard precisely because of her popular influence.[24]

However, Hasbrouck turns what she sees as Stone's failure into a lesson for her readers: "Perhaps Lucy can reconcile her conscience to the course she has taken; if so she has a more accommodating one than ourself [*sic*]. We are sure we could never hold our head up amongst reformers or claim to be one of them, should we do as she has done." Hasbrouck exhorts her audience to show more dedication than one of the century's most noted Woman's Rights campaigners. In order to remain within the reform community of the newspaper's readership, they must rise to the occasion. Hasbrouck is clearly concerned that the defection of a celebrity from dress reform may hurt the movement, and she emphatically declares, "We wish the world to know that our strength is not from her." Rather, Hasbrouck identifies the provenance of her cause's strength as the cadre of dedicated women reformers who make up the readership of the *Sibyl.*[25]

The *Sibyl*'s version of sisterhood differs sharply from the editorial sisterhood created by mainstream publications like *Godey's Lady's Book.* In her analysis of a range of nineteenth-century mainstream women's periodicals, Patricia Okker identifies "the sisterly editorial voice" as a common rhetorical strategy: "This voice is characterized by a relative informality and an assumed equal and personal relationship between editor and reader" (23). Okker suggests that the sisterly editorial voice "assumes a friendly, even intimate relationship with her readers who share 'mutual interests.'" Although the *Sibyl* seeks to unite a scattered community of women reformers, as the above discussion of Lucy Stone illustrates, the newspaper carefully outlines criteria for membership among its list of reformers. While the newspaper offers support to readers like O. D. from La Grange, New York, who vows to "continue [to wear reform dress] as long as I can have *The Sibyl* to bear me company," her inclusion in the community created by the paper is not based solely on her gender or even her sympathy with the cause, but with her commitment to adhering to and promoting reform dress.[26]

An editorial titled "Pecuniary Dependence," written by "Sister Fannie," demonstrates the *Sibyl*'s application of exacting standards to all its potential members, regardless of practical concerns. In response to a reader who cannot obtain a lucrative teaching position because she wears reform dress, Sister Fannie counsels steely determination and unwavering dedication to reform dress, encouraging "that genuine martyr spirit that one who would be of the highest service to the world should possess." Fannie cushions her strict advice by saying, "I cannot tell another's duty, nor do I know how weak and irresolute I might be in the cause, had I not fully committed myself," thereby effectively representing any practical concessions to fashionable dress as an indication of a flawed character. Although Fannie superficially employs a sisterly voice similar to the one Okker identifies in mainstream women's magazines, Fannie does not offer actual sisterly sympathy, instead issuing a call to moral duty. In order to be worthy of Fannie's approbation and that of her fellow sisters reading the *Sibyl*, Fannie counsels that the would-be teacher should

> persevere in the course her conscience approves. If employment suited to her wishes cannot be obtained, she can perform any labor, however disagreeable under ordinary circumstances, which will enable her to support herself . . . Yet if she can consent to bear the present disappointment, she will do the world quite as much, I think more good, by this act of heroism, by showing the world that she will never surrender a principle for its favor of patronage.

Casting dedication to dress reform as heroism, Fannie honors the readers of the *Sibyl* by aggrandizing their political and social resistance work. Her column suggests the small distance between insiders and outsiders—ideological agreement must be supported with action or women risk rejection. Hence, despite the paper's often-insightful critiques of the economic pressures their readers face gaining and keeping employment due to their gender, that sophisticated analysis is displaced by the call to reform at any cost.[27]

Holmes is aware of the *Sibyl*'s version of sisterhood, and because she has proven her mettle as a dedicated reform-dress activist, she can become a spokeswoman. She not only chooses the *Sibyl* as the appropriate venue to publish her travelogue (other local publications were interested in accounts of the Lawrence Party; in fact Holmes's mother published a letter written by Holmes about the trip in the *Lawrence Republican*), but she also specifically addresses her narrative to "my sisters in reform, the readers of *The Sibyl*" (521). Holmes is not interested in non-reform-minded women; she targets an audience of women committed to the cause she shares, whom she can reach through a periodical that has helped both to create and to connect that community.[28]

Holmes reinforces her status as an insider in the *Sibyl*'s reform community by means of contrast with the other female member of the wagon train, whom she initially hopes to befriend: "I was much pleased to learn on my arrival, that the company contained a lady, and rejoiced at the prospect of having a female companion on such a long journey" (522). The prospect of shared friendship, however, much less a sympathetic audience for her reform agenda, vanishes in the very next sentence: "But my hopes were disappointed. I soon found that there could be no congeniality between us. She proved to be a woman unable to appreciate freedom or reform, affected that her sphere denied her the liberty to roam at pleasure, and confined herself the long days to feminine impotence in the hot covered wagon" (522). Politics quickly divide the only two female members of the Lawrence Party and just as quickly reveal the limits of the rhetoric of sisterhood among all women.

Holmes does make a final effort to convert her would-be female ally to reform with unsuccessful results. After the woman suggests to Holmes, "If you have a long dress with you, do put it on for the rest of the trip, the men talk so much about you," it is fairly clear that she is unlikely to change her position on Woman's Rights (522). Nonetheless, Holmes includes her version of their spirited debate on the reform question:

> I then endeavored to explain to her the many advantages which the reform dress possesses over the fashionable one but failed to make her appreciate my views. She had never found her dress to be the least inconvenient, she said; she could walk as much in her dress as she wanted to, or as was proper for a woman among so many men. I rejoiced that I was independent of such little views of propriety. (522)

Holmes fails to add another member to the roster of women reformers, although this "failure" allows her to be the first Woman's Rights supporter to accomplish and chronicle her Western journey. Instead of presenting a successful conversion of her opponent, Holmes designs this passage to elicit a response from the readers of the *Sibyl*. By representing the irrationality of this conservative woman (who, after all, fails to appreciate the many logical arguments Holmes presents, which she does not need to rehearse for her proreform audience) and her defiant backwardness in disregarding her own comfort and independence in favor of "propriety," Holmes demonstrates her insider status with the *Sibyl*'s audience. The conservative woman effectively highlights Holmes's dedication to the reform cause as well as the ridiculousness of the opposition.

Both the editors of and contributors to the *Sibyl*, as well as Holmes's unconventional travel writing, spoke to women's increasing participa-

tion in traditionally masculine aspects of public life. As women readers traveled across the pages of the *Sibyl*, travel writing with a feminist
agenda reinforced a view of white, middle-class women as capable
of moving about in the public world. Although the newspaper and
Holmes each suggested the possibilities of women's increased autonomy, they also problematically limited membership in the feminist
reform community. Ideological fervor at times eclipsed practical discussions of negotiations women may have been forced to make—negotiations stemming from the subordinate social status of women that
the *Sibyl* so cogently analyzed. Despite its rural audience and its occasionally insightful critique of economic injustice, the *Sibyl* demanded
a level of commitment and dedication that may have been possible
only for privileged middle-class women. Alliances across class and race
lines were unlikely with this exclusionary notion of reform community
membership. In fact, the *Sibyl*'s exclusive sisterhood foreshadowed the
later exclusion of African-American women from suffrage activism. The
Sibyl staunchly supported abolition, and features called for emancipation from the beginning to the end of its publication run. However,
a closer inspection of the newspaper's limited view of appropriately
reform-minded readers presages later conflicts between black and
white women over suffrage, and suggests the problematic nature of
sisterhood and alliance defined in such narrow and exclusive terms.

Conclusions: Travel Writing and the Feminist Press

Two months later the *Sibyl* published another travel account, although
much briefer and not featured as prominently as Holmes's narrative.
Titled "Our Visit Home," Louisa T. Whittier's letter to the *Sibyl* describes
her relocation to teach, her adoption of "Bloomer Dress as our universal
dress, having only worn it to work in before," and finally her trip by
"the cars" and omnibus from Palmyra, Wisconsin, to Brandon, Wisconsin. Whittier's letter offers a condensed version of many of the themes
raised by Holmes, including women's travel as liberating, the utility
of reform dress, the link between bloomers and Woman's Rights, and
encounters with those unfamiliar with and potentially hostile to dress
reform and feminism. The letter focuses on bloomers as a means to
white, middle-class women's autonomy and mobility: "With perfect
confidence in our ability to travel alone and unmolested in our favorite
costume, we bid good-bye to loved friends, for a few weeks, stepped

aboard the cars at Palmyra—our home by adoption—and with no fearful encounters to break the monotonous ride, soon found ourselves at
our great western emporium, Milwaukee." Whittier and her fellow
female companion gain a spirit of independence and self-assuredness
from their practical dress, which also provides practical benefits, since
they are unencumbered, "holding in [their] hands a shawl and book,
instead of, as formerly, dress, crinoline and skirts." Without elaborate
hoops and skirts, Whittier and company are able to act on their "disposition to help themselves," and they decline offers of aid and extra
attention from both the omnibus driver and the male innkeeper. Like
Holmes, Whittier constructs herself as a woman without need of assistance while at the same time revealing the sexism underlying notions
of chivalry. In response to the innkeeper, who wants to know "whether
we were man or woman" because "it was customary to pay a little
more attention to ladies," Whittier declines the innkeeper's pampering
while critiquing gender inequity: "We told him wherever he saw this
style of dress, there he would find that little gallantries were not needed
or desired, and might have added, that they could not atone for rights
denied and unjust power usurped." Despite this opportunity to educate the antireform innkeeper, Whittier's journey is largely uneventful,
marked by competence and self-assuredness rather than by a series of
difficulties. What her letter suggests is that with the proper attire and an
acceptance of female competence, travel by women alone can eventually become a nonevent, even boring and commonplace (like the train
ride to Milwaukee).[29]

Nevertheless, Whittier's local travel and Holmes's more-adventur-
ous climb up Pikes Peak both speak to women's increasing participation in public life. The *Sibyl*'s vision of reform does not stop at women
living more-comfortable and healthier lives at home. Wearing reform
dress and reading the *Sibyl* will fit women for public participation and
ultimately full and active citizenship. Travel writing with a feminist
agenda reinforces this view of white, middle-class women as capable of
moving about in the public world. Both accounts look toward the day
when women's travel will be mundane, and when Woman's Rights will
be fully claimed.

The *Sibyl* finds in Holmes an exemplar of its feminism put into
practice, and the partnership of travel writer and feminist press suggests travel writing as a suitable and useful genre for reform periodicals. Travel writing is often thought of as closely related to journalism
(although *Traveling Economies* demonstrates how many literary strate-

gies and techniques women authors use to color their presentations of the "facts" of the places they visit), and it is not surprising that many of the authors studied so far continued their public writing in newspapers. Anne Royall founded and edited *Paul Pry* and the *Huntress;* Mary Ann Shadd Cary published her travel editorials in the pages of her own newspaper, the *Provincial Freeman* (the first newspaper in North America to be owned and edited by an African-American woman); and Frances Wright owned and edited the *Free Enquirer.* All of these women began their careers with travel writing and sought the expanded audience and greater voice in public debates that newspapers offered. Woman's Rights activists also recognized the power of the press to spread their messages and founded numerous feminist newspapers at midcentury. Holmes specifically chose one such newspaper to print her travelogue, and as a result she offers us a fascinating case study of an explicitly feminist traveler and of the audience for travel writing with a Woman's Rights agenda. In her analysis of Holmes's feminist rhetoric, historian Margaret Solomon finds a vision of "the feminist as lonely outcast," an argument that does not take into account Holmes's sense of the community to which she was connecting through the pages of the *Sibyl.* The columns that appeared alongside Holmes's narrative offer unique insight into the close-knit reform community that newspapers like the *Sibyl* linked across a wide geographic area. As Ellen Gruber Garvey argues, it is the role of periodical editors to be "generators of community, inviting readers to see themselves as gathered around the magazine." Garvey goes on to suggest that "membership in theses imagined readerly communities was often active and contested," and the *Sibyl,* with its strict policing of reform membership, offers an example of just how contested readerly communities could be, with the surprising twist that the limitations of audience could come from the publication itself. Unfortunately, the vision of both Holmes and the *Sibyl* did not extend beyond the privileged middle class. Holmes's and the *Sibyl*'s "sisters in reform" were a small group indeed and, while dedicated, may have found themselves alone on mountain peaks, rather than leading mainstream America toward fully realized Woman's Rights.[30]

· *Afterword* ·

A delightful thought has struck me; it has positively illumined the blank of existence! Why should I not follow in the glowing footsteps of 'Eôthen' [a book of Middle Eastern travel]? Why should I not bask in the rays of Eastern suns, and steep my drooping spirits in the reviving influences of their magical mirages? The idea was an inspiration! I instantly rang for my faithful Minikin [the author's best friend], and bade her prepare for Eastern travel at the shortest notice. I shall not dread the wrench from old associations; familiar faces can make any land a home. Dear little Bijou [her dog]! Neither shall you be left behind.[1]
—Lady Dufferin, "An Unprotected Female in the East" (1863)

So at the end of our journey, we return to the Honorable Miss Impulsia Gushington, the heroine of *Harper's New Monthly Magazine*'s parody of women's solo travel, whom we met in the introduction on her runaway camel. Confiding her impulsive decision to travel to the pages of her journal (which well-meaning friends encourage her to publish on her return), the fictional Impulsia provides a stark contrast to the thoughtful, competent, ragged-edge travelers we have met in *Traveling Economies.* Ridiculous from the start, Impulsia imagines herself a romantic travel heroine, and indulges herself not just with the trip itself, but with bringing her dog along with her mountains of luggage. In Cairo, Bijou succumbs to the "ferocious nature of the indigenous dogs," his "ears and tail alone remain[ing] to tell [the] terrible story" to his distraught mistress (439). Bijou's death means that Impulsia is truly traveling alone, without "the only link between [her] and home," because her friend and companion, Minikin, abandons her as soon as their steamer has landed at the first Eastern port, Alexandria, the prospect of riding a donkey having frightened Minikin straight back home (438). Minikin's desertion and Bijou's death are but the beginning of Impulsia's travel misadventures—handsome but thieving guides; obnoxious, dishonest, and drunken traveling companions; locals who literally steal the dress off her back; runaway camels; confidence men and women posing as relatives; and gold-digging suitors all get the better of the hopelessly romantic and unfailingly inexperienced Impulsia. Richly illustrated, Impulsia's foibles are even more comic when events like her runaway camel ride are caricatured with flying dress and desperate grasping to keep hold of the saddle. The effect is a vivid portrait of women's traveling incompetence; Impulsia's repeated victimization emphasizes the myriad hazards that threatened traveling women and spotlights the "weaker" sex's inability to successfully negotiate the obstacle course of travel.[2]

Readers are invited to laugh out loud at Impulsia's pretensions to travel and independence. Expounding about the "freedom" and "charm" of travel, Impulsia follows her romantic notions to disastrous effect. What is being mocked here is tourist literature, with its "gushing," sentimental, romantic language that tries to evoke for both the tourist and the reader the flood of emotions that foreign sites and experiences are supposed to produce. Following a standard route through a standard set of places and "adventures," tourist authors have to make their account of the same places compelling for readers who have already read about them. Parodies like the one in *Harper's* show how by 1863 there was already an avalanche of women's tourist writing and how making fun of it convinced audiences that tourist accounts were all the women's travel writing there was. That avalanche effectively buried the cultural criticism and political commentary found in the travel narratives of the women studied in *Traveling Economies*.

Also erased were the successful and competent travels of earlier women. The text and illustration of Impulsia's wild camel ride emphasize the vulnerability and out-of-placeness of her traveling female body. Similar (although not ridiculous or parodic) scenes of physical danger found in the travel writing of Amy Morris Bradley, Nancy Prince, and Frances Wright highlight the risks of travel that they successfully survived—be they cliff-side mule rides, threatened beating and enslavement by Southern slaveholders, or a near tumble down a waterfall. A crucial missing element of Impulsia's narrative is the inclusion of corresponding scenes of strength and competence designed to show readers that women are more than able to meet the challenges of travel. Travel-savvy Anne Royall would never have been so easily parted from her luggage (not to mention her dress!), and indomitable Mary Seacole would have handled the runaway camel ride as easily as she dodged bullets on the Crimean battlefront. Julia Archibald Holmes would have found her bloomer much more suited to riding her camel astride, and Mary Ann Shadd Cary would have used a trip on the Nile to evaluate possible emigration to Africa and the column inches of *Harper's* to bring her discussions of black nationalism to a wider audience.

So why, when there were such gripping stories of women's travel to tell, did *Harper's* spend twenty pages mocking the putative idiocy of women travelers in general and Impulsia Gushington in particular? The lampooning of suffragettes and women wearing bloomers (discussed in chapter 5) follows a similar pattern to the *Harper's* parody of women travelers. Anxiety about women's increasing participation in public life fueled these kinds of mocking parodies. It was not women's silliness but women travelers' independence and mobility that was the problem. The venom of the parody reveals the deep cultural fear about how to keep women at home. As we have seen again and again in *Traveling Economies,* when women traveled and wrote, they often challenged social power structures and worked to change the places they visited and the places from which they started. In fact, antebellum women travelers were not ridiculous Impulsias who traveled on a whim and were completely unprepared for their journeys. Neither were they Gushingtons who merely babbled effusively about pyramids, camels, and bargains to be had at local bazaars. The women travel authors featured in *Traveling Economies* carefully weighed the risks and rewards of travel and set forth not out of boredom, but for a range of reasons including work, racism, and reform efforts. They are deliberate authors who craft careful representations of themselves, their destinations, and the "homes" they leave behind. Telling their stories would have made much better copy for *Harper's* and will make much better theories of women's writing and experience for students and scholars today.

· Notes ·

Introduction

1. Lady Dufferin, "An Unprotected Female in the East," *Harper's New Monthly Magazine* 160.27 (September 1863): 433–54. The *Harper's* feature is most likely a parody of Anthony Trollope's 1861 short story, "An Unprotected Female at the Pyramids." Gushington is supposed to be British, but publication of the piece in the popular American magazine clearly comments on American women travelers as well. Ibid., 443.

2. Ibid., 444.

3. For sources on tourism, see Dean MacCannell, *The Tourist: A New Theory of the Leisure Class* (New York: Schocken Books Inc., 1989); James Buzard, *The Beaten Track: European Tourism, Literature, and the Ways of Culture, 1800–1918* (Oxford: Clarendon Press, 1993); Judith Adler, "Origins of Sightseeing," *Annals of Tourism Research* 16 (1989) 7–29; Stephanie Cary, "The Tourist Moment," *Annals of Tourism Research* 31.1 (2004) 61–77; Patrick Holland and Graeme Huggan, *Tourists with Typewriters: Critical Reflections on Contemporary Travel Writing* (Ann Arbor, MI: University of Michigan Press, 2000); Adrian Franklin, *Tourism: An Introduction* (London: Sage Publications, 2003); Mark Rennella and Whitney Walton, "Planned Serendipity: American Travelers and the Transatlantic Voyage in the Nineteenth and Twentieth Centuries," *Journal of Social History* 38.2 (2004): 365–83.

4. Susan Bordo, *Unbearable Weight: Feminism, Western Culture, and the Body* (Berkeley, CA: University of California Press, 1993). Rosemarie Garland Thomson, introduction to *Freakery: Cultural Spectacles of the Extraordinary Body* (New York: New York University Press, 1996). Jennifer Terry and Jacqueline Urla, "Introduction: Mapping Embodied Deviance," in *Deviant Bodies: Critical Perspectives on Difference in Science and Popular Culture,* eds. Jennifer Terry and Jacqueline Urla (Bloomington: Indiana University Press, 1995), 2.

5. My formulation builds on Judith Butler's insights into the performative nature of gender roles featured in *Gender Trouble: Feminism and the Subversion of Identity* (New York: Routledge, 1990). I will discuss this at length in chapter 4.

6. "A Downright Gabbler, or a Goose That Deserves to Be Hissed," New

York Historical Society, reprinted in Celia Morris Eckhardt, *Fanny Wright Rebel in America* (Cambridge, MA: Harvard University Press, 1984), 192; "Female Infidelity," *Advocate of Moral Reform*, August 1, 1836, quotes *Ladies' Morning Star; New York Commercial Advertiser*, January 12, 1829; Catharine Beecher quoted in *The Limits of Sisterhood: The Beecher Sisters on Woman's Rights and Woman's Sphere*, eds. Jeanne Boydston, Mary Kelley, and Anne Margolis, (Chapel Hill, NC: The University of North Carolina Press, 1988), 236–37.

7. For discussions of the limitations of the model of separate spheres, see Linda Kerber, "Separate Spheres, Female Worlds, Woman's Place: The Rhetoric of Women's History," *Journal of American History* 75 (1988): 9–39; Gillian Brown, *Domestic Individualism: Imagining Self in Nineteenth-Century America* (Berkeley and Los Angeles: University of California Press, 1990); You-me Park and Gayle Walk, "Native Daughters in the Promised Land: Gender, Race, and the Question of Separate Spheres," in *No More Separate Spheres! . . . A Next Wave American Studies Reader*, eds. Cathy Davidson and Jessamyn Hatcher (Durham, NC: Duke University Press, 2002); Amy Kaplan, "Manifest Domesticity," in *The Anarchy of Empire in the Making of U.S. Culture* (Cambridge, MA: Harvard University Press, 2002), 23–50; Monika Elbert, ed., *Separate Spheres No More* (Tuscaloosa, AL: University of Alabama Press, 2000.

8. Farah Griffin and Cheryl Fish, eds., *A Stranger in the Village: Two Centuries of African-American Travel Writing* (Boston: Beacon Press, 1998); R. Victoria Arana, "Introduction: Black Travel Writing, A Kaleidoscopic Genre," *BMa: The Sonia Sanchez Literary Review* 9.1 (Fall 2003), 1; Jennifer Young, "'We Sweep the Liquid Plain': Wheatley's Travel Poems about the Sea," *BMa: The Sonia Sanchez Literary Review* 9.1 (Fall 2003): 33–49; Kenneth Speirs, "Strategies of Approximation in *The Life and Adventures of Nat Love*," *BMa: The Sonia Sanchez Literary Review* 9.1 (Fall 2003): 71–89; Kimberly Blockett, "Moving Subjectivities in the Evangelical Narrative of Zilpha Elaw," *BMa: The Sonia Sanchez Literary Review* 9.1 (Fall 2003): 103–111; Jennifer Steadman, "Traveling Uplift: Mary Ann Shadd Cary Creating and Connecting Black Communities," *BMa: The Sonia Sanchez Literary Review* 9.1 (Fall 2003): 119–37. Problematically, the recent special issue of the *Yearbook of English Studies*, "Nineteenth-Century Travel Writing," featured no articles on black authors (there were eighteen articles included, only three of which were on women authors). "Nineteenth-Century Travel Writing," Special Issue, *Yearbook of English Studies*, 34 (2004).

9. Cheryl Fish, "Voices of Restless (Dis)continuity: The Significance of Travel for Free Black Women in the Antebellum Americas," *Women's Studies—An Interdisciplinary Journal* 25.5 (1997): 485.

10. Nancy Garner Prince, *A Narrative of the Life and Travels of Mrs. Nancy Prince, Written by Herself*, 2nd ed. (1853; reprint, New York: Oxford University Press, 1988).

11. Mary Suzanne Schriber, *Writing Home: American Women Abroad, 1830–1920* (Charlottesville, VA: University Press of Virginia, 1997), 23–24.

12. Arguing for the same level of complexity I want applied to the women in *Traveling Economies*, critics Mark Rennella and Whitney Walton find that narratives dismissed as mass tourism can offer authors "the opportunity to engage in a constructive questioning and self-examination," rather than only a chance to

rehearse middle-class values (365). Mark Rennella and Whitney Walton, "Planned Serendipity: American Travelers and the Transatlantic Voyage in the Nineteenth and Twentieth Centuries," *Journal of Social History* 38.2 (2004): 365–83.

13. For a discussion of women traveling and working with their husbands, see Molly M. Wood, "A Diplomat's Wife in Mexico: Creating Professional, Political, and National Identities in the Early Twentieth Century," *Frontiers: A Journal of Women Studies* 25.3 (2004): 104–33.

14. Amy Schrager Lang, *The Syntax of Class: Writing Inequality in Nineteenth-Century America* (Princeton, NJ: Princeton University Press, 2003), 18.

15. Amy Morris Bradley, Amy Morris Bradley Papers, Manuscript Collection, William R. Perkins Library, Duke University.

16. Marion Tinling, introduction to *Women into the Unknown: A Sourcebook on Women Explorers and Travelers* (New York: Greenwood Press, 1989) xxiv–xxv; Catherine Stevenson, *Victorian Women Travel Writers in Africa* (Boston: Twayne, 1982); Jane Robinson, *Wayward Women: A Guide to Women Travellers* (New York: Oxford University Press, 1990).

17. Mary Suzanne Schriber, *Writing Home: American Women Abroad, 1830–1920* (Charlottesville, VA: University Press of Virginia, 1997). Mary Louise Pratt, *Imperial Eyes: Travel Writing and Transculturation* (New York: Routledge, 1992), 159. Lorenza Steven Berbineau, *From Beacon Hill to the Crystal Palace: The 1851 Travel Diary of a Working-Class Woman*, ed. Karen L. Kilcup (Iowa City, IA: University of Iowa Press, 2002). Cheryl Fish, "Voices of Restless (Dis)continuity: The Significance of Travel for Free Black Women in the Antebellum Americas," *Women's Studies—An Interdisciplinary Journal* 25.5 (1997). Sandra Gunning, "Nancy Prince and the Politics of Mobility, Home and Diasporic (Mis)Identification," *American Quarterly* 53.1 (March 2001): 32–69. Sandra Gunning, "Traveling with Her Mother's Tastes: The Negotiation of Gender, Race, and Location in *Wonderful Adventures of Mrs. Seacole in Many Lands*," *Signs* 26.4 (Summer 2001): 949–82.

18. Eric J. Leed, *The Mind of the Traveler: From Gilgamesh to Global Tourism* (New York: Basic Books Inc., 1991), 286.

19. Schriber, 58.

20. Julia Archibald Holmes, "A Journey to Pikes Peak and New Mexico," pts. 1 and 2, *Sibyl*, March 15, 1859: 521–23; April 1, 1859: 529–31. *Sibyl* (1856–64).

21. Mary G. Mason, "Travel as Metaphor and Reality in Afro-American Women's Autobiography, 1850–1972," *Black American Literature Forum* 24.2 (Summer 1990): 339. Julie E. Hall's recent work on Sophia Hawthorne argues that Hawthorne uses the travel genre to gain access to literary expression, rather than to the political voice Shadd Cary and Royall gain by using the genre. All three women point to travel writing as a genre open to women and perceived to be a route to authority in other cultural conversations. Julie E. Hall, "'Coming to Europe,' Coming to Authorship: Sophia Hawthorne and Her *Notes in England and Italy*," *Legacy* 19.2 (2002): 137–51.

22. Amy Kaplan, "Manifest Domesticity," *The Anarchy of Empire in the Making of U.S. Culture* (Cambridge, MA: Harvard University Press, 2002), 23–50.

23. Anne Newport Royall, *Sketches of History, Life, and Manners in the United States, by a Traveller* (1826; reprint, New York: Johnson Reprint Corporation, 1970).

24. Mae M. Ngai, "Transnationalism and the Transformation of the 'Other': Response to the Presidential Address," *American Quarterly* 57.1 (March 2005): 60.

25. Mary Seacole, *Wonderful Adventures of Mrs. Seacole in Many Lands* (1857; reprint, New York: Oxford University Press, 1988).

26. Tiffany Ruby Patterson and Robin D. G. Kelley, "Unfinished Migrations: Reflections on the African Diaspora and the Making of the Modern World," *African Studies Review* 43.1 (April 2000): 20.

27. Mary Ann Shadd Cary, *A Plea for Emigration, or Notes of Canada West* (1852; reprint, ed. Richard Almonte, Toronto: Mercury Press, 1998). Travel editorials published in *Provincial Freeman* (1853–60).

28. Paul Lauter, *From Walden Pond to Jurassic Park* (Durham, NC: Duke University Press, 2001), 11.

29. For a discussion of how women's travel writing can be both transgressive and supportive of status quo social hierarchies, see Brigette Bailey, "Gender, Nation, and the Tourist Gaze in the European 'Year of Revolutions': Kirkland's *Holidays Abroad*," *American Literary History* 14.1 (Spring 2002): 60–82.

Chapter One

1. Bradley's papers are held by Duke University's Special Collections Library and include correspondence and journals (collection I.D. # ADH-9963). This study focuses on Bradley's journal kept during her visit to Costa Rica (1854–58), which is the volume designated "Diary and Letterbook, November 6, 1853–September 12, 1865." In her journal, Bradley mixes diary entries with copies of correspondence she sent and received, and the dates of entries do not proceed in strict chronological order. I will indicate diary journal entries by date, copied letters in the journal by "copy of letter" with the correspondent's name and the date, and correspondence with correspondent's name and date. AMB is the abbreviation I will use for Amy Morris Bradley.

2. Nancy Prince, *Narrative of the Life and Travels of Mrs. Nancy Prince, Written by Herself.* 2nd ed. (Boston: published by the author, 1853; reprint, *Collected Black Women's Narratives* [New York: Oxford University Press, 1988]), 20.

3. Lilian Leland, *Traveling Alone: A Woman's Journey Around the World* (New York: Press of John Polhemus, 1890), 358.

4. Schriber suggests that Leland's text may be a spoof, since she can find no census records of Leland and since Leland's hyperbole and Twain-speak suggest parody. Schriber concludes, and I agree, that even if the text is a fake, it nevertheless speaks to the cultural obsession and familiarity with the middle-class female traveler in the late-nineteenth century (164–65). I will return to this idea and elaborate at the end of the chapter. Mary Suzanne Schriber, *Writing Home: American Women Abroad, 1830–1920* (Charlottesville, VA: University Press of Virginia, 1997).

5. For further discussion of how tourism works as performance of class status, see Schriber, Dean MacCannell, *The Tourist: A New Theory of the Leisure Class* (New York: Schocken Books Inc., 1989); James Buzard, *The Beaten Track: European*

Tourism, Literature, and the Ways of Culture, 1800–1918 (Oxford: Clarendon Press, 1993); Judith Adler, "Origins of Sightseeing," *Annals of Tourism Research* 16 (1989): 7–29; Stephanie Hom Cary, "The Tourist Moment," *Annals of Tourism Research* 31.1 (2004): 61–77; and Adrian Franklin, *Tourism: An Introduction* (London: Sage Publication, 2003).

6. Schriber, 39–40.

7. The final section of this chapter will discuss how Bradley's semipublic diary reaches an audience consisting of her younger female cousins and relatives.

8. Lorenza Steven Berbineau, *From Beacon Hill to the Crystal Palace: The 1851 Travel Diary of a Working-Class Woman*, ed. Karen L. Kilcup (Iowa City, IA: University of Iowa Press, 2002).

9. Linda Kerber, "Separate Spheres, Female Worlds, Woman's Place: The Rhetoric of Women's History," *Journal of American History* 75 (1988): 9–39; Gillian Brown, *Domestic Individualism: Imagining Self in Nineteenth-Century America* (Berkeley and Los Angeles: University of California Press, 1990); Amy Kaplan, "Manifest Domesticity," *No More Separate Spheres! . . . A Next Wave American Studies Reader*, eds. Cathy Davidson and Jessamyn Hatcher (Durham, NC: Duke University Press, 2002).

10. Amy Lang, *The Syntax of Class: Writing Inequality in Nineteenth-Century America* (Princeton, NJ: Princeton University Press, 2003), 15.

11. AMB journal entry, January 20, 1852.

12. Lang, 15.

13. Letter from AMB to Sarah Baxter, April 1, 1851. Historian Nancy Cott describes "women's second-class position in the economy" in New England in the first half of the nineteenth century as such: "There was only a limited number of paid occupations generally open to women, in housework, handicrafts and industry, and school-teaching. Their wages were one-fourth to one-half what men earned in comparable work." Despite her hard work, Bradley struggles as a result of these limited opportunities and low wages. Expectations that women like Bradley would marry actually further reduce their wage-earning potential, as Cott explains: "Wage rates reflected the expectation that [middle-class white women] would rely on men as providers." Finally, Bradley's family's financial position does not allow them to provide her with financial assistance, which would have been her other possible resource. Nancy F. Cott, *The Bonds of Womanhood: "Woman's Sphere" in New England, 1780–1835* (New Haven, CT: Yale University Press, 1977). Letter from AMB to Elijah Bradley, August 1851.

14. Letter from AMB to Jeremy Jones, July 20, 1851; ibid.; letter from AMB to William C. Fuller, November 22, 1851.

15. Sandra Myres, introduction to *Ho for California! Women's Overland Diaries from the Huntington Library*, ed. Sandra Myres (San Marino, CA: Huntington Library, 1980), 1.

16. Letter from AMB to William C. Fuller, November 22, 1851.

17. AMB journal entry, copy of letter from Stacy Baxter, November 6, 1853; ibid.

18. AMB journal entry, January 2, 1856; AMB journal entry, copy of letter from Stacy Baxter, November 6, 1853; ibid.

176 • Notes to Chapter One

19. Cheryl Fish, "Voices of Restless (Dis)continuity: The Significance of Travel for Free Black Women in the Antebellum Americas," *Women's Studies—An Interdisciplinary Journal* 26.5 (1997): 475; Paul Gilroy, *The Black Atlantic: Modernity and Double Consciousness* (Cambridge, MA: Harvard University Press, 1993), 4. Critics Gretchen H. Gerzina and Sandra Gunning discuss Prince's Russian travel in terms of its provocative expansion of the Black Atlantic, extending the formulation of diaspora to include blacks in Russia. For this discussion, see Gretchen H. Gerzina, "Mobility in Chains: Freedom of Movement in the Early Black Atlantic," *South Atlantic Quarterly* 100.1 (Winter 2001): 41–59; and Sandra Gunning, "Nancy Prince and the Politics of Mobility, Home, and Diasporic (Mis)Idenitification," *American Quarterly* 53.1 (March 2001): 32–69.

20. Cheryl Fish, *Black and White Women's Travel Narratives: Antebellum Explorations* (Gainesville, FL: University Press of Florida, 2004), 40–41.

21. Frances Smith Foster, in *Written by Herself* (1993), emphasizes the importance of Prince's representation of her marital status: "As implied by her self-designation as 'Mrs. Nancy Prince,' Nancy Prince was very careful to establish herself as a respectable woman" (85). Foster suggests that Prince's insistence on respectability and propriety reinforced her authority as a traveler and a writer, even as her behavior challenged the limits of traditional gender roles (85). See also Frances Smith Foster, "Adding Color and Contour to Early American Self-Portraitures: Autobiographical Writings of Afro-American Women," in *Conjuring: Black Women, Fiction, and Literary Tradition*, eds. Marjorie Pryse and Hortense Spillers (Bloomington, IN: Indiana University Press, 1985), 25–38. Sandra Gunning makes a distinction between Foster's reading of Prince's avoidance of publicity as a strategy for securing respectability and what Gunning sees as Prince's "judicious" construction of her own "public image" ("Nancy Prince" 49). In either case, the salient features of Prince's emphasis on respectability for this study are the class ramifications of asserting her own worthiness for middle-class standing, juxtaposed with the denial of that standing based solely on her race.

22. Allison Blakely, in *Russia and the Negro: Blacks in Russian History and Thought* (Washington DC: Howard University Press, 1986), notes that the inclusion of blacks in the Russian imperial court began during the reign of Peter the Great: "In 1697, Peter hired at least one black servant" (14). Black servants lent exoticism and interest to the court, as Blakely suggests: "[Peter the Great] later acquired a number of Negroes to embellish his court, in the manner that was fashionable in the rest of Europe at the time" (14). Blakely cites Prince's narrative as "the most revealing account available of these [black] servants' life in Russia" (17). Blakely credits Prince's husband, Nero Prince, with recruiting American blacks into service in the Russian imperial court: "As a leading mason, Prince was certainly a possible link between the tsar's court and certain Negro circles in America" (16).

23. Fish, "Restless," 484.

24. Fish, "Restless," 485.

25. Jennifer Terry and Jacqueline Urla, "Introduction: Mapping Embodied Deviance," in *Deviant Bodies: Critical Perspectives on Difference in Science and Popular Culture*, eds. Jennifer Terry and Jacqueline Urla (Bloomington, IN: Indiana University Press, 1995), 2. Kristi Siegel, "Women's Travel and the Rhetoric of Peril:

It Is Suicide to Be Abroad," in *Gender, Genre, and Identity in Women's Travel Writing,* ed. Kristi Siegel (New York: Peter Lang, 2004), 61. I will discuss the rhetoric of peril in more depth in chapter 4.

26. Mary Seacole, *Wonderful Adventures of Mrs. Seacole in Many Lands* (1857; reprint, New York: Oxford University Press, 1988), 5.

27. Myres, 1.

28. Mrs. D. B. Bates, *Incidents on Land and Water, or Four Years on the Pacific Coast* (1858; reprint, New York: Arno Press, 1974).

29. AMB journal entry, January 2, 1856.

30. Diane Cobb Cashman, *Headstrong: The Biography of Amy Morris Bradley, 1823–1904: A Life of Noblest Usefulness* (Wilmington, NC: Broadfoot Publishing Company, 1990), 73.

31. AMB journal entry, January 2, 1856.

32. AMB journal entry, copy of letter to Sarah Bradley Homans, January 1, 1854.

33. AMB journal entry, copy of letter to Dr. Hogan, January 5, 1854. By means of a loan from a friend, Bradley is able to repay the Medinas for her passage to Costa Rica and travel to San Jose, where she takes up residence (Cashman 77).

34. AMB journal entry, copy of letter to Sarah Bradley Homans, January 1, 1854; Cashman, 78; AMB journal entry, September 8, 1856; Cashman, 86.

35. AMB journal entry, copy of letter to her father, Abiud Bradley, December 24, 1853.

36. Fish similarly argues that Prince focuses on representing her working and mobile black female body and that this theme is reinforced through her representation of working black bodies she encounters on her travels (Fish, *Black and White,* 58).

37. Gunning, 44.

38. Gunning, 45; ibid., 45. Gunning qualifies her comparison, saying, "She was not entirely comparable to the elite white tourists to whom Buzard refers" (45). She further contends that "the 'escape' achieved by Prince in Europe—or more appropriately, achieved in the retelling of her transformative journey within *Life and Travels*—involved much higher stakes than those faced by middle-class white travelers who would have exemplified the name 'tourist' in nineteenth-century Europe" (46). Nevertheless, Gunning argues that Prince's choice of writing in the travel genre problematically participates in discourses "that functioned as the pillars of western imperialism" (39). *Traveling Economies* foregrounds the importance differences between the material conditions of Prince's travel from that of elite white tourists and the significant revision of the genre that her travel text constitutes.

39. Peter Kolchin, *Unfree Labor: American Slavery and Russian Serfdom* (Cambridge, MA: The Belknap Press of Harvard University Press, 1994), 42.

40. For further information on Prince's biography during this hiatus in her travels, see Fish, *Black and White,* 48–52.

41. Prince's uplift work in Jamaica has been treated at some length by Foster, Fish, and Gunning; *Traveling Economies* will focus on her return journey from Jamaica as an example of the extreme risk Prince runs as a black female traveler.

42. Fish, "Restless," 485.

43. Carla L. Peterson, *"Doers of the Word": African-American Women Speakers and Writers in the North (1830–1880)* (New York: Oxford University Press, 1995), 20.

44. Peterson, 88; ibid., 90.

45. Fish, "Restless," 483.

46. Peterson, 5.

47. "Book Reviews: Briefer Notice," *Overland Monthly and Out West Magazine* 16.91 (July 1890): 112; "A Yankee Ida Pfieffer, Going Round the World." *New York Daily Tribune,* February 14, 1890, page 10, column 1.

48. Schriber, 164–65.

49. AMB journal entry, copy of a letter to Betsey and Elizabeth Bradley, January 21, 1858.

50. AMB journal entry, January 1, 1856. Bradley also includes a copy of a letter addressed to her cousins Betsey and Elisabeth Bradley in her January 1, 1858 journal entry.

51. "The Emigration Scheme," *The Colored American,* November 13, 1841.

52. Ads for Prince's Russian lectures appeared in the March 8, 1839 *Liberator,* and she advertised the sale of her Jamaican pamphlet in the November 12, 1841 *Liberator.*

Chapter Two

1. (Harrisburg) *Intelligencer,* August 4, 1829, reprinted from the *New York Commercial Advertiser,* quoted in Bessie Rowland James, *Anne Royall's U.S.A.* (New Brunswick, NJ: Rutgers University Press, 1972), 260.

2. Ibid., 260; ibid., 262.

3. Ibid., 261. For a discussion of Royall's "apocalyptic" language, see Karen Ramsay Johnson and Joseph Keller, "Anne Royall's Apocalyptic Rhetoric: Politics and the Role of Women," *Women's Studies* 31 (2002): 671–88.

4. Phren and Logos, letter to the editor, *New York Commercial Advertiser,* July 31, 1829, quoted in James, 255. Phrenology was a pseudoscience of studying the bumps on the head to diagnose disease—it was an eighteenth-century fad that continued to be popular into the nineteenth century.

5. James, 256–57.

6. James, 259.

7. Two recent articles by Elizabeth J. Clapp call attention to the political content of Royall's travel writing and focus on her travel writing after *Sketches.* Elizabeth J. Clapp, "Black Books and Southern Tours: Tone and Perspective in the Travel Writing of Anne Royall," *Yearbook of English Studies* 34 (2004): 61–73; and Elizabeth J. Clapp, "The Boundaries of Femininity: The Travels and Writings of Mrs. Anne Royall, 1823–31," *American Nineteenth-Century History* 4.3 (Fall 2003): 1–28. *Traveling Economies* focuses on Royall's first published travel book, and chapter 2, along with the following chapters on Mary Ann Shadd Cary, Frances Wright, and Julia Archibald Holmes, answers Clapp's call for a new theory of women's political travel writing.

8. Anne Newport Royall, *Sketches of History, Life, and Manners in the United States, by a Traveller* (1826; reprint, New York: Johnson Reprint Corporation, 1970).

9. Anne Newport Royall, *Letters from Alabama, 1817–1822* (1830; reprint, ed. Lucille Griffith, Tuscaloosa, AL: University of Alabama Press, 1969), 238. Although Royall wrote *Letters from Alabama* between 1817 and 1822 as a series of letters to a friend, these letters were not published until 1830. For further information on Anne Royall's biography, see Sarah Harvey Porter, *Life and Times of Anne Royall* (Cedar Rapids, IA: Torch Press Book Shop, 1909); George S. Jackson, *Uncommon Scold: The Story of Anne Royall* (Boston: Bruce Humphries Inc., 1937); Bessie Rowland James, *Anne Royall's U.S.A.* (New Brunswick, NJ: Rutgers University Press, 1972); and Marion B. Dunlevy and Alice S. Maxwell, *Virago!: The Story of Anne Newport Royall (1769–1854)* (Jefferson, NC: McFarland & Company Inc., 1985).

10. Porter, 39; ibid.; ibid.

11. Anne Royall, *Mrs. Royall's Pennsylvania, or Travels Continued in the United States*, Volume 1, 86–87.

12. James, 108.

13. Royall, *Pennsylvania*, Volume 1, 3.

14. Maria Cummins, *The Lamplighter* (1854; reprint, with an introduction by Nina Baym, New Brunswick, NJ: Rutgers University Press, 1988), 70.

15. "Editor's Table," *Godey's Lady's Book* 16 (May 1838): 239.

16. Mary Suzanne Schriber, *Writing Home: American Women Abroad, 1830–1920* (Charlottesville, VA: University Press of Virginia, 1997), 4.

17. Schriber, *Writing Home*, 2.

18. "Editor's Table," *Godey's Lady's Book* 22 (January 1841): 46.

19. Jackson, 70; (Albany) *Daily Advertiser*, February 12, 1825.

20. Mrs. Johnstone, "Lady Travellers" (book review), *The Living Age* 6.68 (August 30, 1845): 423–24.

21. All of the texts Mrs. Johnstone discusses are published by European women; she does not recognize the growing number of American women travel writers.

22. Marion Tinling, introduction to *Women into the Unknown: A Sourcebook on Women Explorers and Travelers* (New York: Greenwood Press, 1989), xxiv–xxv; Mary Suzanne Schriber, introduction to *Telling Travels: Selected Writings by Nineteenth-Century American Women Abroad* (DeKalb, IL: Northern Illinois University Press, 1995), xxvii.

23. Mrs. Johnstone, 427.

24. Schriber, in *Writing Home, American Women Abroad, 1830–1920* (1997), cites Margaret Fuller, Mary Hannah Krout, Kate Field, Nellie Bly, and Lillian Leland (whom we met in the first chapter) as examples of women authors writing "travel-as-politics." Mary Louise Pratt's discussion of elite women traveling in South America, whom she terms *"exploratrices socials,"* similarly touches on the unexpectedly political content of "bourgeois women's travel writing" in the early nineteenth century. Complementing Schriber's and Pratt's analysis of overt political content, critics approaching women's travel writing from a postcolonial perspective, such as Sara Mills, Shirley Foster, Susan Kollin, and Chu-Chueh Cheng, trace the link between middle-class white women's travel writing and

the maintenance and dissemination (and occasional subversion) of proimperialist rhetoric. Mary Suzanne Schriber, *Writing Home: American Women Abroad 1830–1920* (Charlottesville, VA: University Press of Virginia, 1997), 137; Mary Louise Pratt, *Imperial Eyes: Travel Writing and Transculturation* (New York: Routledge, 1992), 155; Sara Mills, *Discourses of Difference: An Analysis of Women's Travel Writing and Colonialism* (New York: Routledge, 1991); Shirley Foster, "Colonialism and Gender in the East: Representations of the Harem in the Writings of Women Travellers," *Yearbook of English Studies* 34 (2004): 6–18; Susan Kollin, "'The First White Woman in the Last Frontier': Writing Race, Gender, and Nature in Alaskan Travel Narratives," *Frontiers: A Journal of Women's Studies* 18.2 (1997): 105–24; Chu-Chueh Cheng, "Frances Trollope's America and Anna Leonowen's Siam: Questionable Travel and Problematic Writing," in *Gender, Genre, and Identity in Women's Travel Writing*, ed. Kristi Siegel (New York: Peter Lang, 2004), 123–66.

25. Pratt, 160.

26. Pratt, 162.

27. James, vii.

28. Johnstone, 431.

29. For a discussion of how literary and mass culture representations of male "fops" express cultural anxiety about changing notions of masculinity during the transition from an agrarian to a business economy, see E. Anthony Rotundo, *American Manhood: Transformations in Masculinity from the Revolution to the Modern Era* (New York: Basic Books, 1993).

30. James, 307; ibid., 308.

Chapter Three

1. Mary Ann Shadd, "Hints to the Colored People of the North" (1849), quoted in J. B. Y., "Miss Shadd's Pamphlet," *North Star*, June 8, 1849.

2. Mary Ann Shadd Cary, *A Plea for Emigration, or Notes from Canada West* (1852; reprint, ed. Richard Almonte, Toronto: Mercury Press, 1998), 71.

3. Mary Ann Shadd Cary, "Our Tour," *Provincial Freeman*, July 22, 1854; emphasis in original.

4. Jim Bearden and Linda Jean Butler's recovery of Shadd Cary, *Shadd: The Life and Time of Mary Shadd Cary* (Toronto: N.C. Press Ltd., 1977); Carla Peterson's chapter "'Colored Tourists': Nancy Prince, Mary Ann Shadd Cary, Ethnographic Writing, and the Question of Home," in *"Doers of the Word": African-American Women Speakers and Writers in the North (1830–1880)* (New Brunswick, NJ: Rutgers University Press, 1995); Shirley Yee's critique of Shadd Cary's integrationist philosophy, "Finding a Place: Mary Ann Shadd Cary and the Dilemmas of Black Migration to Canada, 1850–1870," *Frontiers: A Journal of Women's Studies* 18.3 (1997); Jane Rhodes's excellent biography, *Mary Ann Shadd Cary: The Black Press and Protest in the Nineteenth Century* (Bloomington, IN: Indiana University Press, 1998); Richard Almonte's reprint of Shadd Cary's *A Plea for Emigration, or Notes from Canada West* (1852; reprint, ed. Richard Almonte, Toronto: Mercury Press, 1998); and my own article in the first edition of an academic journal entirely devoted to black travel writing, Jennifer Steadman, "Traveling Uplift: Mary Ann Shadd Cary Creating and Connecting Black Communities," *BMa: The Sonia San-*

chez Literary Review Special Issue on Black Travel Writing 9.1 (Fall 2003): 119–38, are among the recent scholarly treatments of Shadd Cary that attempt to remedy this neglect.

5. Tiffany Ruby Patterson and Robin D. G. Kelley, "Unfinished Migrations: Reflections on the African Diaspora and the Making of the Modern World," *African Studies Review* 43.1 (April 2000): 20.

6. Alexander Crummell, "The Relations and Duties of Free Colored Men in America to Africa," in *The Future of Africa, Being Addresses, Sermons, etc. Delivered in the Republic of Liberia by Rev. Alexander Crummell* (1860; reprint, *A Stranger in the Village: Two Centuries of African-American Travel Writing,* eds. Farah Griffin and Cheryl Fish [Boston: Beacon Press, 1998]), 124–36; W. E. B. DuBois, "Little Portraits of Africa" (1924; reprint, *A Stranger in the Village: Two Centuries of African-American Travel Writing,* eds. Farah Griffin and Cheryl Fish [Boston: Beacon Press, 1998]), 146–50.

7. Maria W. Stewart, *Religion and the Pure Principles of Morality, the Sure Foundation on Which We Must Build, Productions from the Pen of Mrs. Maria W. Steward* [sic], *Widow of the Late James W. Steward, of Boston* (reprint, *Words of Fire: An Anthology of African-American Feminist Thought,* ed. Beverly Guy-Sheftall [New York: The New Press, 1995]), 29.

8. Peterson, 9.

9. Peterson, 9. For further discussion of the black middle class see James Oliver Horton, *Free People of Color: Inside the African American Community* (Washington, DC: Smithsonian Institute Press, 1993).

10. Rhodes, 5.

11. As Jane Rhodes suggests, "Her father's close association with Philadelphia's black elite may have paved the way for [Shadd Cary] to participate in that world as well" (18).

12. Letter from A. D. Shadd to Mary Ann Shadd, December 8, 1844, Mary Ann Shadd Cary Papers, Manuscript Division, Moorland-Spingarn Research Center, Howard University.

13. Rhodes, 26.

14. Rhodes, 22; Mary Ann Shadd, "Hints to the Colored People of the North" (1849), quoted in J. B. Y., "Miss Shadd's Pamphlet," *North Star,* June 8, 1849.

15. Rhodes, 33–34.

16. Almonte, Introduction, 26.

17. Peterson, 107; ibid., 108; Elizabeth McHenry, *Forgotten Readers: Recovering the Lost History of African American Literary Societies* (Durham, NC: Duke University Press, 2002), 128.

18. The British and Foreign Anti-Slavery Society appointed John Scoble Secretary of Dawn. Robin Winks characterizes him as "a white liberal of the most paternalistic sort, who could not tolerate sharing responsibility with black men" (202). The Dawn Settlement was initially one of the most successful black settlements in Canada West, but it ultimately resulted in "ignominious and public failure" (Winks 204). Robin Winks, *The Blacks in Canada* (New Haven, CT: Yale University Press, 1971).

19. Begging was one of the most hotly contested issues among Canadian emigrants. Those who adopted a probegging philosophy sought charitable support from individuals and organizations in Canada and particularly from abolitionist

groups back in the United States. Blacks like Shadd Cary who opposed begging thought that communities should develop self-sufficiency, and that begging reinforced stereotypes of blacks as lazy and incompetent.

20. Shirley Yee discusses Shadd Cary's position on integration in her article "Finding a Place: Mary Ann Shadd Cary and the Dilemmas of Black Migration to Canada, 1850–1870," and argues that Shadd Cary was politically conservative. However, Richard Almonte, in his introduction to *Notes*, suggests a more-complicated reading of Shadd Cary's integrationist stance. According to Almonte: "We must remember her motives. When compared to a country where Blacks had no rights, where many lived as slaves without freedom, Canada appeared a haven. The fact that Shadd stresses conservative assimilationist values needs to be read with the volatile background of American slavery in mind. [S]hadd hopes Blacks will assimilate so that they can *benefit* from Canadian-British institutions. This is about repudiating a troubling past to make a better present. In other words, a strictly utilitarian decision" (29).

21. Todd Vogel, Introduction, *The Black Press: New Literary and Historical Essays,* ed. Todd Vogel (New Brunswick, NJ: Rutgers University Press, 2001), 2.

22. Robin Winks, *The Blacks in Canada* (New Haven, CT: Yale University Press, 1971); William H. Pease and Jane H. Pease, *Black Utopia* (Madison, WI: State Historical Society of Wisconsin, 1963); Jason H. Silverman, *Unwelcome Guests: Canada West's Response to American Fugitive Slaves, 1800–1865* (Millwood, NY: Associated Faculties Press, 1985). Peterson, 109.

23. Katherine Bassard, *Spiritual Interrogations: Culture, Gender, and Community in Early African American Women's Writing* (Princeton, NJ: Princeton University Press, 1999), 128; McHenry, 102.

Chapter Four

1. The *New York Evening Post* (January 26, 1829) referred to Wright as a "singular spectacle of a female, publicly and ostentatiously proclaiming doctrines of atheistical fanaticism, and even the most abandoned lewdness."

2. Catharine Esther Beecher, *Letters on the Difficulties of Religion,* 1836, selections reprinted in *The Limits of Sisterhood: The Beecher Sisters on Women's Rights and Woman's Sphere,* eds. Jeanne Boydston, Mary Kelley, and Anne Margolis (Chapel Hill, NC: The University of North Carolina Press, 1988), 236–37.

3. Celia Morris Eckhardt, *Fanny Wright Rebel in America* (Cambridge, MA: Harvard University Press, 1984), 244; ibid., 3.

4. Frances Wright, *Views of Society and Manners in America: In a Series of Letters from That Country to a Friend in England, During the Years 1818, 1819, and 1820* (1821; reprint, ed. Paul Baker, Cambridge, MA: The Belknap Press of Harvard University Press, 1963).

5. Jeanne Boydston, Mary Kelley, and Anne Margolis, introduction to *The Limits of Sisterhood: The Beecher Sisters on Women's Rights and Woman's Sphere* (Chapel Hill, NC: The University of North Carolina Press, 1988), 13.

6. "A Downright Gabbler, or a Goose That Deserves to Be Hissed," New York Historical Society, reprinted in Celia Morris Eckhardt, *Fanny Wright Rebel in*

America (Cambridge, MA: Harvard University Press, 1984), 192; "Female Infidelity," *Advocate of Moral Reform,* August 1, 1836, quotes *Ladies' Morning Star; New York Commercial Advertiser,* January 12, 1829.

7. *New York Evening Post,* January 26, 1829.

8. Lori D. Ginzberg, "'The Hearts of Your Readers Will Shudder': Fanny Wright, Infidelity, and American Freethought," *American Quarterly* 46.2 (June 1994): 206; ibid, 197.

9. Ginzberg, 195–203.

10. Recasting travel as "peaceful," Wright's formulation of travel is no less powerful than the violence of conquering male explorers and imperialists. As critic Mary Louise Pratt observes, the act of looking constitutes a crucial first step to the conquest of land and people by "seeing-men," the male explorers and travelers who serve as agents of would-be colonizing nations. For a discussion of "seeing-man," consult Mary Louise Pratt, *Imperial Eyes: Travel Writing and Transculturation* (New York: Routledge, 1992), 202.

11. Paul Baker, introduction to *Views of Society and Manners in America: In a Series of Letters from That Country to a Friend in England, During the Years 1818, 1819, and 1820,* by Frances Wright (1821; reprint, ed. Paul Baker, Cambridge, MA: The Belknap Press of Harvard University Press, 1963), xiii.

12. Jennifer Terry and Jacqueline Urla, "Introduction: Mapping Embodied Deviance," in *Deviant Bodies: Critical Perspectives on Difference in Science and Popular Culture,* eds. Terry and Urla (Bloomington, IN: Indiana University Press, 1995), 4.

13. Judith Butler explains the performative nature of gender roles in this manner: "There is no gender identity behind the expression of gender; that identity is performatively constituted by the very 'expressions' that are said to be its results." Judith Butler, *Gender Trouble: Feminism and the Subversion of Identity* (New York: Routledge, 1990), 25.

14. Kristi Siegel, "Women's Travel and the Rhetoric of Peril: It Is Suicide to Be Abroad," in *Gender, Genre, and Identity in Women's Travel Writing,* ed. Kristi Siegel (New York: Peter Lang, 2004), 61.

15. In one instance, Seacole is denied passage on an American steamer en route from Panama to Jamaica. After interrogating Seacole about her intentions to travel aboard the steamer, her fellow white female passengers declare their objection, saying, "I never travelled with a nigger yet, and I expect I shan't begin now" (57). A stewardess tells Seacole that she "can't expect to stay with the white people, that's clear. Flesh and blood can stand a good deal of aggravation; but not that" (58). In a toast ostensibly in her honor, a "thin sallow-looking American" berates Seacole for her race and gender (47). The American acknowledges her medical skill, "what she's done for us—, when the cholera was among us," but his faint praise is quickly overshadowed by his disparagement of her as a "yaller woman" (47). "Vexed" that Seacole is "not wholly white," the speaker "rejoice[s]" that as a mulatto, Seacole is "so many shades removed from being entirely black" (47). Indicating the extreme extent of the social prejudice Seacole faces because of her race, the speaker sarcastically suggests that to "bleach her by any means" is the only way to "make her as acceptable in any company as she deserves to be" (47). Mary Seacole, *Wonderful Adventures of Mrs. Seacole in Many Lands* (1857;

reprint, New York: Oxford University Press, 1988).

16. Seacole, 12–13.

17. Critic Cheryl Fish discusses Seacole's gendered laboring body in her chapter "Traveling Medicine Chest: Mary Seacole 'Plays Doctor' at Colonial Crossroads in Panama and the Crimea," in *Black and White Women's Travel Narratives: Antebellum Explorations* (Gainesville, FL: University Press of Florida, 2004): 65–96.

18. Recent criticism of Mary Seacole includes Ziggi Alexander and Audrey Dewjee, introduction to *Wonderful Adventures of Mrs. Seacole in Many Lands* (London: Falling Wall Press, 1984): 9–45; Cheryl Fish, "Voices of Restless (Dis)continuity: The Significance of Travel for Free Black Women in the Antebellum Americas," *Women's Studies—An Interdisciplinary Journal* 25.5 (1997): 475–95; Cheryl Fish, "Traveling Medicine Chest: Mary Seacole 'Plays Doctor' at Colonial Crossroads in Panama and the Crimea," in *Black and White Women's Travel Narratives: Antebellum Explorations* (Gainesville, FL: University Press of Florida, 2004): 65–96; Sandra Gunning, "Traveling with Her Mother's Tastes: The Negotiation of Gender, Race, and Location in *Wonderful Adventures of Mrs. Seacole in Many Lands*," *Signs* 26.4 (Summer 2001): 949–82; Bernard McKenna, "'Fancies of Exclusive Possession': Validation and Dissociation in Mary Seacole's England and Caribbean," *Philological Quarterly* 76.2 (Spring 1997): 219–40; Sandra Pouchet Paquet, "The Enigma of Arrival: *The Wonderful Adventures of Mrs. Seacole in Many Lands*," *African-American Review* 26.4 (Winter 1992): 651–63; and Amy Robinson, "Authority and the Public Display of Identity: *Wonderful Adventures of Mrs. Seacole in Many Lands*," *Feminist Studies* 20.3 (Fall 1994): 537–57.

19. Carolyn Karcher, "Frances Wright of the *Free Enquirer*: Woman Editor in a Man's World," in *Blue Pencils and Hidden Hands: Women Editing Periodicals, 1830–1910*, ed. Sharon M. Harris (Boston: Northeastern University Press, 2004), 83.

20. Anne Newport Royall, *Sketches of History, Life, and Manners in the United States, by a Traveller* (1826; reprint, New York: Johnson Reprint Corporation, 1970).

21. Mary Suzanne Schriber, *Writing Home: American Women Abroad, 1830–1920* (Charlottesville, VA: University Press of Virginia, 1997), 88–89.

22. Terry and Urla, 1.

23. Farah Griffin and Cheryl Fish, eds. *A Stranger in the Village: Two Centuries of African-American Travel Writing* (Boston: Beacon Press, 1998), 4.

24. Terry and Urla, 5.

25. Schriber, 23.

26. Nancy Cott, *The Bonds of Womanhood: "Woman's Sphere" in New England, 1780–1835* (New Haven, CT: Yale University Press, 1977), 220.

27. Anne Newport Royall, *Letters from Alabama, 1817–1822* (1830; reprint, ed. Lucille Griffith, Tuscaloosa, AL: University of Alabama Press, 1969).

28. For a discussion of the "Jezebel" stereotype, see Deborah Gray White, *Ar'n't I a Woman?: Female Slaves in the Plantation South* (New York: W. W. Norton & Company, 1985): 27–61.

29. "Female Infidelity," *Advocate of Moral Reform*, August 1, 1836, quotes *Ladies' Morning Star*.

30. Frances Trollope, a famous nineteenth-century travel writer whom Wright convinced to relocate from Europe to Nashoba, describes her first impression of the location: "The forest became thicker and more dreary-looking every mile we advanced; but our ever-grinning negro declared it was a right good road, and that we should be sure to get to Nashoba: and so we did . . . and one glance sufficed to convince me that every idea I had formed of the place was as far as possible from the truth. Desolation was the only feeling—the only word that presented itself." For Trollope, the "savage aspect of the scene" of the settlement in "this wilderness" was devoid of even the "minor comforts which ordinary minds class among the necessaries of life." Frances Trollope, *Domestic Manners of the Americans* (1832; reprint, London: George Routledge and Sons Ltd., 1927), 23–24.

31. Excerpts from the "Nashoba Book," published in Benjamin Lundy's *Genius of Universal Emancipation* in July 1827, shocked abolitionists by revealing physical and sexual abuses occurring at Nashoba. Trustee James Richardson kept the journal of everyday life in the community and, for unknown reasons, forwarded excerpts to Lundy. The "Nashoba Book" revealed that despite Nashoba's dedication to principles of "human liberty and equality" (Wright, "Explanatory Notes"), the reality of life in the community was marked by violence and exploitation ("Nashoba Book," *The Genius of Universal Emancipation*, July 28, 1827: 29–30).

32. Frances Wright, "Explanatory Notes, Respecting the Nature and Objects of the Institution of Nashoba," *The New Harmony Gazette*, January 30, 1828; February 6 & 13, 1828.

33. Elizabeth Ann Bartlett, *Liberty, Equality, Sorority: The Origins and Interpretation of American Feminist Thought: Frances Wright, Sarah Grimke, and Margaret Fuller* (Brooklyn, NY: Carlson Publishing Inc., 1994), 49; ibid.; Wright, "Explanatory Notes"; ibid.

34. Wright, "Explanatory Notes."

35. "Nashoba Book," 30.

36. White, 29.

37. Frances Wright, *England, the Civilizer*, quoted in Eckhardt, 281.

38. Eckhardt, 290.

39. Alexander and Dewjee, 31–34.

40. Alexander and Dewjee, 37.

41. Alexander and Dewjee, 37–38.

42. Alexander and Dewjee, 40.

43. For a discussion of Seacole and Nightingale, see Cheryl Fish, *Black and White Women's Travel Narratives: Antebellum Explorations* (Gainesville, FL: University Press of Florida, 2004), 65–96.

Chapter Five

1. Julia Archibald Holmes, "A Journey to Pikes Peak and New Mexico," *Sibyl*, March 15, 1859; 521–23. Holmes's travel text consists of two letters published serially, "A Journey to Pikes Peak and New Mexico," pts. 1 and 2, *Sibyl*, March 15, 1859: 521–23; and April 1, 1859: 529–31. All subsequent references to Holmes are to this version and will be cited internally.

2. Agnes Wright Spring, ed., *A Bloomer Girl on Pikes Peak, 1858: Julia Archibald Holmes, First White Woman to Climb Pikes Peak* (Denver, CO: Denver Public Library, 1949), 9.

3. The men were her husband, James H. Holmes; J. C. Miller, a Lawrence Party member who had made the ascent a few days before and served as a guide; and George Peck, another member of the Lawrence Party (Spring 30, footnote).

4. Susan Kollin, "'The First White Women in the Last Frontier': Writing Race, Gender, and Nature in Alaskan Travel Narratives," *Frontiers: A Journal of Women's Studies* 18.2 (1997): 108; ibid., 108–9.

5. Late-twentieth-century retellings certainly trade on the sensationalism of Holmes's 1858 summiting of the Peak; *A Bloomer Girl on Pikes Peak*, the title of Agnes Wright Spring's edited reprint of Holmes's narrative, and "A Bloomer Girl Conquers Pikes Peak," the title of Margaret Solomon's profile of Holmes for *American History Illustrated*, both highlight the quirkiness of bloomers and the achievement of being the first woman to climb the mountain. Nowhere does Holmes refer to herself as a "girl," and neither does the *Sibyl* refer to its readers as anything other than reform-minded women.

6. Kollin, 105.

7. Mary Louise Pratt, *Imperial Eyes: Travel Writing and Transculturation* (New York: Routledge, 1992), 7; ibid., 202; ibid., 7.

8. Spring, 38.

9. Spring, 48.

10. Mary Suzanne Schriber, *Writing Home: American Women Abroad, 1830–1920* (Charlottesville, VA: University Press of Virginia, 1997), 135–36; ibid., 137.

11. Jean Fagan Yellin, *Women & Sisters: The Antislavery Feminists in American Culture* (New Haven, CT: Yale University Press, 1989), 171–75.

12. Victoria Lamont, "Cattle Branding and the Traffic in Women in Early Twentieth-Century Westerns by Women," *Legacy* 22.1 (2005): 31.

13. Lamont, 31.

14. Lydia Sayer Hasbrouck, "Remarks," *Sibyl*, April 1, 1859: 533; ibid., 533; Patricia Smith Butcher, *Education for Equality: Women's Rights Periodicals and Women's Higher Education, 1849–1920* (Westport, CT: Greenwood Press, 1989), ix.

15. Gary L. Bunker, "Antebellum Caricature and Woman's Sphere," *Journal of Women's History* 3 (Winter 1992): 29.

16. Anonymous, "Miss Alice," *Sibyl*, March 15, 1859: 521; Madge Moody, "Madge Moody's Lectures, No. 7," *Sibyl*, April 15, 1859: 537.

17. Lori Duin Kelly, "Bipeds in Bloomers: How the Popular Press Killed the Dress Reform Movement," *Studies in Popular Culture* 13.2 (1991): 73.

18. Bunker, 17.

19. D. D., "Educational Development," *Sibyl*, April 15, 1859: 541; Luna, "Equal Political Rights," *Sibyl*, May 15, 1859: 557.

20. *Sibyl*, April 15, 1859: 538; Carroll Smith-Rosenberg, *Disorderly Conduct: Visions of Gender in Victorian America* (New York: Oxford University Press, 1985), 117–18; Sister Fannie, "Pecuniary Dependence," *Sibyl*, April 1, 1859: 534; "A Chance for a Dress Reformer," *Sibyl*, April 1, 1859: 533

21. *Sibyl*, July 1, 1856: 3; ibid., 3; Kathleen L Endes and Therese L. Lueck, "*The Sibyl*," in *Women's Periodicals in the United States: Social and Political Issues*, eds. Kathleen L Endes and Therese L. Lueck (Westport, CT: Greenwood Press, 1996),

350. Frank Luther Mott, *A History of American Magazines,* Vol. 2, 1850–1865 (Cambridge, MA: Harvard University Press, 1938), 51. Amy Beth Aronson, "America's First Feminist Magazine: Transforming the Popular to the Political," in *Nineteenth-Century Media and the Construction of Identities,* eds. Laurel Brake, Bill Bell, and David Finkelstein (London: Palgrave, 2000), 198.

22. Mary F. Craig, "Our Cause in Iowa," *Sibyl,* March 15, 1859: 528. Data on letters to the editor gathered from a survey of issues of the *Sibyl,* July 1, 1856 to May 15, 1859. Guila, "Extracts from Correspondence," *Sibyl,* August 1, 1856: 19. John W. Hasbrouck, "*The Sibyl:* A Semi-Monthly Journal of Eight Pages, Devoted to Reforms in Every Department of Life," August 1, 1856: 24. Hasbrouck authors this statement of the *Sibyl*'s mission, but he makes clear that his wife, Lydia Sayer Hasbrouck, will serve as editor.

23. Fidelia R. Harris, "Letter from Miss Fidelia R. Harris, MD, Beaver Dam, Wisconsin," *Sibyl,* March 15, 1859: 526.

24. Lydia Sayer Hasbrouck, "Lucy Stone's Position," *Sibyl,* April 15, 1859: 540.

25. Ibid., 540; ibid.

26. Patricia Okker, *Our Sister Editors: Sarah J. Hale and the Tradition of Nineteenth-Century American Women Editors* (Athens, GA: The University of Georgia Press), 1995: 23; O. D., "After Our Own Heart," *Sibyl,* March 15, 1859: 528.

27. Sister Fannie, 534; ibid.; ibid.

28. Jane Archibald, Holmes's mother, forwarded a letter she received from Holmes to the *Lawrence* (Kan.) *Republican,* which published it on October 7, 1858.

29. Louisa T. Whittier, "Our Visit Home," *Sibyl,* May 15, 1859: 555.

30. Margaret Solomon, "A Study of Feminism as a Motif in 'A Journey to Pikes Peak and New Mexico,' by Julia Archibald Holmes," in *Women and Western American Literature,* eds. Helen Winter Stauffer and Susan J. Rosowski (Troy, NY: The Whitston Publishing Company, 1982), 31; Ellen Gruber Garvey, foreword to *Blue Pencils and Hidden Hands: Women Editing Periodicals, 1830–1910,* eds. Sharon M. Harris with Ellen Gruber Garvey (Boston: Northeastern University Press, 2004), xii; ibid.

Afterword

1. Lady Dufferin, "An Unprotected Female in the East," *Harper's New Monthly Magazine* 160.27 (September 1863): 434–35.

2. See the fourth chapter's discussion of the "rhetoric of peril," Kristi Siegel's term for the strategies and ideologies used to threaten women into staying at home. Kristi Siegel, "Women's Travel and the Rhetoric of Peril: It Is Suicide to Be Abroad," in *Gender, Genre, and Identity in Women's Travel Writing,* ed. Kristi Siegel (New York: Peter Lang, 2004), 1–15.

· Bibliography ·

Ada. "The Panic." *Free Enquirer,* February 8, 1829.

Adler, Judith. "Origins of Sightseeing." *Annals of Tourism Research* 16 (1989): 7–29.

Alexander, Ziggi and Audrey Dewjee. Introduction. *Wonderful Adventures of Mrs. Seacole in Many Lands.* (1857) Edited by Ziggi Alexander and Audrey Dewjee. London: Falling Wall Press, 1984. 9–45.

Almonte, Richard. Introduction. *A Plea for Emigration, or Notes from Canada West.* 1852. Edited by Richard Almonte. Toronto: Mercury Press, 1998. 9–41.

Amy Morris Bradley Papers. Manuscript Collection. William R. Perkins Library, Duke University.

Anonymous. "Miss Alice." *Sibyl,* March 15, 1859, page 521.

Arana, R. Victoria. "Introduction: Black Travel Writing, a Kaleidoscopic Genre." *BMa: The Sonia Sanchez Literary Review* 9.1 (Fall 2003): 1–11.

Archibald, Jane. Letter to the Editor. *Lawrence* (Kan.) *Republican,* October 7, 1858.

Armstrong, Nancy. *Desire and Domestic Fiction: A Political History of the Novel.* New York: Oxford University Press, 1987.

Aronson, Amy Beth. "America's First Feminist Magazine: Transforming the Popular to the Political." In *Nineteenth-Century Media and the Construction of Identities,* edited by Laurel Brake, Bill Bell, and David Finkelstein, 197–219. London: Palgrave, 2000.

Bailey, Brigette. "Gender, Nation, and the Tourist Gaze in the European 'Year of Revolutions': Kirkland's *Holidays Abroad.*" *American Literary History* 14.1 (Spring 2002): 60–82.

Baker, Paul. Introduction. *Views of Society and Manners in America: In a Series of Letters from That Country to a Friend in England, During the Years 1818, 1819, and 1820.* 1821. Edited by Paul Baker. Cambridge, MA: The Belknap Press of Harvard University Press, 1963. ix–xxiv.

Bartlett, Elizabeth Ann. *Liberty, Equality, Sorority: The Origins and Interpretation of American Feminist Thought: Frances Wright, Sarah Grimke, and Margaret Fuller.* Brooklyn, NY: Carlson Publishing Inc., 1994.

Bassard, Katherine. *Spiritual Interrogations: Culture, Gender, and Community in Early African American Women's Writing*. Princeton, NJ: Princeton University Press, 1999.

Bates, D. B., Mrs. *Incidents on Land and Water, or Four Years on the Pacific Coast*. 1858. New York: Arno Press, 1974.

Bearden, Jim and Linda Jean Butler. *Shadd: The Life and Time of Mary Shadd Cary*. Toronto: N.C. Press Ltd., 1977.

Beecher, Catharine Esther. *Letters on the Difficulties of Religion*. 1836. Selections reprinted in *The Limits of Sisterhood: The Beecher Sisters on Women's Rights and Woman's Sphere*. Edited by Jeanne Boydston, Mary Kelley, and Anne Margolis. Chapel Hill, NC: The University of North Carolina Press, 1988. 236–37.

Berbineau, Lorenza Steven. *From Beacon Hill to the Crystal Palace: The 1851 Travel Diary of a Working-Class Woman*. Edited by Karen L. Kilcup. Iowa City, IA: University of Iowa Press, 2002.

Blakely, Allison. *Russia and the Negro: Blacks in Russian History and Thought*. Washington DC: Howard University Press, 1986.

Blockett, Kimberly. "Moving Subjectivities in the Evangelical Narrative of Zilpha Elaw." *BMa: The Sonia Sanchez Literary Review* 9.1 (Fall 2003): 103–11.

"Book Reviews: Briefer Notice." *Overland Monthly and Out West Magazine* 16.91 (July 1890): 112.

Bordo, Susan. *Unbearable Weight: Feminism, Western Culture, and the Body*. Berkeley, CA: University of California Press, 1993.

Boydston, Jeanne, Mary Kelley, and Anne Margolis. *The Limits of Sisterhood: The Beecher Sisters on Women's Rights and Woman's Sphere*. Chapel Hill, NC: The University of North Carolina Press, 1988.

Boydston, Jeanne. "To Earn Her Daily Bread: Housework and Antebellum Working-Class Subsistence." In *Unequal Sisters: A Multicultural Reader in U.S. Women's History*, edited by Vicki L. Ruiz and Ellen Carol DuBois, 44–56. New York: Routledge, 1994.

Brooks, Gwendolyn. *Report from Part One*. Detroit: Broadside Press, 1972.

Brown, Gillian. *Domestic Individualism: Imagining Self in Nineteenth-Century America*. Berkeley and Los Angeles: University of California Press, 1990.

Brown, William Wells. *The Travels of William Wells Brown*. (1852). Edited by Paul Jefferson. New York: Markus Wiener Publishing Inc., 1991.

Bunker, Gary L. "Antebellum Caricature and Woman's Sphere." *Journal of Women's History* 3.3 (Winter 1992): 6–43.

Butcher, Patricia Smith. *Education for Equality: Women's Rights Periodicals and Women's Higher Education, 1849–1920*. Westport, CT: Greenwood Press, 1989.

Butler, Judith. *Gender Trouble: Feminism and the Subversion of Identity*. New York: Routledge, 1990.

Buzard, James. *The Beaten Track: European Tourism, Literature, and the Ways of Culture, 1800–1918*. Oxford: Clarendon Press, 1993.

Campbell, Robert. *A Pilgrimage to My Motherland: An Account of a Journey among the Egbas and Yorubas of Central Africa, 1855–1860*. New York: Thomas Hamilton, 1861.

Cary, Stephanie Hom. "The Tourist Moment." *Annals of Tourism Research* 31.1 (2004): 61–77.

Cashman, Diane Cobb. *Headstrong: The Biography of Amy Morris Bradley, 1823–1904: A Life of Noblest Usefulness.* Wilmington, NC: Broadfoot Publishing Company, 1990.

"A Chance for a Dress Reformer." *Sibyl,* April 1, 1859, page 533.

Cheng, Chu-Chueh. "Frances Trollope's America and Anna Leonowen's Siam: Questionable Travel and Problematic Writing." In *Gender, Genre, and Identity in Women's Travel Writing,* edited by Kristi Siegel, 123–66. New York: Peter Lang, 2004.

Child, Lydia Maria. *Letters from New York.* Freeport, NY: Books for Libraries Press, 1970.

Clapp, Elizabeth J. "Black Books and Southern Tours: Tone and Perspective in the Travel Writing of Anne Royall." *The Yearbook of English Studies* 34 (2004): 61–73.

———. "The Boundaries of Femininity: The Travels and Writings of Mrs. Anne Royall, 1823–31." *American Nineteenth-Century History* 4.3 (Fall 2003): 1–28.

Cott, Nancy F. *The Bonds of Womanhood: "Woman's Sphere" in New England, 1780–1835.* New Haven, CT: Yale University Press, 1977.

———. "Passionlessness: An Interpretation of Victorian Sexual Ideology, 1790–1850." *Signs* 4.2 (1978): 219–36.

Craig, Mary F. "Our Cause in Iowa." *Sibyl,* March 15, 1859, page 528.

Cuffe, Paul. *A Brief Account of the Settlement and Present Situation of the Colony of Sierra Leone, in Africa.* New York: Samuel Wood, 1812.

Cummins, Maria. *The Lamplighter.*1854. Reprint, with an introduction by Nina Baym. New Brunswick, NJ: Rutgers University Press, 1988.

D'Arusmont, Frances Wright. *Life, Letters and Lectures, 1834–1844, Frances Wright D'Arusmont.* Reprint of *Course of Popular Lectures: With Three Addresses, on Various Public Occasions, and a Reply to the Charges Against the French Reformers of 1789.* 1834. Supplement Course of Lectures. 1834. *Biography, Notes, and Political Letters of Frances Wright D'Arusmont.* 1844. Arno's American Women: Images and Realities. New York: Arno Press, 1972.

Davidson, Cathy N. and Jessamyn Hatcher, eds. *No More Separate Spheres!: A Next Wave American Studies Reader.* Durham, NC: Duke University Press, 2002.

Delaney, Martin R. *Official Report of the Niger Valley Exploring Party.* New York: Thomas Hamilton, 1861.

DuBois, Ellen Carol. "Working Women, Class Relations, and Suffrage Militance: Harriot Stanton Blatch and the New York Woman Suffrage Movement, 1894–1909." In *Unequal Sisters: A Multicultural Reader in U.S. Women's History,* 2nd ed., edited by Vicki L. Ruiz and Ellen Carol DuBois, 228–46. New York: Routledge, 1994.

DuBois, W. E. B. "Little Portraits of Africa." *The Crisis* 276 (1924): 273–74.

Dufferin, Lady. "An Unprotected Female in the East." *Harper's New Monthly Magazine* 160.27 (September 1863): 433–54.

Dunlevy, Marion B. and Alice S. Maxwell. *Virago!: The Story of Anne Newport Royall (1769–1854).* Jefferson, NC: McFarland & Company Inc., 1985.

Eckhardt, Celia Morris. *Fanny Wright: Rebel in America.* Cambridge, MA: Harvard University Press, 1984.

"Editor's Table." *Godey's Lady's Book* 16 (May 1838): 239.

————. *Godey's Lady's Book* 22 (January 1841): 46.

"The Emigration Scheme." *The Colored American*, November 13, 1841.

Endes, Kathleen L. and Therese L. Lueck. *"The Sybil."* In *Women's Periodicals in the United States: Social and Political Issues*, edited by Kathleen L. Endes and Therese L. Lueck, 346–51. Westport, CT: Greenwood Press, 1996.

Engle, Anna. "Depictions of the Irish in Frank Webb's *The Garies and Their Friends* and Frances E. W. Harper's *Trial and Triumph*." *MELUS* 26.1 (2001): 151–71.

Fish, Cheryl. "Voices of Restless (Dis)continuity: The Significance of Travel for Free Black Women in the Antebellum Americas." *Women's Studies—An Interdisciplinary Journal* 26.5 (1997): 475–95.

————. *Black and White Women's Travel Narratives: Antebellum Explorations*. Gainesville, FL: University Press of Florida, 2004.

Foster, Frances Smith. "Adding Color and Contour to Early American Self-Portraitures: Autobiographical Writings of Afro-American Women." In *Conjuring: Black Women, Fiction, and Literary Tradition*, edited by Marjorie Pryse and Hortense Spillers, 25–38. Bloomington, IN: Indiana University Press, 1985.

————. *Written By Herself: Literary Production by African American Women, 1746—1892*. Bloomington, IN: Indiana University Press, 1993.

Foster, Shirley. "Colonialism and Gender in the East: Representations of the Harem in the Writings of Women Travellers." *The Yearbook of English Studies* 34 (2004): 6–18.

Franklin, Adrian. *Tourism: An Introduction*. London: Sage Publication, 2003.

Garvey, Ellen Gruber. Foreword. *Blue Pencils and Hidden Hands: Women Editing Periodicals, 1830–1910*. Edited by Sharon M. Harris and Ellen Gruber Garvey. Boston: Northeastern University Press, 2004. xi–xxiv.

Georgi-Findlay, Brigitte. *The Frontiers of Women's Writing: Women's Narratives and the Rhetoric of Westward Expansion*. Tucson, AZ: University of Arizona Press, 1996.

Gerzina, Gretchen Holbrook. "Mobility in Chains: Freedom of Movement in the Early Black Atlantic." *South Atlantic Quarterly* 100.1 (Winter 2001): 41–59.

Ginzberg, Lori D. *Women and the Work of Benevolence: Morality, Politics, and Class in the Nineteenth-Century United States*. New Haven, CT: Yale University Press, 1990.

————. "'The Hearts of Your Readers Will Shudder': Fanny Wright, Infidelity, and American Freethought." *American Quarterly* 46.2 (June 1994):195–226.

Griffin, Farah and Cheryl Fish, eds. *A Stranger in the Village: Two Centuries of African-American Travel Writing*. Boston: Beacon Press, 1998.

Guila. "Extracts from Correspondence." *Sibyl*, August 1, 1856, page 19.

Gunning, Sandra. "Nancy Prince and the Politics of Mobility, Home, and Diasporic (Mis)Identification." *American Quarterly* 53.1 (March 2001): 32–69.

————. "Traveling with Her Mother's Tastes: The Negotiation of Gender, Race, and Location in *Wonderful Adventures of Mrs. Seacole in Many Lands*." *Signs* 26.4 (Summer 2001): 949–82.

Hall, Julie E. "'Coming to Europe,' Coming to Authorship: Sophia Hawthorne and Her *Notes in England and Italy*." *Legacy* 19.2 (2002): 137–51.

Harris, Fidelia R. "Letter from Miss Fidelia R. Harris, MD, Beaver Dam, Wisconsin." *Sibyl*, March 15, 1859, page 526.

Hasbrouck, John W. *"The Sibyl:* A Semi-Monthly Journal of Eight Pages, Devoted to Reforms in Every Department of Life." *Sibyl,* August 1, 1856, page 24.

Hasbrouck, Lydia Sayer. "Lucy Stone's Position." *Sibyl,* April 15, 1859, page 540.

———. "Remarks." *Sibyl,* April 1, 1859, page 533.

Holland, Patrick and Graeme Huggan. *Tourists with Typewriters: Critical Reflections on Contemporary Travel Writing.* Ann Arbor, MI: University of Michigan Press, 2000.

hooks, bell. *Yearning: Race, Gender, and Cultural Politics.* Boston: South End Press, 1990.

Horton, James Oliver. *Free People of Color: Inside the African American Community.* Washington DC: Smithsonian Institute Press, 1993.

Jackson, George S. *Uncommon Scold: The Story of Anne Royall.* Boston: Bruce Humphries Inc., 1937.

James, Bessie Rowland. *Anne Royall's U.S.A.* New Brunswick, NJ: Rutgers University Press, 1972.

Johnson, Karen Ramsay and Joseph Keller. "Anne Royall's Apocalyptic Rhetoric: Politics and the Role of Women." *Women's Studies* 31 (2002): 671–88.

Johnstone, Mrs. "Lady Travellers." *The Living Age* 6.68 (August 30, 1845): 423–24.

Jordan, June. "Report from the Bahamas." *Moving Towards Home: Political Essays.* London: Virago Press, 1989.

Kaplan, Amy. "Manifest Domesticity." In Davidson and Hatcher, *No More Separate Spheres!,* 183–208.

Karcher, Carolyn. "Frances Wright of the *Free Enquirer:* Woman Editor in a Man's World." In *Blue Pencils and Hidden Hands: Women Editing Periodicals, 1830–1910,* edited by Sharon M. Harris and Ellen Gruber Garvey, 80–95. Boston: Northeastern University Press, 2004.

Kelly, Lori Duin. "Bipeds in Bloomers: How the Popular Press Killed the Dress Reform Movement." *Studies in Popular Culture* 13.2 (1991): 67–76.

Kerber, Linda. "Separate Spheres, Female Worlds, Woman's Place: The Rhetoric of Women's History." *Journal of American History* 75 (1988): 9–39.

Kolchin, Peter. *Unfree Labor: American Slavery and Russian Serfdom.* Cambridge, MA: The Belknap Press of Harvard University Press, 1987.

Kollin, Susan. "'The First White Women in the Last Frontier': Writing Race, Gender, and Nature in Alaskan Travel Narratives." *Frontiers: A Journal of Women's Studies* 18.2 (1997): 105–24.

Lamont, Victoria. "Cattle Branding and the Traffic in Women in Early Twentieth-Century Westerns by Women." *Legacy* 22.1 (2005): 30–46.

Lang, Amy Schrager. *The Syntax of Class: Writing Inequality in Nineteenth-Century America.* Princeton, NJ: Princeton University Press, 2003.

Lauter, Paul. *From Walden Pond to Jurassic Park: Activism, Culture, and American Studies.* Durham, NC: Duke University Press, 2001.

Lawrence, Karen R. *Penelope Voyages: Women and Travel in the British Literary Tradition.* Ithaca, NY: Cornell University Press, 1994.

Leed, Eric J. *The Mind of the Traveler from Gilgamesh to Global Tourism.* New York, NY: Basic Books, Harper Collins Publishers, 1991.

Leland, Lilian. *Traveling Alone: A Woman's Journey Around the World.* New York, NY: Press of John Polhemus, 1890.

MacCannell, Dean. *The Tourist: A New Theory of the Leisure Class.* New York: Schocken Books Inc., 1989.

Mary Ann Shadd Cary Papers. Moorland-Spingarn Research Center. Howard University.

Mason, Mary G. "Travel as Metaphor and Reality in Afro-American Women's Autobiography, 1850–1972." *Black American Literature Forum* 24.2 (Summer 1990): 337–56.

McElroy, Colleen. *A Long Way from St. Louie.* Minneapolis, MN: Coffee House Press, 1997.

McHenry, Elizabeth. *Forgotten Readers: Recovering the Lost History of African American Literary Societies.* Durham, NC: Duke University Press, 2002.

McKenna, Bernard. "'Fancies of Exclusive Possession': Validation and Dissociation in Mary Seacole's England and Caribbean." *Philological Quarterly* 76.2 (Spring 1997): 219–40.

Mills, Sara. *Discourses of Difference: An Analysis of Women's Travel Writing and Colonialism.* New York: Routledge, 1991.

Monika Elbert, ed. *Separate Spheres No More.* Tuscaloosa, AL: University of Alabama Press, 2000.

Moody, Madge. "Madge Moody's Lectures, No. 7." *Sibyl,* April 15, 1859, page 537.

Mott, Frank Luther. *A History of American Magazines.* Vol. 2, *1850–1865.* Cambridge, MA: Harvard University Press, 1938.

Myres, Sandra L., ed. *Ho for California! Women's Overland Diaries from the Huntington Library.* San Marino, CA: Huntington Library, 1980.

New York Evening Post, January, 26, 1829.

O. D. "After Our Own Heart." *Sibyl,* March 15, 1859, page 528.

Okker, Patricia. *Our Sister Editors: Sarah J. Hale and the Tradition of Nineteenth-Century American Women Editors.* Athens, GA: The University of Georgia Press, 1995.

Paquet, Sandra Pouchet. "The Enigma of Arrival: *The Wonderful Adventures of Mrs. Seacole in Many Lands.*" *African-American Review* 26.4 (Winter 1992): 651–63.

Park, You-me and Gayle Walk. "Native Daughters in the Promised Land: Gender, Race, and the Question of Separate Spheres." In Davidson and Hatcher, *No More Separate Spheres!,* 263–90.

Payne-Gaposchkin, Cecilia Helena, ed. "The Nashoba Plan for Removing the Evil of Slavery: Letters of Frances and Camilla Wright, 1820–1829." Pts. 1 and 2. *Harvard Library Bulletin* 23.3 (July 1975): 221–51; 23.4 (October 1975): 429–61.

Pease, William H. and Jane H. Pease. *Black Utopia.* Madison, WI: State Historical Society of Wisconsin, 1963.

Perkins, A. J. G. and Theresa Wolfson. *Frances Wright, Free Enquirer: The Study of a Temperament.* New York: Harper & Brothers, 1939.

Peterson, Carla L. *"Doers of the Word": African-American Women Speakers and Writers in the North (1830–1880).* New York: Oxford University Press, 1995.

Poovey, Mary. "Speaking of the Body: Mid-Victorian Constructions of Female Desire." In *Body/Politics: Women and the Discourses of Science,* edited by Mary Jacobus, Evelyn Fox Keller, and Sally Shuttleworth, 29–46. New York: Routledge, 1990.

Porter, Sarah Harvey. *Life and Times of Anne Royall.* Cedar Rapids, IA: Torch Press Book Shop, 1909.

Pratt, Mary Louise. *Imperial Eyes: Travel Writing and Transculturation.* New York: Routledge, 1992.

Prince, Nancy Garner. *A Narrative of the Life and Travels of Mrs. Nancy Prince, Written by Herself.* 1853. 2nd ed. Collected Black Women's Narratives, edited by Henry Louis Gates Jr. New York: Oxford University Press, 1988.

———. *The West Indies, Being a Description of the Islands, Progress of Christianity, Education, and Liberty Among the Colored Population Generally, by Mrs. Nancy Prince.* Boston: Dow & Jackson Printers, 1841.

Provincial Freeman. (1853–1860).

Reid, Hiriam A. "Words of Good Cheer." *Sibyl,* May 1, 1859, page 548.

Rennella, Mark and Whitney Walton. "Planned Serendipity: American Travelers and the Transatlantic Voyage in the Nineteenth and Twentieth Centuries." *Journal of Social History* 38.2 (2004): 365–83.

Rhodes, Jane. *Mary Ann Shadd Cary: The Black Press and Protest in the Nineteenth Century.* Bloomington, IN: Indiana University Press, 1998.

Robinson, Amy. "Authority and the Public Display of Identity: *Wonderful Adventures of Mrs. Seacole in Many Lands.*" *Feminist Studies* 20.3 (Fall 1994): 537–57.

Robinson, Jane. *Wayward Women: A Guide to Women Travellers.* New York: Oxford University Press, 1990.

Roediger, David. *The Wages of Whiteness: Race and the Making of the American Working Class.* New York: Verso, 1991.

Rotundo, E. Anthony. *American Manhood: Transformations in Masculinity from the Revolution to the Modern Era.* New York: Basic Books, 1993.

Royall, Anne Newport. *Letters from Alabama, 1817–1822.* 1830. Edited by Lucille Griffith. Tuscaloosa, AL: University of Alabama Press, 1969.

———. *Mrs. Royall's Pennsylvania, or Travels Continued in the United States, Volume 1.* 1829. *Volume 2.* 1829.

———. *Mrs. Royall's Southern Tour, or Second Series of the Black Book, In Three or More Volumes.* 1830–31.

———. *The Black Book, or A Continuation of Travels, in the United States, Volume 1.* 1828. *Volume 2* 1828. *Volume 3.* 1829. Washington DC, 1828.

———. *The Tennesseean: A Novel Founded on Facts.* 1827.

———. *Sketches of History, Life, and Manners in the United States, by a Traveller.* 1826. New York: Johnson Reprint Corp., 1970.

Schriber, Mary Suzanne, ed. *Telling Travels: Selected Writings by Nineteenth-Century American Women Abroad.* DeKalb: Northern Illinois University Press, 1995.

———. *Writing Home: American Women Abroad 1830–1920.* Charlottesville, VA: University Press of Virginia, 1997.

Seacole, Mary. *Wonderful Adventures of Mrs. Seacole in Many Lands.* 1857. New York: Oxford University Press, 1988.

Shadd, Mary Ann. "Hints to the Colored People of the North." Quoted in J. B. Y. "Miss Shadd's Pamphlet." *North Star,* June 8, 1849.

———. *A Plea for Emigration, or Notes from Canada West.* 1852. Edited by Richard Almonte. Toronto: Mercury Press, 1998.

Sibyl. (1856–64).

Siegel, Kristi. Introduction. *Gender, Genre, and Identity in Women's Travel Writing.* Edited by Kristi Siegel. New York: Peter Lang, 2004. 1–15.

———. "Women's Travel and the Rhetoric of Peril: It Is Suicide to Be Abroad." In *Gender, Genre, and Identity in Women's Travel Writing*, edited by Kristi Siegel, 55–72. New York: Peter Lang, 2004.

Silverman, Jason H. *Unwelcome Guests: Canada West's Response to American Fugitive Slaves, 1800–1865*. Millwood, NY: Associated Faculties Press, 1985.

Sister Fannie. "Pecuniary Dependence." *Sibyl*, April 1, 1859, page 534.

Smith-Rosenberg, Carroll. *Disorderly Conduct: Visions of Gender in Victorian America*. New York: Knopf, 1985.

Solomon, Margaret. "A Bloomer Girl Conquers Pikes Peak." *American History Illustrated* 18.9 (January 1984): 40–47.

———. "A Study of Feminism as a Motif in 'A Journey to Pikes Peak and New Mexico,' by Julia Archibald Holmes." In *Women and Western American Literature*, edited by Helen Winter Stauffer and Susan J. Rosowski, 28–39. Troy, NY: The Whitston Publishing Company, 1982.

Speirs, Kenneth. "Strategies of Approximation in *The Life and Adventures of Nat Love*." *BMa: The Sonia Sanchez Literary Review* 9.1 (Fall 2003): 71–89.

Spring, Agnes Wright, ed. *A Bloomer Girl on Pikes Peak, 1858, Julia Archibald Holmes First White Woman to Climb Pikes Peak*. Denver: Denver Public Library, 1949.

Stansell, Christine. *City of Women: Sex and Class in New York, 1789–1860*. Urbana, IL: University of Illinois Press, 1987.

Stanton, Elizabeth Cady, Susan B. Anthony, and Matilda Joslyn Gage, eds. *History of Woman Suffrage*. New York: Fowler & Wells, 1881.

Steadman, Jennifer. "Traveling Uplift: Mary Ann Shadd Cary Creating and Connecting Black Communities." *BMa: The Sonia Sanchez Literary Review* 9.1 (Fall 2003): 119–37.

Stevenson, Catherine. *Victorian Women Travel Writers in Africa*. Boston: Twayne, 1982.

Terry, Jennifer and Jacqueline Urla. "Introduction: Mapping Embodied Deviance." *Deviant Bodies: Critical Perspectives on Difference in Science and Popular Culture*. Edited by Jennifer Terry and Jacqueline Urla. 1–18. Bloomington, IN: Indiana University Press, 1995.

Thomson, Rosemarie Garland. Introduction. *Freakery: Cultural Spectacles of the Extraordinary Body*. Edited by Rosemary Garland Thomson. New York: New York University Press, 1996. 1–22.

Tinling, Marion. *Women into the Unknown: A Sourcebook on Women Explorers and Travelers*. New York: Greenwood Press, 1989.

Trollope, Frances. *Domestic Manners of the Americans*. 1832. London: George Routledge and Sons, Ltd., 1927.

Vogel, Todd. Introduction. *The Black Press: New Literary and Historical Essays*. Edited by Todd Vogel. New Brunswick, NJ: Rutgers University Press, 2001. 1–16.

Waterman, William Randall. *Frances Wright*. New York: Columbia University Press, 1924.

White, Deborah Gray. *Ar'n't I a Woman?: Female Slaves in the Plantation South*. New York: W. W. Norton & Company, 1985.

Whittier, Louisa T. "Our Visit Home." *Sibyl*, May 15, 1859.

Winks, Robin. *The Blacks in Canada*. New Haven: Yale University Press, 1971.

Wood, Molly M. "A Diplomat's Wife in Mexico: Creating Professional, Political, and National Identities in the Early Twentieth Century." *Frontiers: A Journal of Women Studies* 25.3 (2004): 104–33.

Wright, Frances. "Explanatory Notes, Respecting the Nature and Objects of the Institution of Nashoba, and of the Principles upon Which It Is Founded. Addressed to the Friends of Human Improvement, in All Countries and of All Nations." *The New-Harmony Gazette*, January 30, 1828, pages 124–25; February 6, 1828, pages 132–33; February 13, 1828, pages 140–41.

———. *Views of Society and Manners in America: In a Series of Letters from That Country to a Friend in England, During the Years 1818, 1819, and 1820.* 1821. Edited by Paul Baker. Cambridge, MA: The Belknap Press of Harvard University Press, 1963.

Wright, Richard. *Black Power: A Record of Reactions to a Land of Pathos.* New York: Harper & Brothers, 1954.

"A Yankee Ida Pfieffer, Going Round the World." *New York Daily Tribune*, February 14, 1890, page 10, column 1.

Yee, Shirley. "Finding a Place: Mary Ann Shadd Cary and the Dilemmas of Black Migration to Canada, 1850–1870." *Frontiers: A Journal of Women's Studies* 18.3 (1997): 1–16.

Yellin, Jean Fagan. *Women & Sisters: The Antislavery Feminists in American Culture.* New Haven, CT: Yale University Press, 1989.

Young, Jennifer. "'We Sweep the Liquid Plain': Wheatley's Travel Poems about the Sea." *BMa: The Sonia Sanchez Literary Review* 9.1 (Fall 2003): 33–49.

· Index ·

Black Power: A Record of Reactions in a Land of Pathos (Wright), 89

blacks: antebellum culture, 89–90; attitudes toward Shadd Cary, 98–100; civil rights, 96–97; community production and formation, 108–9; emigration, 20, 21, 59, 84, 86–88, 95–99, 101, 107–8; in Jamaica, 52, 59; literary tradition, 88–91, 93, 109–11; middle class, 33, 86–87, 91–95; nationalism, 20–21, 88–91, 99, 107, 109–10; in Russia, 37–38, 48–51, 176n19, 176n22; Shadd Cary on values of, 86, 91; Shadd Cary's portrayal of communities, 109–11; travel as survival strategy of, 87. *See also* black women; slavery

"Black Travel Writing," 11

black women: bodies, 40–41, 48, 52, 54–55, 129, 131, 177n36; cultural attitudes about, 4, 48, 60; on culture of free communities, 90; emigration, 20–21; expectations of, 7, 9, 86, 126–28; femininity, 36, 37, 39; middle class, 33; mobility, 21, 22, 33–34, 52–53, 55–56, 60, 87; nationalism, 20–21; risks, 10–12, 43, 52–56, 88, 95, 125; sexuality, 134–37; and *Sibyl*'s exclusive sisterhood, 164; social deviance, 41–43; stereotypes, 137; use of travel genre, 52; and white middle-class feminists, 151; and Wright, 119. *See also* blacks

Blakely, Allison, 176n22

Blockett, Kimberly, 11

Bloomer, Amelia, 154

"A Bloomer Girl Conquers Pikes Peak" (Solomon), 186n5

A Bloomer Girl on Pikes Peak (Spring), 186n5

bloomers: and physical fitness, 146–47; symbolism, 153–56, 186n5; Whittier on, 164; and Woman's Rights, 143, 153; women climbers in, 149. *See also* dress; dress reform

Bly, Nellie, 179n24

BMa: The Sonia Sanchez Literary Review, 11

bodies: black women's, 40–41, 48, 52, 54–55, 129, 131, 177n36; feminist theory about, 7–8; and morality, 132; and Other's gaze, 116, 132–33; risks, 46–47, 122–24, 131; and Wright, 113–26. *See also* sexuality

Bordo, Susan, 8

Bosphorus, 127

Boston, 36, 37, 60, 75, 91

Boydston, Jeanne, 115

Bradley, Amy Morris: audience, 58–60; background, 29; comparison to Shadd Cary, 110; employment, 30–32, 44–46; finances, 30–32, 44–47, 175n13; mule ride, 47, 123; purpose of travel, 26, 27, 29, 33; risks, 33, 39–40, 46–47, 168; self-presentation, 141; and social class, 12, 14, 28–29, 44–47; travel narrative, 6, 23; treatment by fellow travelers, 43–44, 53, 125; writing technique, 174n1

Bradley, Betsy and Elizabeth, 58, 59

A Brief Account of the Settlement and Present Situation of the Colony of Sierra Leone, in Africa (Cuffe), 88–89

British and Foreign Anti-Slavery Society, 181n18

Brooks, Gwendolyn, 89

Brown, Antoinette, 116

Brown, Gillian, 27–28

Brown, William Wells, 88

Bunker, Gary, 154, 156

Butcher, Patricia Smith, 153

Butler, Judith, 122, 183n13

Butler, Mary, 65–66

Buzard, James, 25, 49, 177n38

California, 31–32, 42

Campbell, Robert, 89

Canada: and black emigration, 20, 21, 84, 86–88, 95–99, 107–8; connection of blacks in, 109, 110; corruption in, 104; economic prospects in, 13; probegging philosophy, 104, 181n19; quality of blacks' life

www.ingramcontent.com/pod-product-compliance
Lightning Source LLC
Chambersburg PA
CBHW031553280326
41928CB00047BA/246